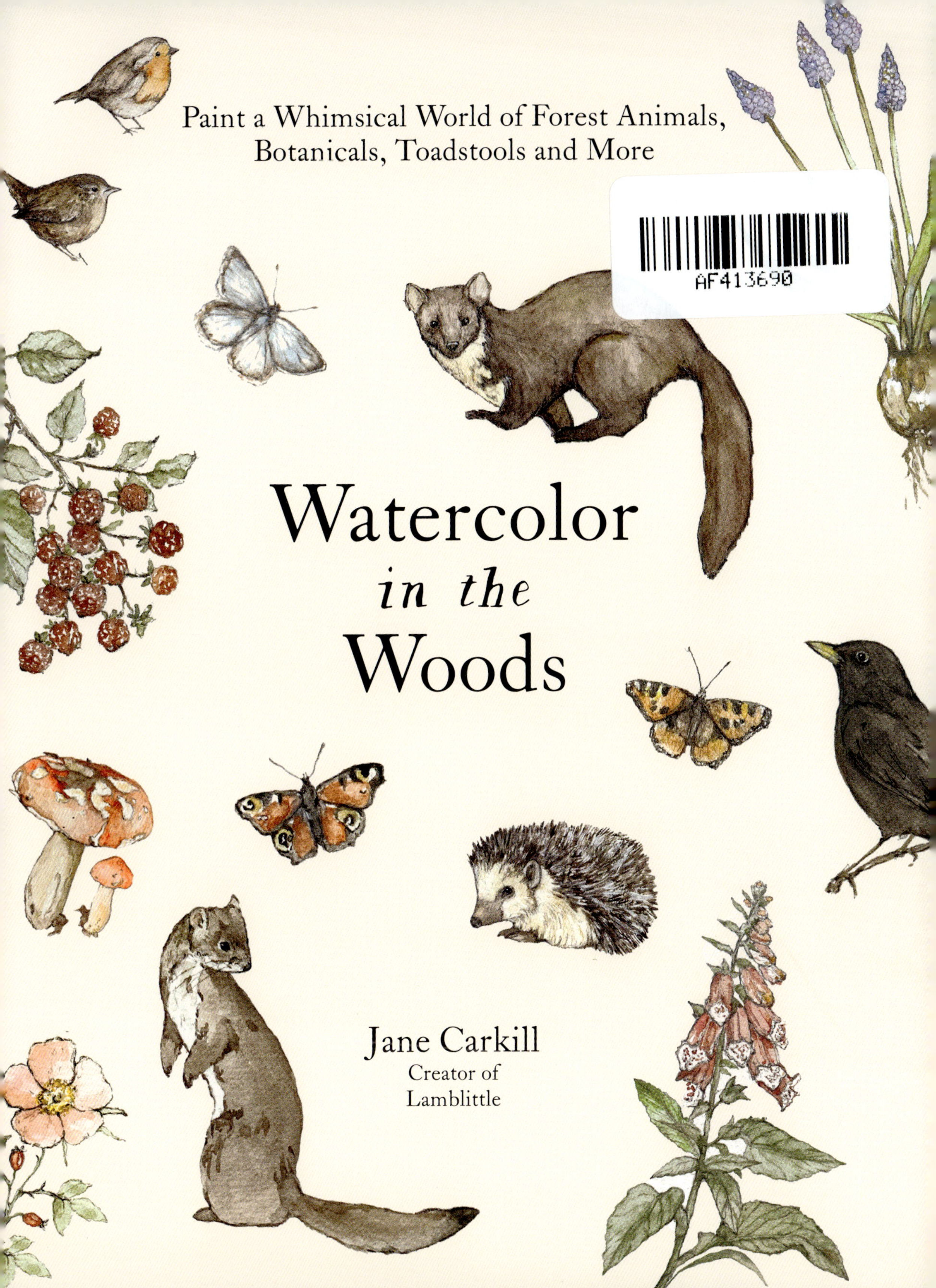

Paint a Whimsical World of Forest Animals, Botanicals, Toadstools and More

# Watercolor
## *in the*
# Woods

Jane Carkill
Creator of
Lamblittle

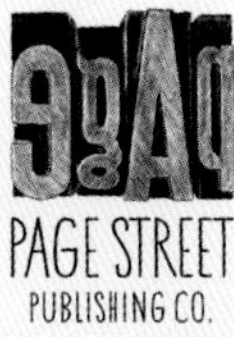

PAGE STREET
PUBLISHING CO.



First published in 2024 by
Page Street Publishing Co.
27 Congress Street, Suite 1511
Salem, MA 01970
www.pagestreetpublishing.com



Distributed by Macmillan, sales in Canada by The Canadian Manda Group.

28  27  26  25          5  6  7  8  9  10

ISBN-13: 979-8-89003-086-3

Library of Congress Control Number: 2023949718

Edited by Krystle Green
Cover and book design by Emma Hardy for Page Street Publishing Co.
Artwork by Jane Carkill

Printed and bound in the United States of America

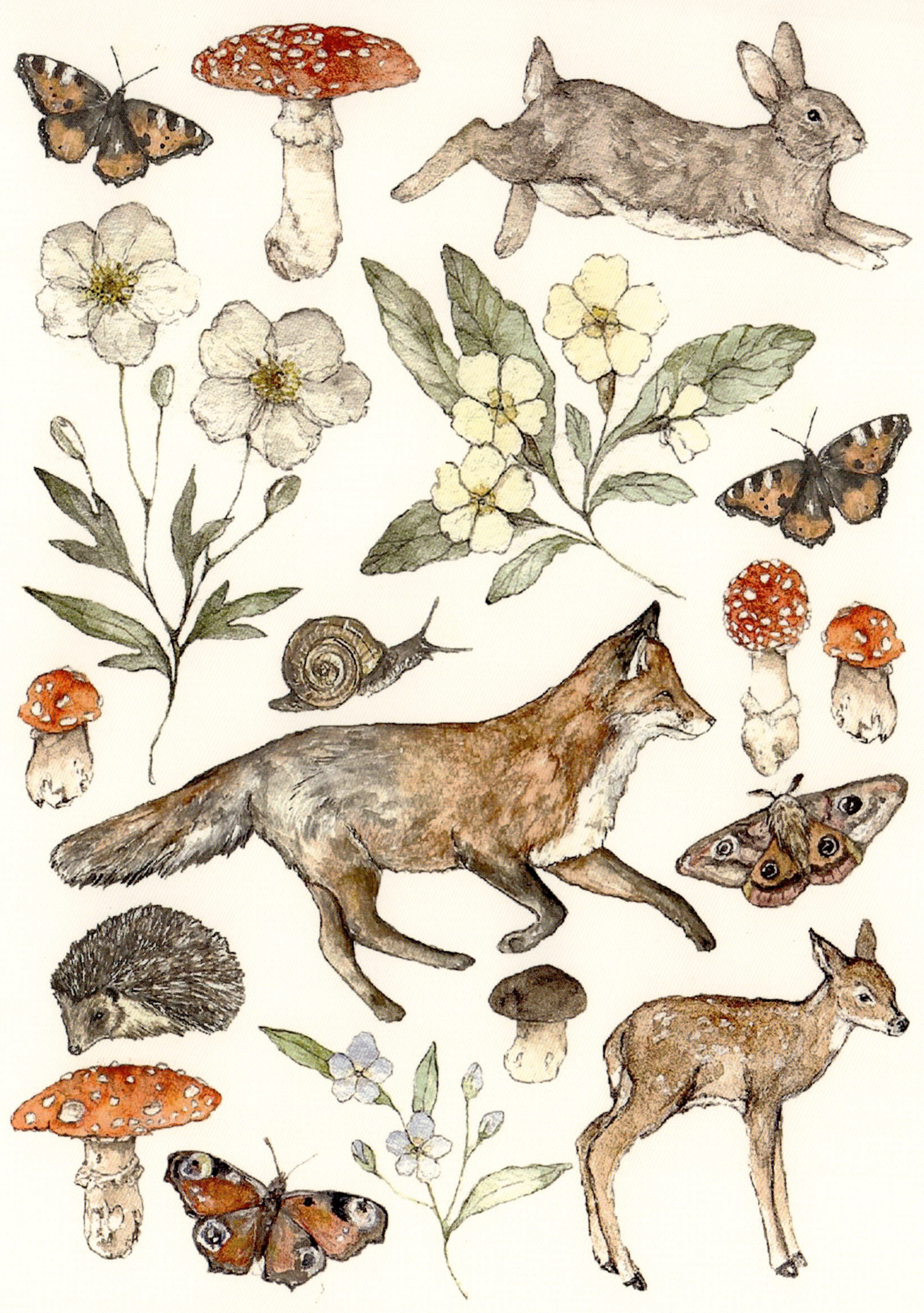

To my friends and family, for their unwavering encouragement
and support for all that I create.

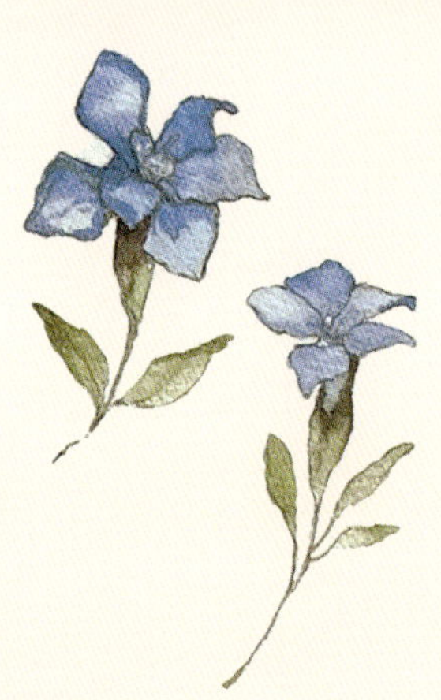

# Table *of* Contents

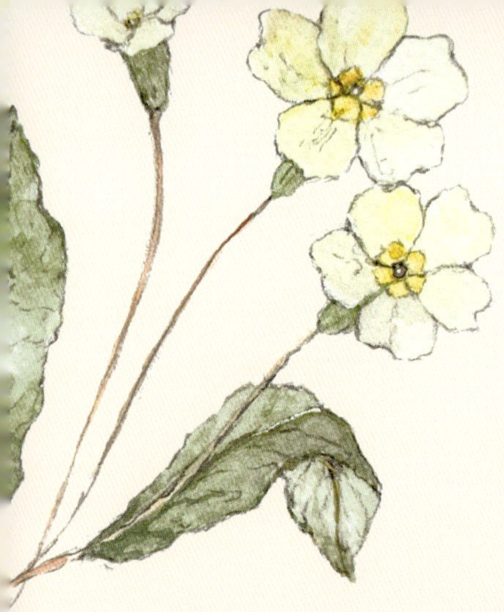



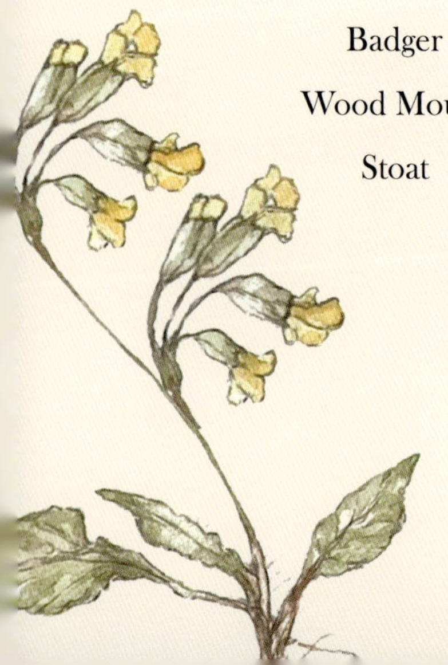

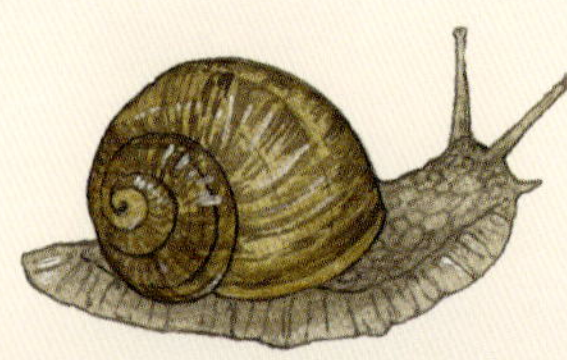

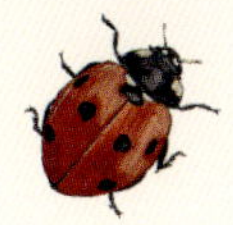

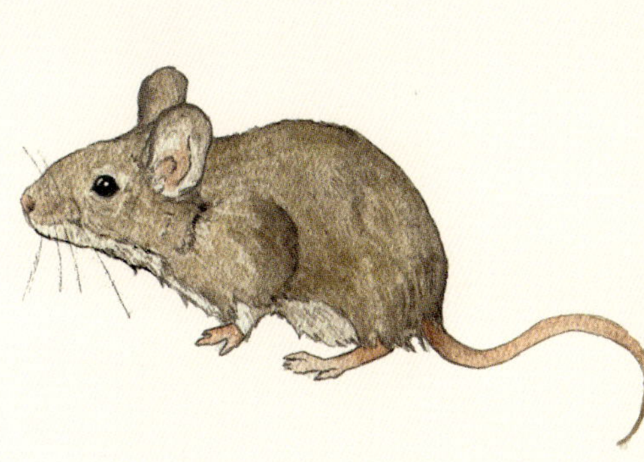

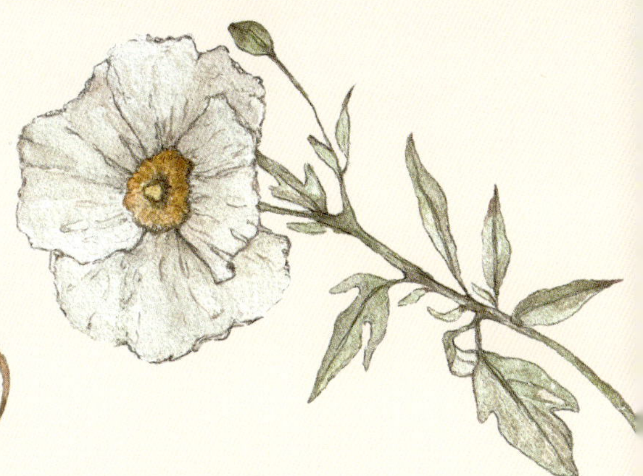

## Woodland Insects · 119



## Forest Flora · 145



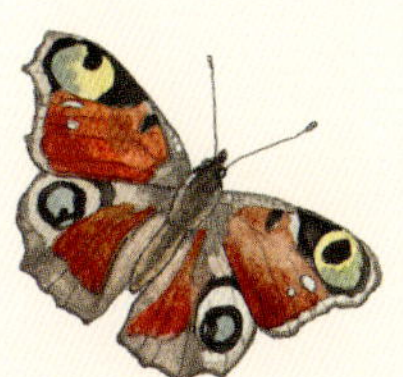

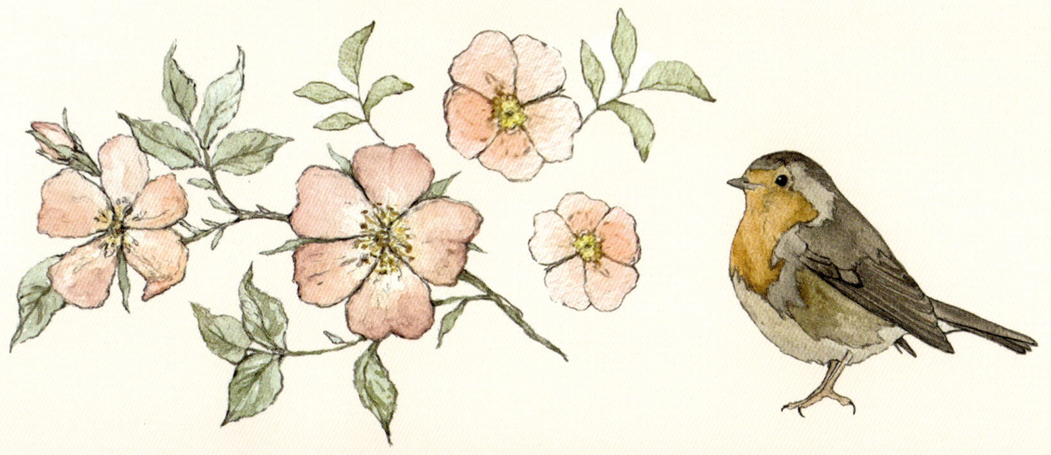

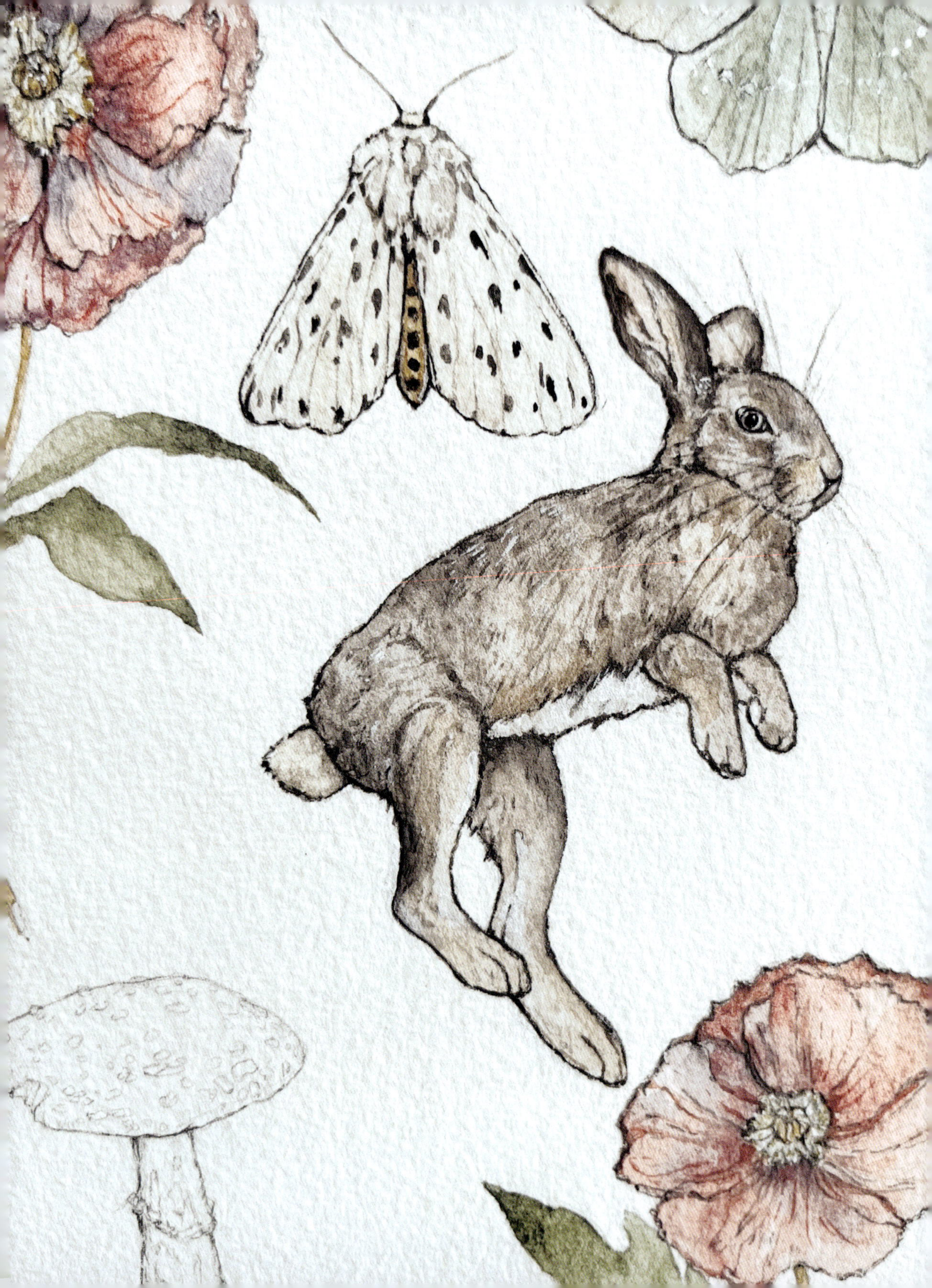

# Introduction

I have always loved drawing and painting. My earliest memories are sitting in a corner of the kitchen as a child—a stack of paper to my side, pencil in hand—and drawing whatever came into my head or asking myself the perpetual question "What shall I draw?" Although I eventually studied textile design, if I am totally honest with myself, the element of preparation for the design of a garment or cloth (e.g., the drawing, painting and illustration) is what I have always truly loved in my heart.

I was drawn to watercolor painting in my own practice due to its unique delicacy and luminous, sparkling transparency. I found that, with practice, I was capable of conjuring up the most fleeting and evanescent effects in nature, which has always been my ultimate inspiration.

The fluidity of watercolor makes the medium an exciting yet equally unpredictable one. And for the inexperienced or beginner artist, this element of uncertainty can be disconcerting. I wanted to write this book as a gentle introduction to the medium that has captivated me throughout the years, to create an invitation to immerse yourself both in the serenity and splendor of the natural world, as well as to break down the barriers of watercolor painting that can be frustrating. Through a series of step-by-step tutorials, you will gain insight on how to capture the delicate interplay of light and shadow, the rich textures of foliage and fur and the tranquil beauty of the patterned wings of insects and birds alike.

Painting and drawing take practice. My best advice is to paint and draw every day, even if it is only for 10 minutes. Each sketch or painting will increase your confidence as well as your abilities. Do not throw any of your studies away—look back over them in a few months' time and you will be amazed by how your skills have improved! If you are feeling apprehensive about your drawing skills, don't worry. I have included some templates at the back of the book (page 166) to help you along, which you can either trace or copy freehand.

Be gentle and have patience with yourself. Watercolor is a challenging medium, but your enthusiasm and confidence will grow once you have achieved a couple of successful washes or completed a corner of a painting that was simple to execute yet magically comes to life!

So, pick up your brushes, set up your palette and join me as we journey into the heart of the woodland. Whether you're seeking to capture the mystery of the barn owl (page 39) or the whimsy of a rabbit peeking out from the underbrush (page 30), this book will inspire and guide you every step of the way.

# Tips & Techniques for Success in Watercolor

Thankfully, when it comes to painting beautiful and realistic flora and fauna in watercolor, you do not need a vast quantity of materials and equipment. When beginning watercolor or any art medium, I would advise to invest in a small amount of the best materials—the better the tools, the better the outcome. Cheap paints are an excellent gateway if you are curious about exploring a medium, but if you find you would like to yield the most realistic results that do not have muted, dull hues, higher quality is always worth the investment. Equally, poor-quality paper and cheaper brushes can be frustrating and may turn you off painting completely under the guise that your skills are at fault!

In the following pages, you will find information and advice to help you choose what you need to feel comfortable and get ready to start exploring your abilities as an artist.

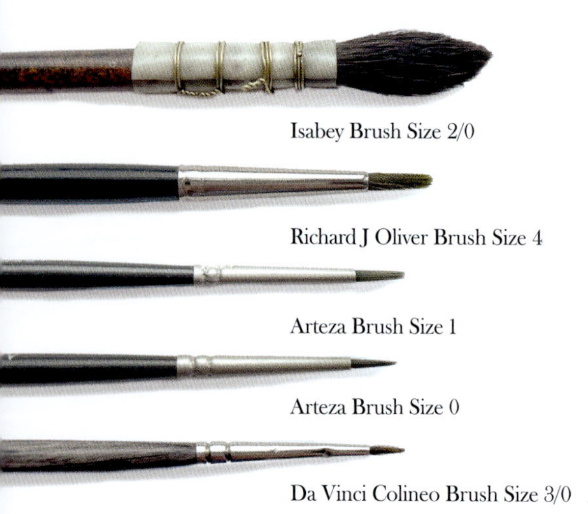

Isabey Brush Size 2/0

Richard J Oliver Brush Size 4

Arteza Brush Size 1

Arteza Brush Size 0

Da Vinci Colineo Brush Size 3/0

## Templates

At the back of this book (page 166), you will find a series of templates that will match the tutorials in each chapter. You can trace over them by placing the template against a light source such as a window or a light box. Using a sharp HB pencil, place a page of watercolor paper over it and trace the outlines and details. Otherwise, you can challenge yourself by drawing the template freehand directly onto your watercolor paper.

## Brushes, Paper and Equipment

### Brushes

Apart from the paints themselves, the most vital pieces of equipment in your artist's toolkit are your brushes. A common mistake that beginners make when starting in watercolor is buying a vast quantity of cheap brushes that do not perform well and quickly wear out. A small quantity of brushes that have springy, resilient bristles, are long-lasting and naturally taper to a fine point will serve you much better in the long term.

In my work and for the projects in this book, I recommend using round brushes. They are extremely versatile, enabling you to make a variety of brushstrokes and to paint fine details, such as fur and leaf veins. Some excellent brands are Winsor & Newton™ Sable series brushes, Arteza® brushes, Richard J Oliver brushes and Isabey® brushes.

These are the brushes that I use often and appear in the projects of this book.

## Brush Care and Maintenance

> Always clean out your brushes at the end of each painting session with clean water. This will extend their lives and ensure they stay in pristine condition.

> Make sure that you rinse out the color in the bristles within the ferrule.

> After washing, gently shape the bristles back into their gathered pointed shape and leave to dry.

> Do not leave the brushes standing on their bristles. This will cause them to get damaged and morph out of shape. While the brushes are drying, they should be laid flat horizontally to avoid water dripping down into the bristles, which can cause damage if done repeatedly.

## Paper

In my experience, the quality of the paper can have a huge effect on the results of your painting. There is a wide range of watercolor papers on the market, varying in weight, texture and quality. Ordinary cartridge paper, although good for drawing, is unsuitable for watercolor, as it lacks strength and texture and will buckle, fold and disintegrate, ruining all of your hard work!

Watercolor paper can be bought in singular sheets, but I often buy watercolor blocks, which consist of sheets of paper gummed around the edge on all four sides. When my painting is finished and dry, the top sheet can be separated and taken off by running a palette knife along the edges.

The surface texture of paper is known as the grain or the tooth. Hot-press paper is smooth, with almost no tooth, and is suitable for fine, detailed work. Cold-press paper has a semi-rough surface quality and pronounced tooth, which allows the washes of paint to sink into the surface and allows the painter—especially beginners—to have more control over layering washes.

Paper weight is traditionally measured in two ways—pounds (lbs) or grams per square meter (gsm). For pounds, the figure denotes how much a ream of 500 sheets of a particular paper would weigh if the sheets are cut to its standard size, which for watercolor paper is 22 x 30 inches (56 x 76 cm).

Traditionally, the lightest watercolor paper is 90 pounds (190 gsm) and the heaviest can be up to 400 pounds (850 gsm).

For the majority of my work, I use cold-press paper at 140 pounds (300 gsm). An excellent brand which I use often and would always recommend is ARCHES®.

## Pencils

My preference when drawing the outline and drafts for my paintings is always a sharp, good-quality HB pencil. I recommend always working with a sharp pencil, as it allows you to achieve the neatest, tightest level of detail without the edges appearing muddied.

## Paper Towel

A paper towel is an excellent and useful tool, as it serves many purposes. I use it to soak up excess water from my paintbrush by dabbing it onto a piece that I keep by my side. It can also be used for various "lifting out" techniques, which are used to create luminous highlights.

## Notebook

Although not a necessity, I always carry a tiny notebook or sketchbook with me to jot down notes and ideas that sprout from events and imagery I see around me that I may forget later.

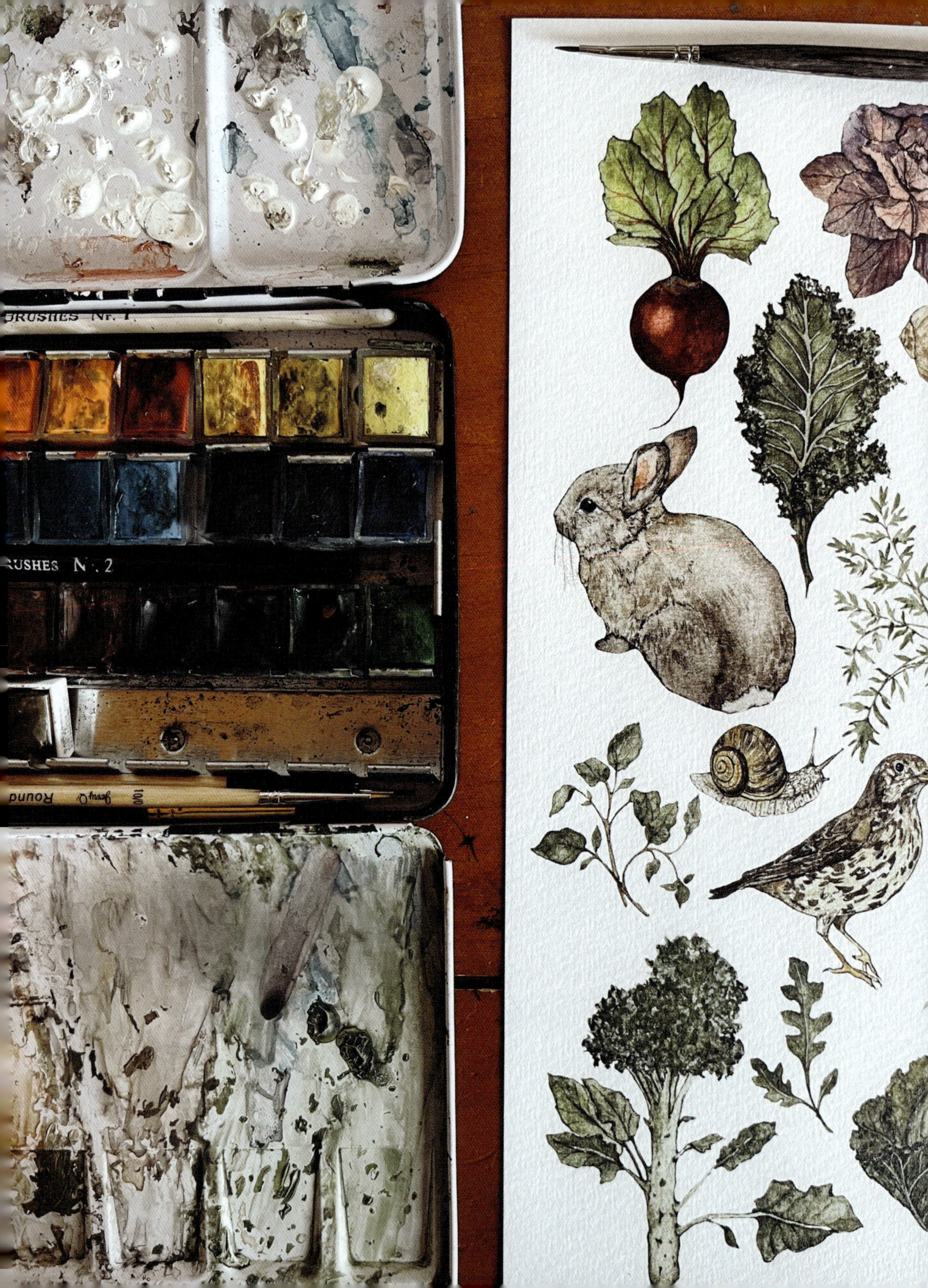

# Paints

Watercolor paint consists of finely ground pigments that are bound together with gum arabic and mixed with glycerin, which acts like a moisturizer. Watercolor paints are available in tubes of thick, moist color and in small blocks called "pans" of semi-moist color. In my own personal work, and for the projects in this book, a pan of watercolors will be used. Tubes of watercolor require a different technique, so I recommend following along with the steps with materials as similar as possible.

Pans are small blocks of semi-moist color that can be bought individually, as well as in specialized boxes with individual slots holding a vast array of colors. The lid opens to form a useful palette to blend and mix colors.

# Mixing Paints

When I first began watercolor painting, I was tempted by the huge range of brilliant colors which were on my palette, and I experimented with trying out new colors and added them to my paintings to see what results they would bring. But after many years of experience and experimentation, I have developed a more refined palette range that I have found achieves the best results.

This color chart references the Winsor & Newton Cotman Watercolour™ palette. You do not have to have the exact matching palette, just try your best to source colors as close as you can.

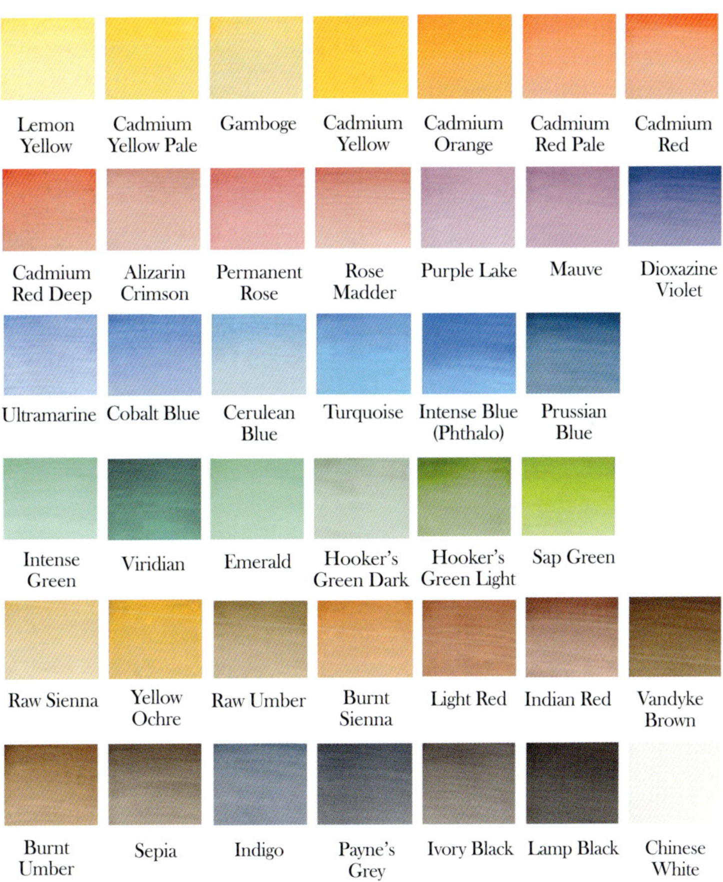

Learning to mix colors and control the saturation of your colors is a vital skill, which you mainly acquire through experimentation and practice. Watercolors are semitransparent, meaning that as they are diluted, their appearance will vastly change.

Tone can also be defined as the degree at which the color is saturated: light saturation, mid saturation and dark saturation.

In this book, I will be referring to three grades of how your paints are diluted: light tone, midtone and dark tone. In the following examples, I mixed various tones of Hooker's green light to show the effects that dilution has on your paint.

### Light Tone

This is a paint solution with the most dilution of water. It will result in a watery consistency and a pale, light saturation of color. This is excellent for creating light shadows and layering washes that cover large areas.

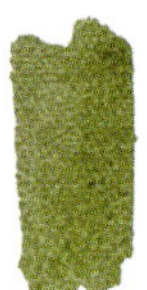

### Midtone

This is a mixture of paint and water that is fluid but not too pale and watery. I would refer to this as a "neutral" mixture, as it is equally not too thick and saturated and not too pale and translucent. This is the basic tone for almost every base layer in my work.

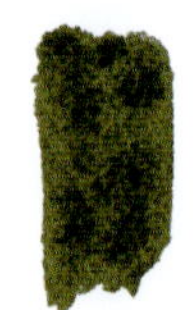

### Dark Tone

This is a highly concentrated solution of paint and water, resulting in a thick, brilliant consistency that gives a matte finish due to less dilution of pigment. This is excellent for painting crisp edges, outlines and fine details such as fur and dark, black pupils.



# Techniques

## Glazing

In the tutorials in this book, you will often see that I refer to the term "glazing." This means covering the area gently with a layer of paint/ water in various degrees of tone, depending on the step.

## Wet-on-Wet

The wet-on-wet technique is a beautiful and expressive one that involves applying each new layer of color while the paper underneath is still damp and not waiting for the earlier layers to dry. This results in the paints spreading naturally together, creating a soft transition with no hard edges or sharp lines. When you drop a new color onto the still wet wash, the weight of the water forces the first color outward, so the colors bleed into one another without actually mixing, causing a natural gradient.

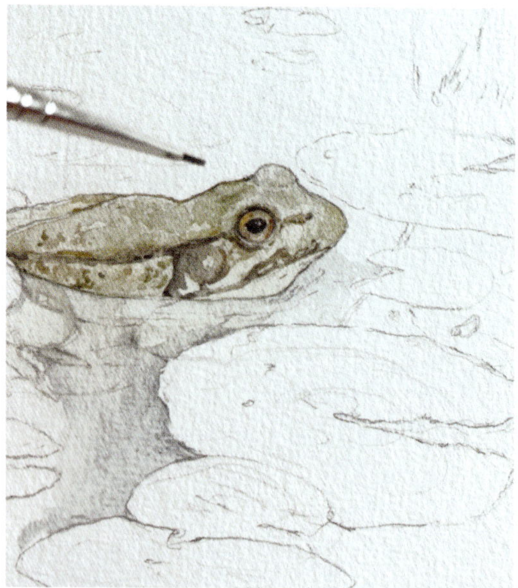

Wet-on-Wet

Another advantage is that this technique can be used to create highlights. As there is a layer of water between the paper and the paint, it is much easier to lift paint off with a clean, damp brush. I will often use the wet-on-wet technique to paint water, as shown in the frog painting on the previous page. I wanted the pond to have a near opaque veil of many different shades of blues and yellows. Glazing the paper first with a clear thin coat of water, then gradually adding layers of light tones of blue, green and yellow helped to achieve a seamless finish like a real pond.

## Wet-on-Dry

This is a classic watercolor technique that I use very often in my work. Paintings are allowed to build up from light to dark by layering successive washes over paint that has been allowed to dry underneath. Wet-on-dry work often leaves crisp, hard edges that form as each layer of color dries. Wet-on-dry work is more predictable and allows for easier control of paint flow.

For the face of the fawn below, especially around the eye, I allowed the base layer of cream to dry before layering on a glaze of earthy tan for the top layer of its coat. This painting technique works very well for creating fur and animal coats because, just like your layers of paint, animals have multiple layers of fur which are various degrees and shades of color sitting atop one another.

## Hard and Soft Edges

The quality and characteristic of the edge is determined by whether you work the paint into damp or dry paper. It can be beneficial to paint a mixture of soft and hard outlines, as this gives your painting more variety. In my work, as I am inspired by drawing and illustration, I find great value in using fine-tipped brushes on dry paper to create hard edges and outlines to define my characters, like the image below of the wild rabbit and the mushroom mouse on the next page. Yet I will equally incorporate soft edges to create seamless blending between paint layers, as seen on the cap of the mushroom (there is a soft gradient of color blending to create light and shadow).

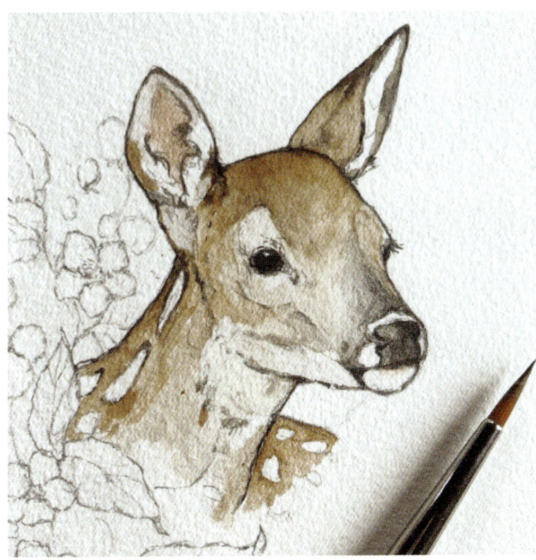

Wet-on-Dry

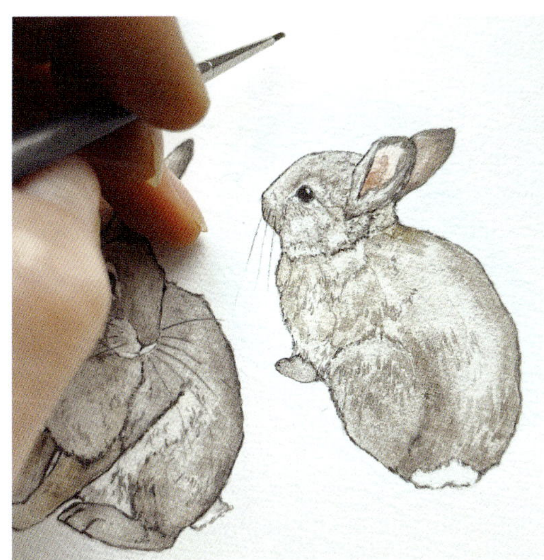

Hard Edges

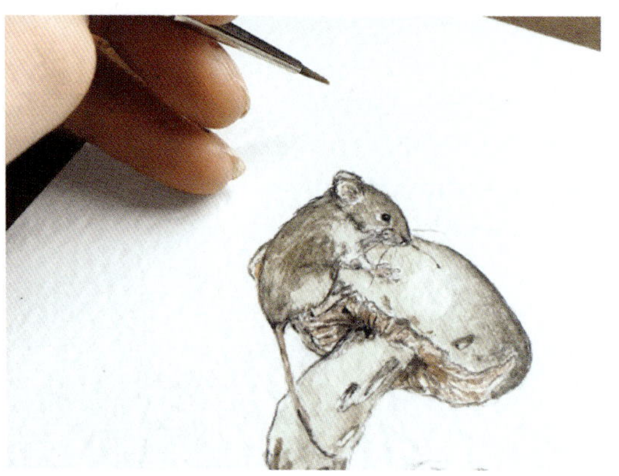

Soft Edges

To soften the edges of your work, you can gently stroke the bristles of a dry, clean brush repeatedly on your paint layer as it is still damp. This will produce an outline that gently fades out rather than stopping sharply and abruptly.

## Drybrushing

Drybrushing is a technique that is used to create pattern and texture. I find that it is an excellent method to suggest the texture of fur, such as the tail of a squirrel or fox. It is done once the background and base layer have been applied and are completely dry. Like all watercolor techniques, drybrushing requires practice. If the paint is too wet, it will go on as a solid wash; if too dry, it will not apply at all. The technique involves a small amount of paint being picked up on the end of a brush that has the bristles slightly splayed to produce a series of fine lines once they are loaded with color. To splay the bristles, I would recommend gently pressing the bristles from the ferrule down against a dry surface as illustrated in the image above to make them spread outward. Unlike hatching or crosshatching in drawing, one color and tone can be laid over another and the brushstrokes can be put on in different directions and the shape—or pattern—of fur growth is suggested.

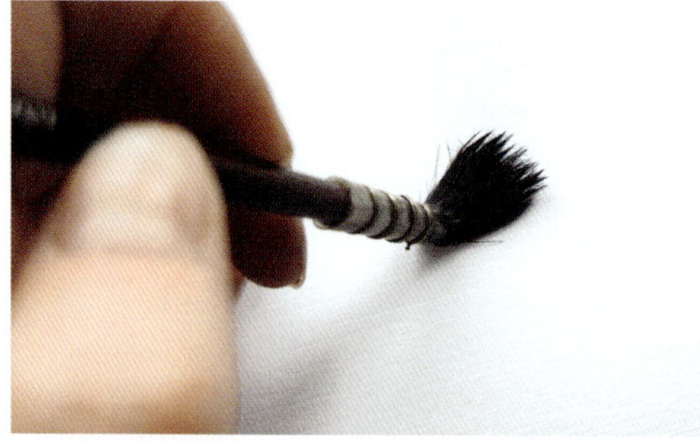

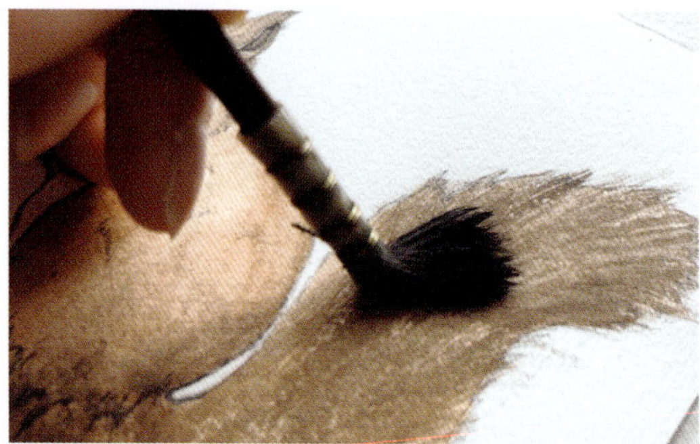

Drybrushing

## Mark Making

In my personal work and for many watercolor artists in general, there is a considerable amount of emphasis placed on the quality of brushstroke, the weight of line that is used and having control over the brush to create neat, tight work. It is a good idea to get familiar with your brushes and the various marks the bristles can make by exercising and practicing with them on a spare piece of paper before any of your work begins.

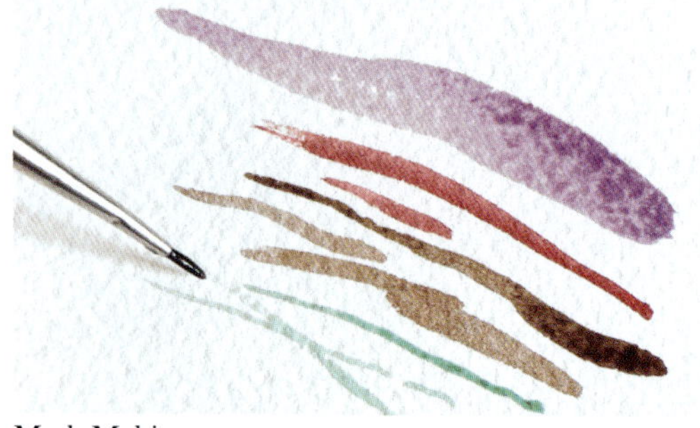

Mark Making

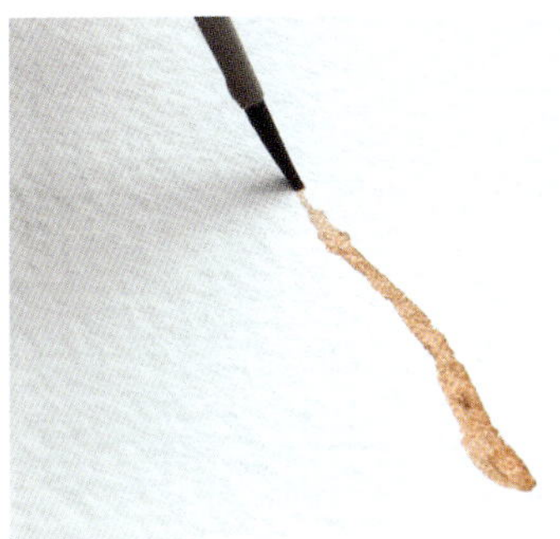
Painting Lines

## Painting Lines

Although watercolor painting may seem like a medium that is unruly and unpredictable, the paint flow is possible to control simply by holding the brush accurately. The more you practice, the more you will see your work becoming more accurate. Holding the brush near the top of the handle gives loose, free stroke lines, while holding the brush tightly close or at the ferrule allows maximum control and can result in tidier brushstrokes.

## Painting Dots

Experiment with painting dots by loading the tip of the brush with paint and lightly applying it to the paper. Practice a variation in the pressure you apply to the paint. Heavier pressure will result in bolder marks, while lighter pressure will result in feathery marks.

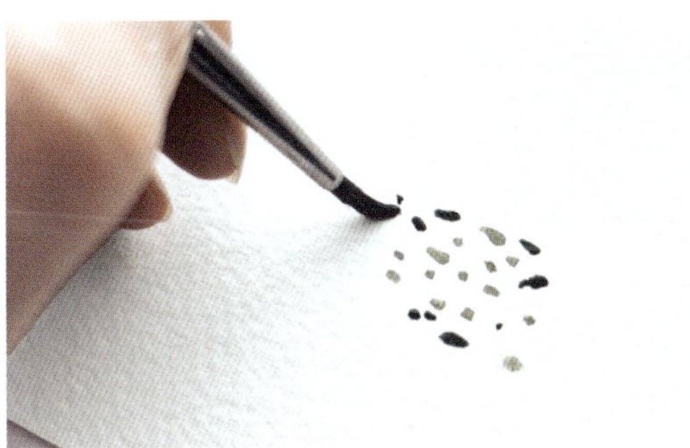
Painting Dots

Splattering is another excellent method of suggesting dotted texture. It is achieved by loading the bristles of the brush with a fluid mixture of paint and flicking or spraying droplets of paint onto the dry surface of paper. I will often use this method when painting the surface of a bird's egg. My favorite way to create the splatter effect is to dip a large brush in paint and to run through the bristles with my finger to release it in miniscule, delicate droplets. A toothbrush can even be used to create a coarser droplet texture!

## Highlights

Highlights represent the points of light that most intensely reflect on the surface of a subject. As watercolor is already quite a luminous medium, it serves as an excellent way to render sparkle and realistic character simply by layering washes of paint. But there are also some easy methods that you can utilize to really emphasize light, giving your paintings a true three-dimensional effect. In my work, highlights are usually created by retaining the natural white color of the paper, by lifting off color or by using another medium such as acrylic or gouache. In the fox painting, you can see various techniques used in one piece: using acrylic for eye highlights, reserving white for the chest and ears and lifting away color on the snout.

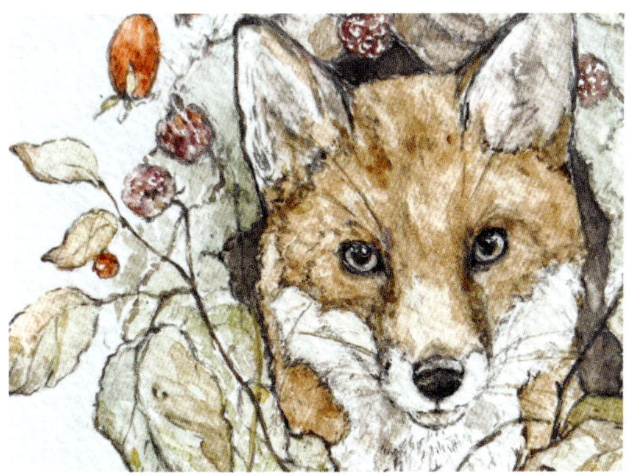
Highlights

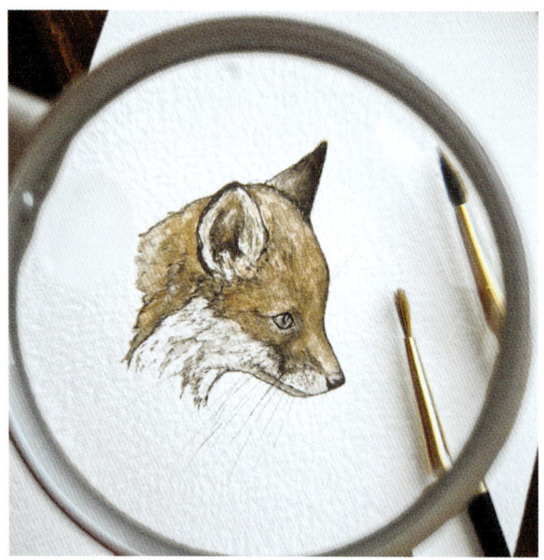

Reserving White

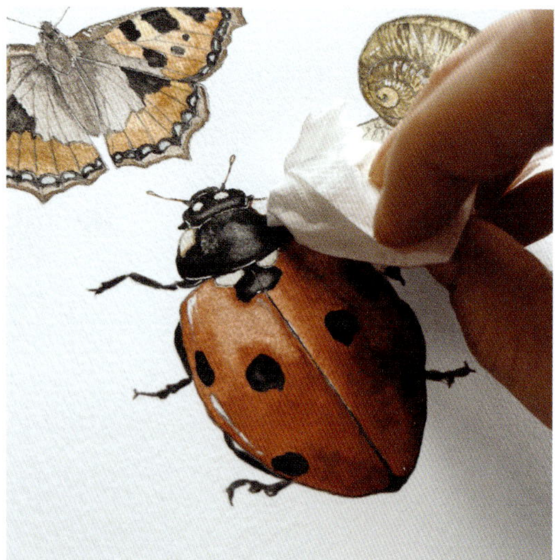

Lifting Out

## Reserving White

The light reflecting from white paper is a very important part of watercolor painting, especially when your paper is of high quality. A very effective way of creating pure, sparkling areas of highlight is to reserve any areas that are to be white by carefully painting around them. You could do this by carefully mapping out your white areas before you begin painting so you know to avoid filling in these areas with a wash of color as you go. I would recommend that, as your paint edges closer to the areas you want to keep white, you paint with a small brush and a controlled hand, holding it close to the ferrule. This ensures that you can keep the most control over the flow of paint and it will not bleed into the "reserved" white areas of blank paper. In the picture, I wanted to keep the front fur on the chest and chin of the fox cub white, so I made sure to keep this area blank and just left the texture and natural color of the paper underneath. Additionally, I used simple short brushstrokes of gray to portray the fur instead of painting in a white or cream base.

## Lifting Out

An alternative method to reserving areas of white or lighter areas is to paint a wash of color and then lift out the sections that you would like to be highlighted.

One way is that, when painting using the wet-on-wet method, you lay down a wash of color. While the paper is still damp, press a dry, clean brush into the sections of paint where you want the color to be lifted. The paint will absorb into the brush, leaving behind a lighter area where the brush was pressed against. This method works wonderfully for small sections and shapes such as lines.

Another method that I apply often is using a paper towel to absorb pigments. I will lay a glaze of color and allow it to dry. Then, I dip my brush into clean water and "wriggle" the bristles in the area I want the color to be lifted. This will agitate the dry color, causing it to be lifted up off of the paper. Then, I will press a piece of paper towel onto this damp section. The color will be absorbed, leaving behind a soft-edge highlight that is very luminous.

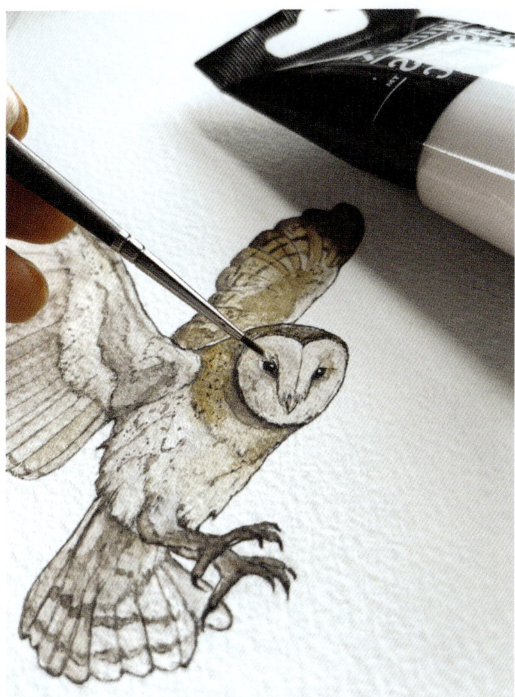
Using Acrylic or Gouache Paint

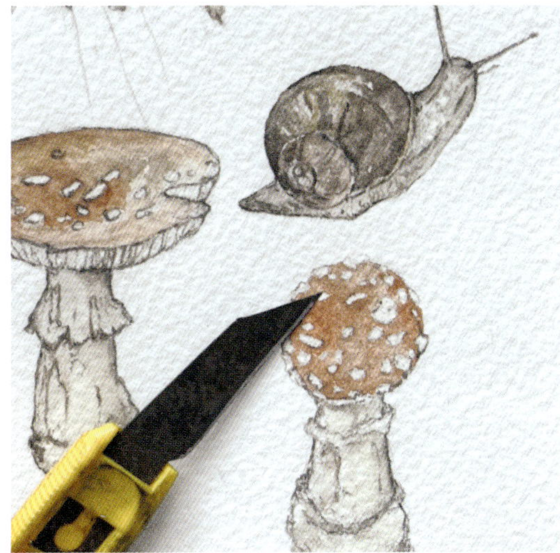
Scratching Out

## Using Acrylic or Gouache Paint

Gouache is the opaque version of watercolor, made by binding the pigments with gum arabic and combining them with white chalk. The paint is thick and dries to an opaque and slightly chalky matte finish, quite different than the delicate transparency of pure watercolor paints. I will often squeeze a tiny blob of either acrylic or gouache paint onto my palette and use a tiny dot painted with the tip of my smallest brush to create a very effective highlight for the eyes of animals, a reflective shine on an insect's wings or a luminous effect on the shell of an acorn. I do have a preference for using acrylic paint, as I find it does have a shinier effect when dry, whereas gouache dries matte and can look dull beside a watercolor wash.

## Scratching Out

This technique, also known as sgraffito, is used to create small, sharp highlights. The most common method involves scraping away at the layer of paint using a sharp tool like a scalpel or card-cutting knife to reveal the bare paper underneath. I don't often use this method as some damage to the painting is inevitable when the surface of the worked paper is scratched, but it can be an interesting way to define the feathers on a bird's wing or the stamen of a flower.

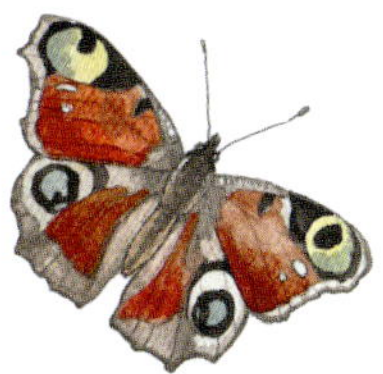

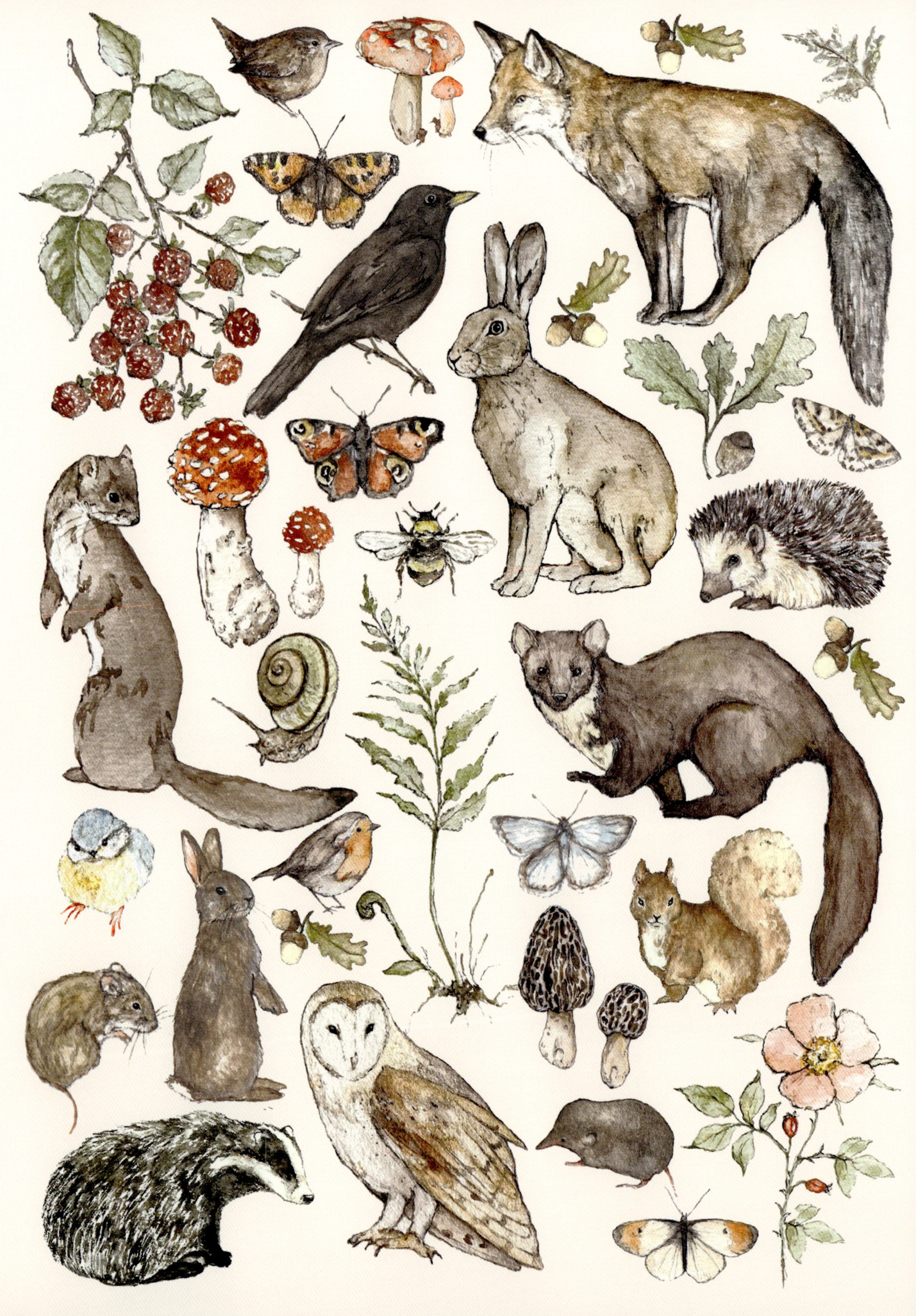

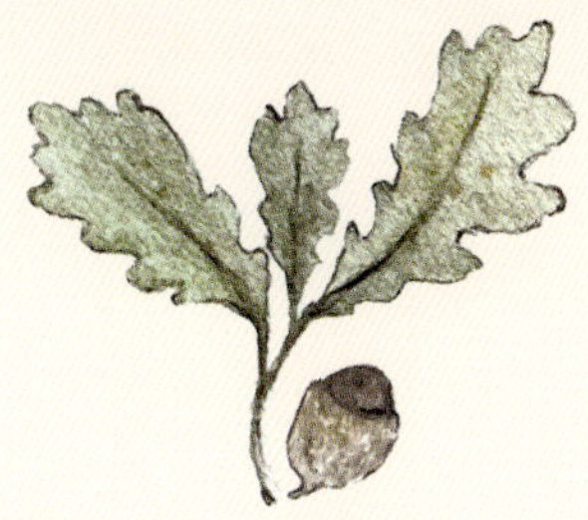

# Fanciful Fauna

We have ventured into the heart of the woodland, where creatures roam amid dappled sunlight and rustling leaves. From the curious nature of the red squirrel (page 35) to the endearing, gentle charm of the hedgehog (page 26), each creature has its own unique personality.

In this chapter, you will learn how to portray the essence of what makes these characters so captivating such as the red fox (page 20), with its sleek body, bushy tail and expressive eyes. We will also focus on capturing the rich earthy hues on the fur of a wild rabbit (page 30), along with the delicate balance of light and shadow and the sense of motion and agility that defines them. Also included are frogs (page 44)—small, agile creatures that present a delightful challenge with their smooth skin, vibrant colors and playful poses. We will explore techniques for creating their glossy appearance, the subtle variations in their greens and browns and the reflections that shimmer on their damp bodies.

And, of course, I had to include one of my personal favorites, the barn owl (page 39). Symbolic of wisdom and mystery, owls are captivating with their large piercing eyes and intricate feather patterns. Learn to portray the texture and detail of their plumage, the depth and intensity of their gaze and the quiet, ethereal presence they command. So, grab your brush and expect to see the paint jump off the page!

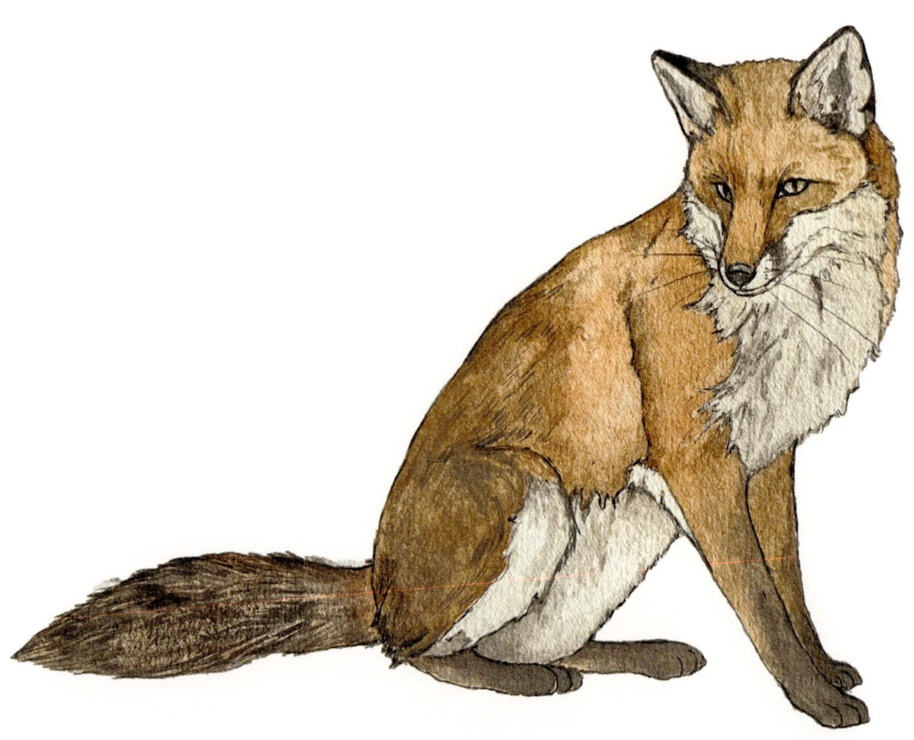

# Red Fox

The red fox is possibly my favorite animal to paint. As a native Irish mammal, it truly holds a special place in my heart, not to mention its amazing palette of fiery orange fur, bushy tail and playful, cunning antics. The fox's resourcefulness and intelligence have gained it a place in the folklore of many cultures, where it is seen as a trickster, outwitting opponents of greater strength. It is even debated that the word "shenanigans," meaning mischief or trickery, may come from the Irish expression "sionnachuighim," meaning "I play the fox" or "I play tricks"!

# Materials Needed

A sheet of cold-press 140-pound (300-gsm) watercolor paper

HB pencil

A piece of paper towel

Brushes

> Size 4

> Size 3/0

> Size 1

> Size 2/0 Isabey

Watercolor paints

> Burnt sienna

> Cadmium orange

> Yellow ochre

> Lamp black

> Chinese white

> Vandyke brown

> Sepia

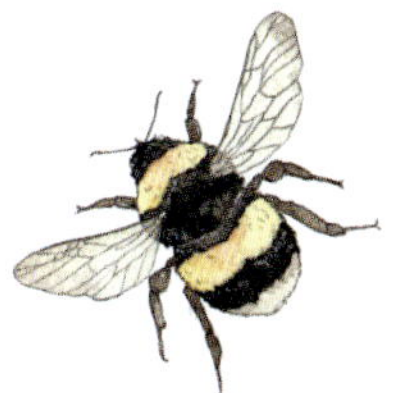

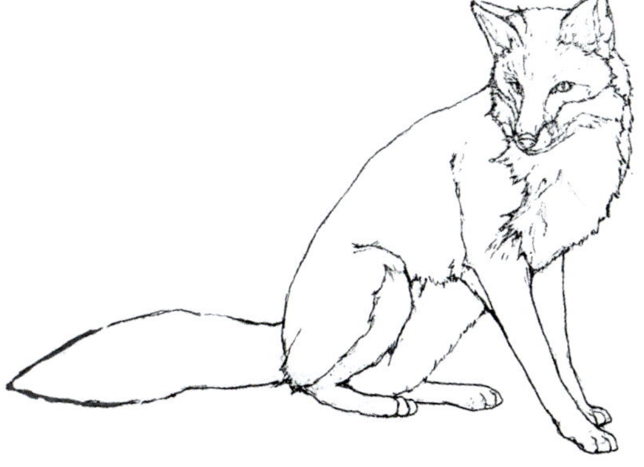

## Step 1: Draw the Outline

Starting on a sheet of cold-press watercolor paper, draw the outline of the fox's body and its fur with a sharp **HB** pencil using the corresponding template located in the back of the book (page 167). Do not worry about the fine bushy details of the tail, as these will be painted later on.

## Step 2: Paint the Base Layer of the Body

To prepare the base layer of color that will fill the head and fur on the fox's body, use a size 4 brush to mix together a midtone solution of burnt sienna with a swirl of cadmium orange hue. We want this color to have a rusty copper hue. Load the paint onto the bristles of the brush and glaze the upper head, outer ears, legs, paws, back and tail with a wash of this warm rusty mixture. Allow the paint to fully dry.

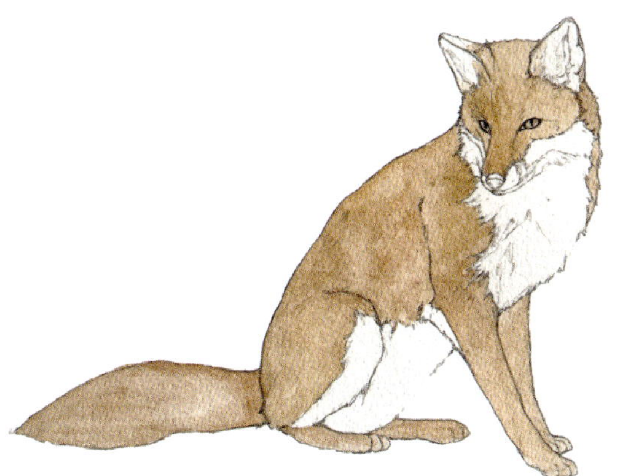

(Continued)

Switch to a size 3/0 brush. Mix a lightly saturated solution of yellow ochre and fill in the iris of both eyes. Allow the paint to fully dry. Clean the bristles of the brush and swirl it into lamp black until the brush is loaded with color. Carefully use the tip to outline the eyes and fill in the pupils with dark inky black.

## Step 3: Paint the Lower Fur Layer

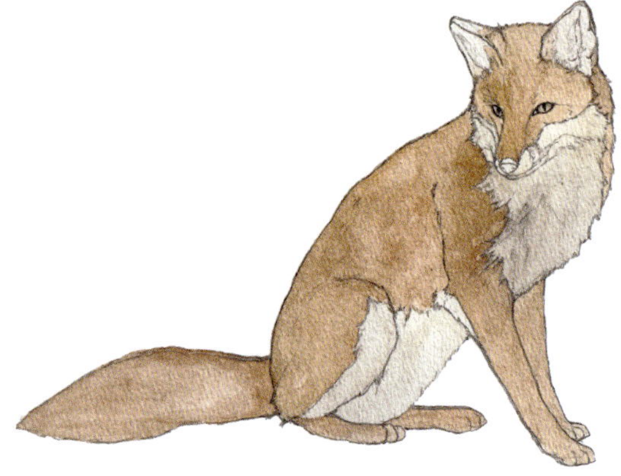

Next, we will paint the fur that runs along the underside of the face, chest and body of the fox. Clean your size 4 brush and mix Chinese white with a tiny dab of Vandyke brown to create a warm cream color. Glaze this color onto the inner ear and the fur on the cheeks, running down onto the front of the chest, the underside of the belly and finally the patch of fur that sits on the bend of the fox's right leg.

While the paint is still damp, mix a lightly saturated sepia using a size 1 brush. Drop this color onto the left-hand side of the fur on the chest and a small dab onto the fur on the fox's right cheek. Let the paint sit and fully dry.

## Step 4: Paint the Face and Upper Chest Fur

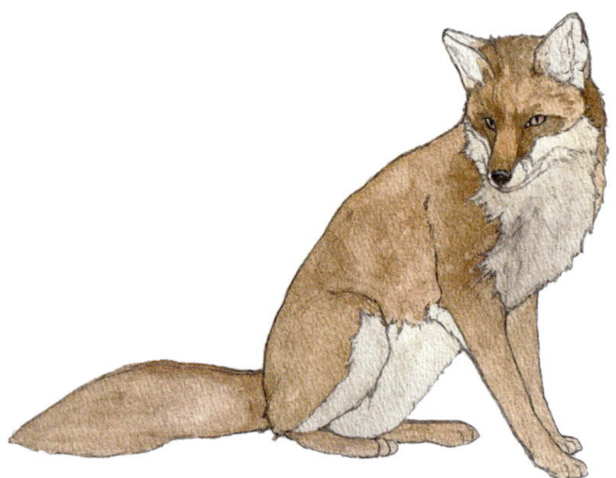

Next, we will begin painting the details on the face. Switch to a size 3/0 brush and mix a lightly saturated solution of burnt sienna with a dab of Vandyke brown. Glaze the sections of the face around the eyes and at the top of the forehead, blending into the bottom of the ears. Use short, quick brushstrokes to fill in the areas of the middle of the head, following the fur growth pattern of curving to the left on the left-hand side and curving to the right on the right-hand side.

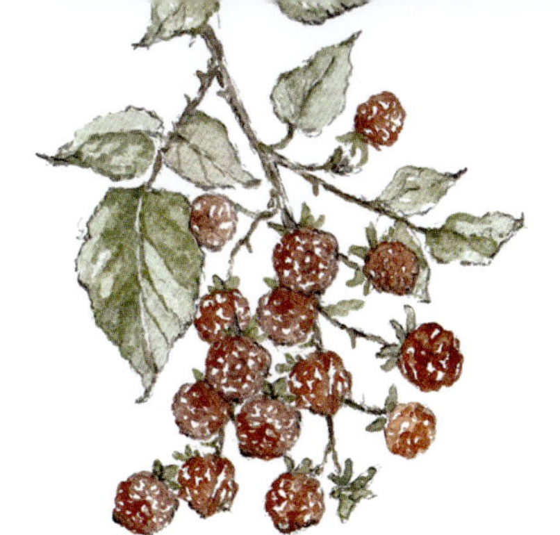

The fur density will be sparser in the middle of the head, so farther spaced brushstrokes are needed versus the top of the forehead and the sections of the cheeks that are on either side of the nose where the fur is more tightly packed together. Add a layer of the dark copper paint to the fur on the right-hand side of the fox's head below the ear.

Clean the brush and load the bristles with a midtone saturation of lamp black to create a gray hue. Fill in the entire nose with this color, and as the paint is drying, add more lamp black to the gray solution to deepen the color to true black. Fill in the front of the nose with this black mix, leaving a strip of gray at the top as a highlight.

## Step 5: Paint the Fine Facial Features

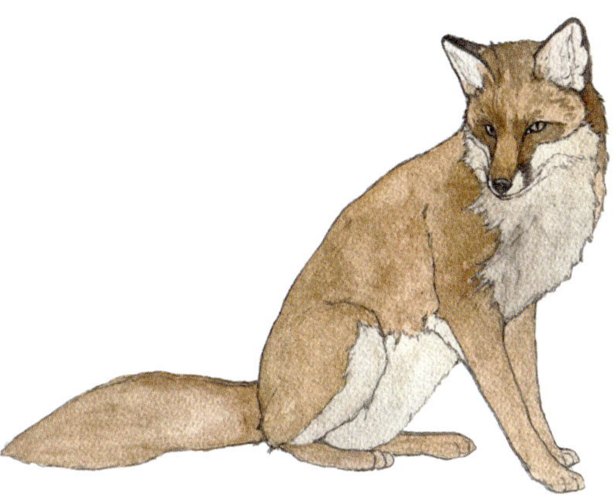

With the same midtone mixture of lamp black we used to darken the front of the nose, use the tip of the size 3/0 brush to trace down either side of the bridge of the nose, extending the black fur outward onto the edge of the mouth on the right-hand side in a small dark patch. Trace along the outlines of the outer ears and follow the contours of the outlines of the orange fur on the face to create greater definition.

## Step 6: Add Shadows and Depth to the Lower-Body Fur

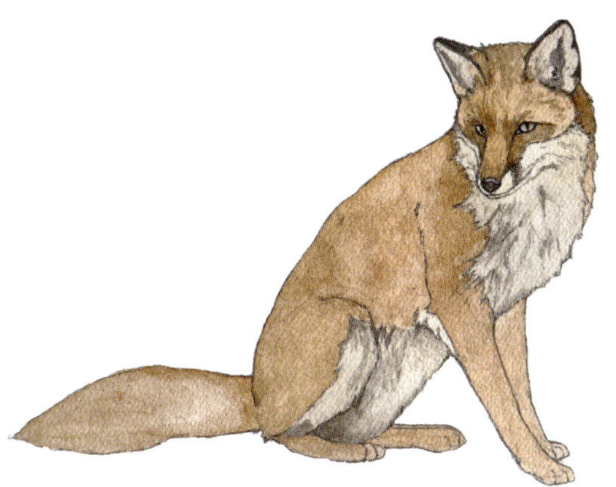

Using the same size 3/0 brush, mix a lightly saturated solution of lamp black and water. This color should be a pale gray. Load the bristles of the brush with this mixture and fill in the center of the inner ears.

(Continued)

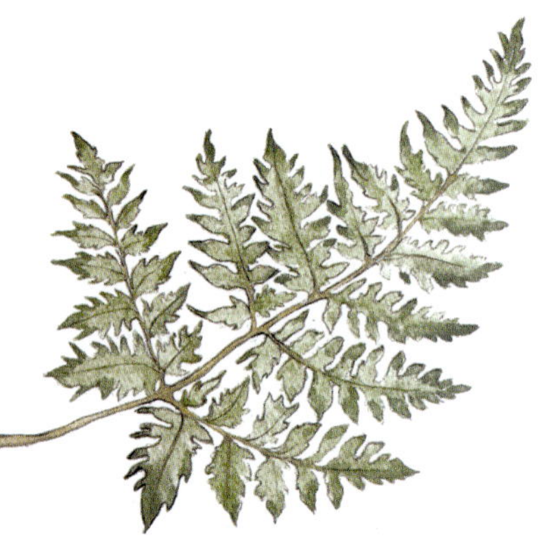

Next, we will give the fur depth and shadow. Using the same brush and pale gray hue, use short, quick and sparse brushstrokes to paint deeper tones of fur on the right cheek. Add a concentration of these strokes along the left-hand side of the fox's chest fur and down the left-hand side of the fur on the lower belly.

Where the lower belly meets the foot, create a layered, dense patch of brushstrokes for a deeper shadow where less light is falling in this fold. Finally, add a sparse patch of short gray brushstrokes to the top of the fox's bent leg. Allow the paint to fully dry.

## Step 7: Add Depth to the Upper-Body Fur

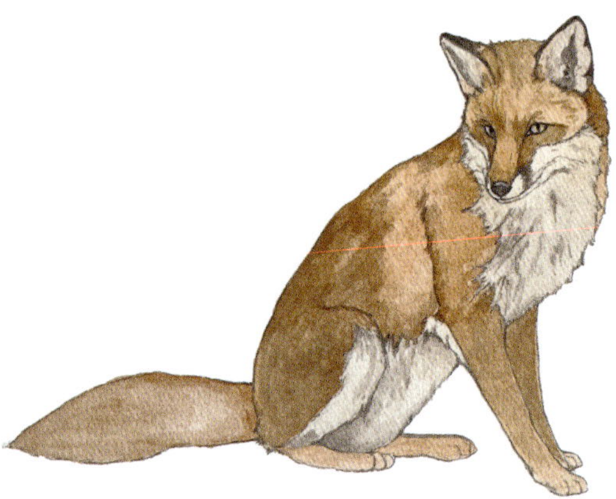

To prepare the color that will be used for the shadows on the fox's upper-body fur, mix a lightly saturated solution of burnt sienna with a dab of Vandyke brown using a size 4 brush. This color will be a warm, deep rust color. Glaze a wash of this hue over the entire curve of the spine, extending into the entire lower back and orange fur on the leg. Add a layer of this color to the legs from the very top of the arm, extending downward to the top of the paws.

## Step 8: Add the Darkest Layers of Fur

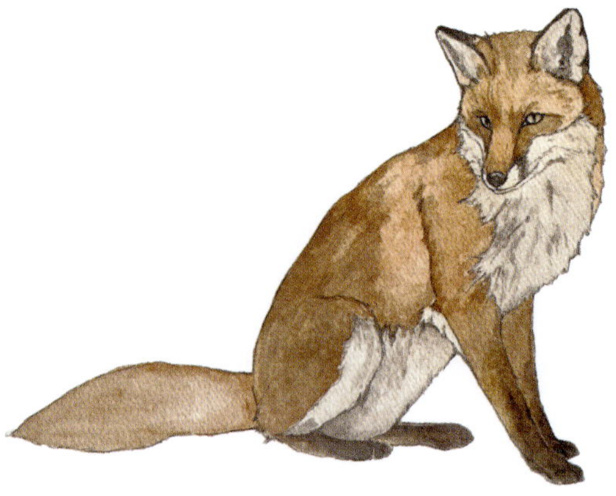

For the darkest layers of fur, use a size 1 brush to mix a midtone solution of sepia. Load the color onto the brush and fill in the front and back paws, extending the paint softly upward along the front legs along the right-hand side. Clean and dry the bristles of the brush and gently stroke the edges of the brown layer we just painted on the front leg upward to soften the edges and allow the dark color to blend seamlessly into the rusty orange fur below it.

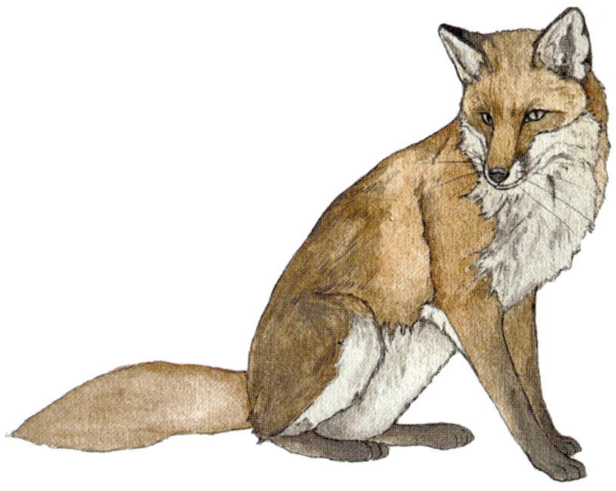

## Step 9: Create Definition on the Fur and Face

Using a size 3/0 brush, mix a midtone solution of sepia with a tiny dab of lamp black to create a deep, rich brown color. Load the tip of the brush with this mixture, and starting at the center of the back, begin to paint in short, quick brushstrokes traveling downward along the contours of the back and the hind leg, filling the patch of rusty orange fur on the back leg with a sparse patch of wiry, dark brown brushstrokes. Use the same brush and dark brown color to outline the contours of the front and back legs, using short, quick brushstrokes to re-create a furry texture. With this dark brown mixture, use the tip of the brush to carefully trace in the whiskers on either side of the cheek.

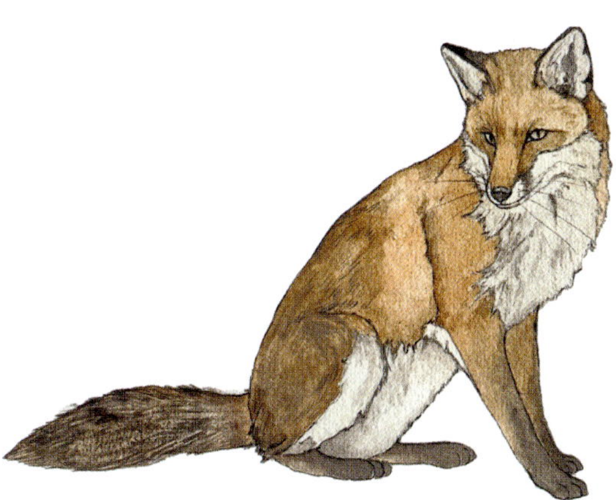

## Step 10: Paint the Tail

Mix a heavily pigmented solution of sepia with a swirl of lamp black to create a dark, rich brown color. Take a dry size 2/0 Isabey brush and swirl the bristles on a piece of dry paper towel. This will separate the bristles outward. Dip the tip of the dry brush into the dark brown solution and very lightly brush the tips of the bristles along the shape of the tail. As the solution is going to be quite dry, you will need to dip and brush repeatedly to build up texture and color on the paper, but this will give a very dry and coarse "bushy" effect. Build up layers of dry color toward the base of the tail where it meets the body. The red fox is now complete!

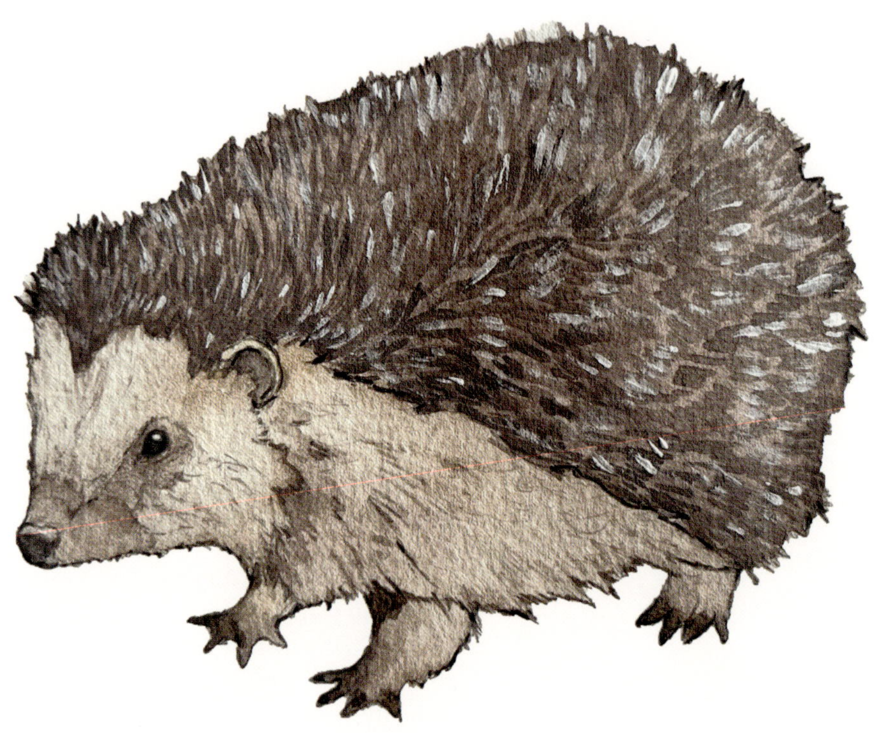

# Hedgehog

Hedgehogs hold a special place in my heart. Even from childhood, their adorable quills and inquisitive expression have been so endearing to me. Early memories of mine are of a family of hedgehogs nesting, year after year, in my grandmother's garden! They are also a joy to capture through painting. All you need is a few repeated delicate brushstrokes and suddenly their essence—spiky, innocent and precious—is on the paper!

# Materials Needed

A sheet of cold-press 140-pound (300-gsm) watercolor paper

HB pencil

Brushes

> Size 4

> Size 3/0

> Size 0

Watercolor paints

> Vandyke brown

> Lamp black

> Sepia

Acrylic white

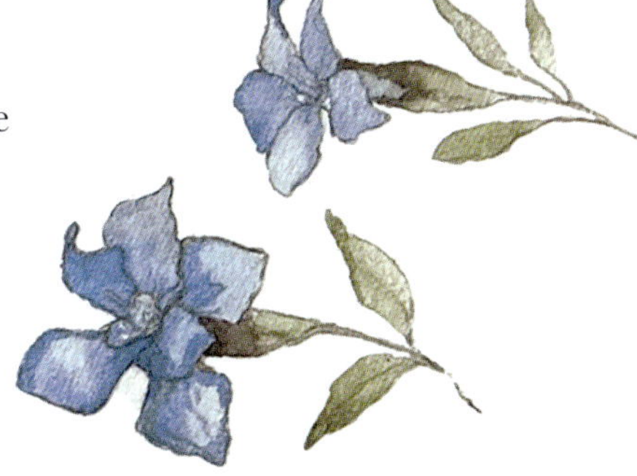

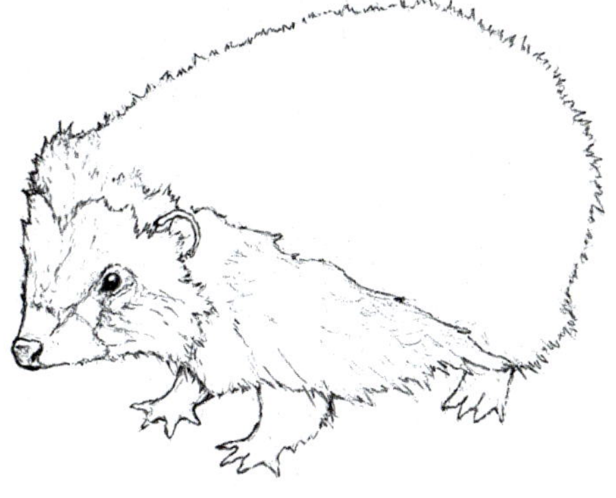

## Step 1: Draw the Outline

Starting on a sheet of cold-press watercolor paper, draw the hedgehog's outline with a sharp HB pencil using the corresponding template located in the back of the book (page 167). Don't worry about filling in the spikes on the body, we will do this later on with paint.

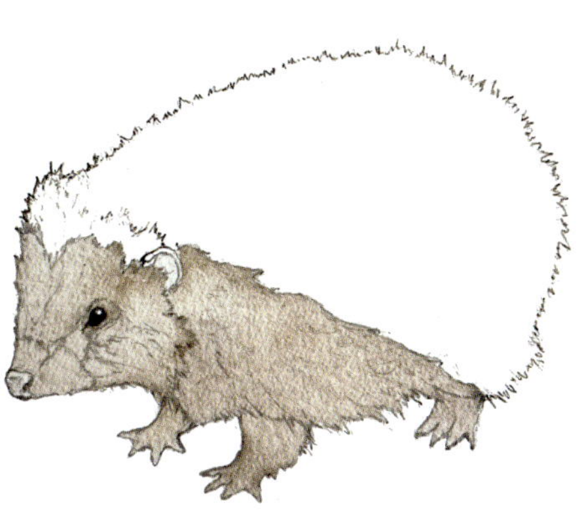

## Step 2: Paint the Body

Using a size 4 brush, prepare your base color by mixing a thin, diluted wash of Vandyke brown and fill in the entire lower body of the hedgehog. While this base layer is still damp, we want to create slight shadowed accents. We will achieve this by layering the same wash of paint on top of our base. Loading your brush with the same wash, layer over the base just above the eye and at the very edge of the cheek, the hedgehog's left paw and right beside the ear. Allow the paint to fully dry.

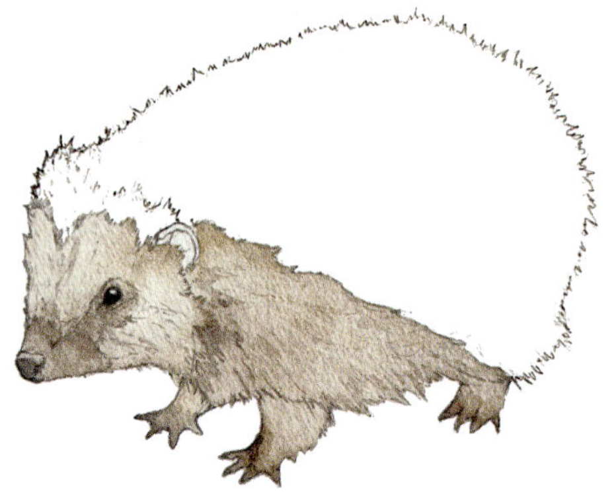

# Step 3: Add the Details

Dip a clean size 3/0 brush into water and then swirl it lightly into lamp black until we have a diluted pale gray-tone solution. Fill in the entire nose section using this wash and allow it to fully dry. We now want to darken this initial solution, so swirl your brush back into lamp black and mix into your diluted solution on your palette until it turns from gray to fully black but still thin in its texture. We will add this solution to the tip of the nose; the initial gray gives the appearance of a highlight.

Now, we will add further shadows to the hedgehog's body. Switch to a clean size 0 brush and make a thin dilution of sepia. Concentrate this wash around the eye, and, bringing it downward to the snout, soften its application as it reaches the tip of the nose. Using just the tip of your brush, create fur on the body by painting very short, straight, sparse tilted lines. These lines do not need to be perfect, as the paint wash is thin. We are creating the appearance of slight texture rather than fine details.

To create shadows, paint the same wash on the tips of the paws and just under the cheek. Allow the paint to fully dry. Then, add another layer of this pale wash to the tips of the paws and just at the top of the snout, being careful to keep the edges softened.

# Step 4: Paint the Upper Body

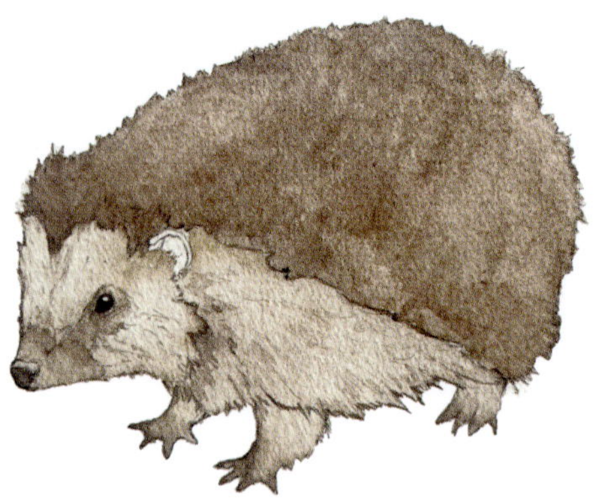

Using a clean size 4 brush, prepare the base color for the upper body of the hedgehog. Create a midtone solution of Vandyke brown. We do not want the consistency of the wash to be so thick and highly pigmented that it does not spread easily, but equally we do not want it extremely pale and almost translucent from water. Fill in the entire upper-body section with this midtone wash of brown and allow it to fully dry.

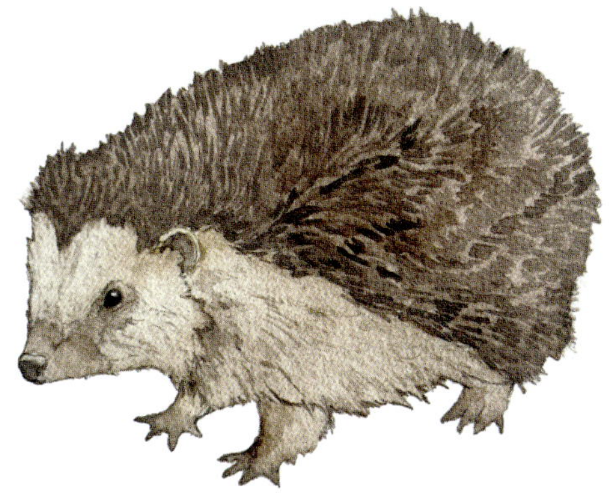

# Step 5: Create the Spikes

Now this is the fun part! Prepare your paint by swirling a clean, wet size 0 brush in sepia. We want this to be a heavily pigmented solution, so load more paint onto the brush versus water. Using short brushstrokes that extend outward and upward, fill in the upper body of the hedgehog. I like to begin at the ear and paint the spikes in a "V" pattern from that point. As the paint will be thick, you may find that your brush is getting dry quickly, so just repeat the beginning of the step. Just ensure that the paint is thick in consistency, but if some spikes appear darker than others due to repeated rounds of mixing, that is fine! This will add more dimension to your hedgehog. Finally, using a clean size 3/0 brush, mix a light-tone solution of sepia and water and fill in the hedgehog's ear. While the paint is still damp, swirl your brush back into sepia, and drop this color on the left-hand side of the inner ear, creating a darker shadow. Soften the edges of this color by lightly blending the paint outward to the right hand side of the inner ear. Allow the paint to dry.

# Step 6: Add the Final Details

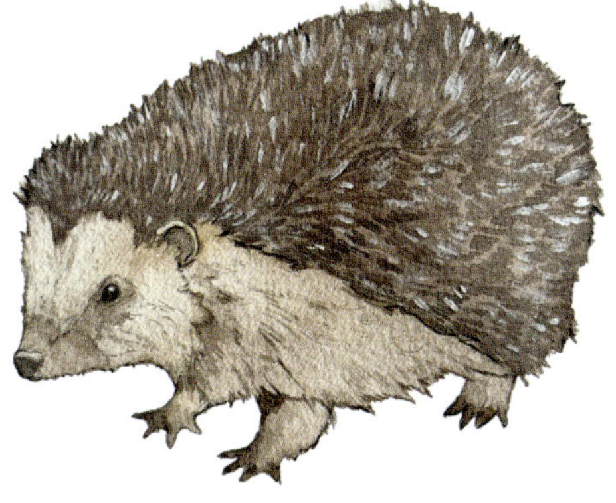

Put a pea-size amount of acrylic white paint onto your palette and dip a clean size 3/0 brush into it. Using the tip of the brush, paint short, straight lines that will act as highlighted spikes on the top of the body. These can be sparse and we also do not want to fully paint the entire space, just a top "coating" of spikes to add a luminous effect.

Clean the same brush with water and mix a midtone dilution of sepia. Use the tip of the brush to fill in shadows at the tips of the paws and at the top left-hand side of the hedgehog's left paw. We want to keep the edges of the shadows soft, so gently blend the paint outward as it goes from the tips of the paws upward. The hedgehog is now complete, well done!

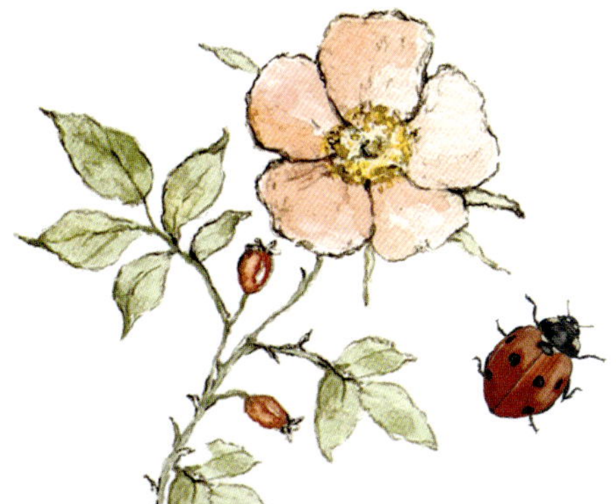

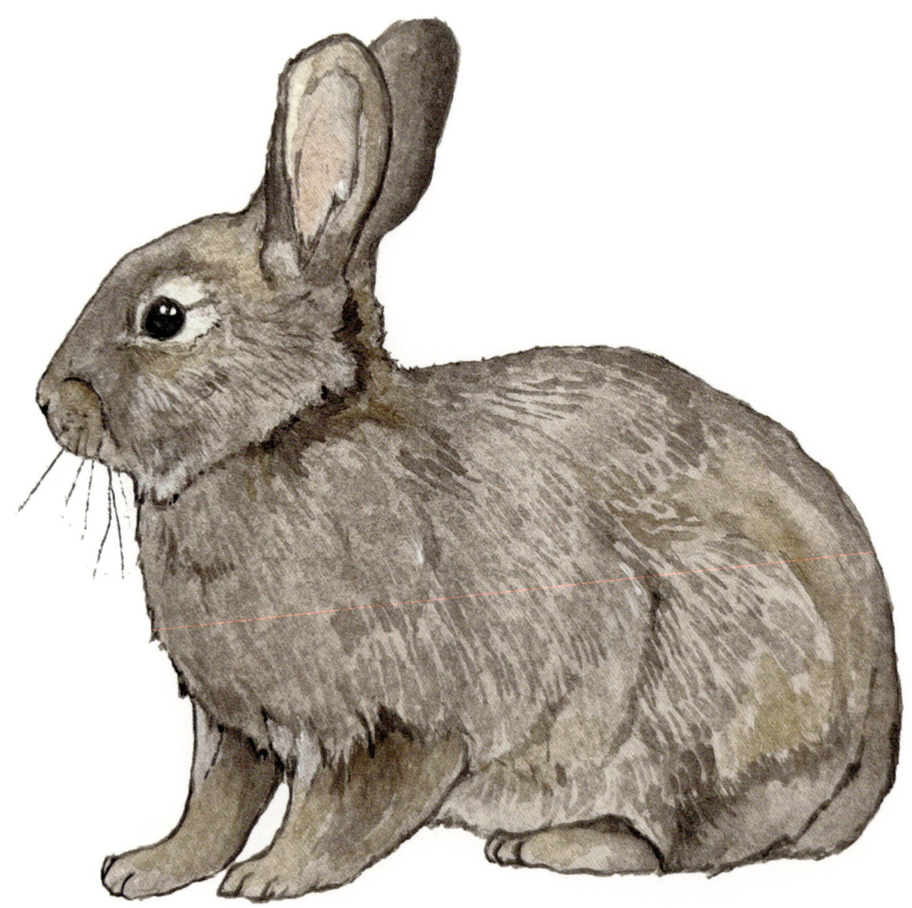

# Wild Rabbit

Wild rabbits are one of the first subjects I ever explored when I began my journey in illustration. I have memories of the innocence and curiosity of soft rabbits appearing in the illustrated pages from my favorite childhood books. And now as an adult, they embody a symbol of both graceful simplicity in their color and nature but also of an enchanting, untamed spirit existing in a landscape.

# Materials Needed

A sheet of cold-press 140-pound (300-gsm) watercolor paper

HB pencil

Brushes

> Size 4

> Size 1

> Size 3/0

Watercolor paints

> Sepia

> Raw sienna

> Vandyke brown

> Light red

> Lamp black

Acrylic white

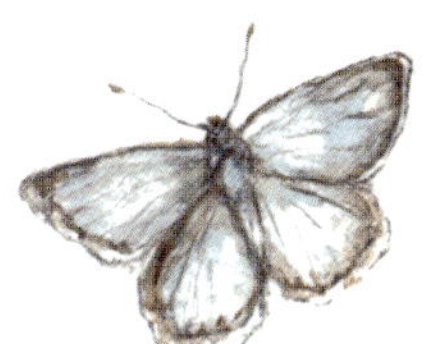

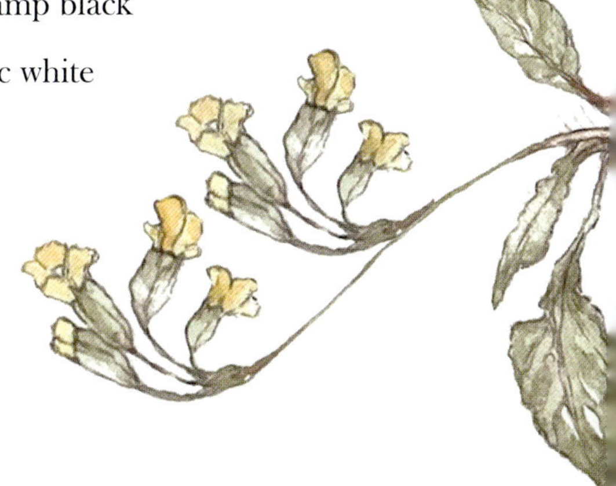

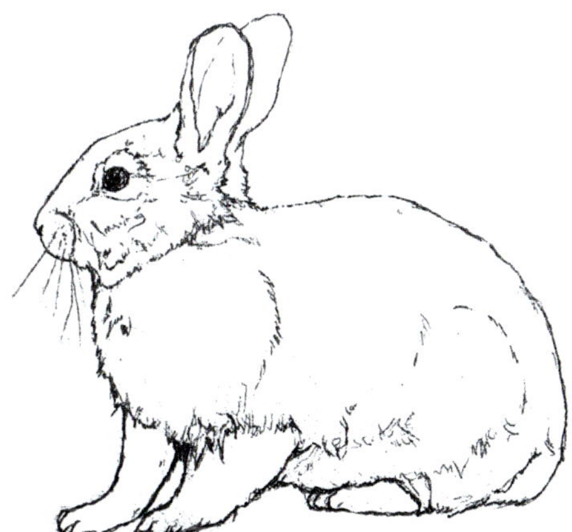

## Step 1: Draw the Outline

Starting on a sheet of cold-press watercolor paper, draw the rabbit's outline and its fur with a sharp HB pencil using the corresponding template located in the back of the book (page 167). Fill in the eye (we will deepen this with black paint later) and make sure to leave two dots for a highlight.

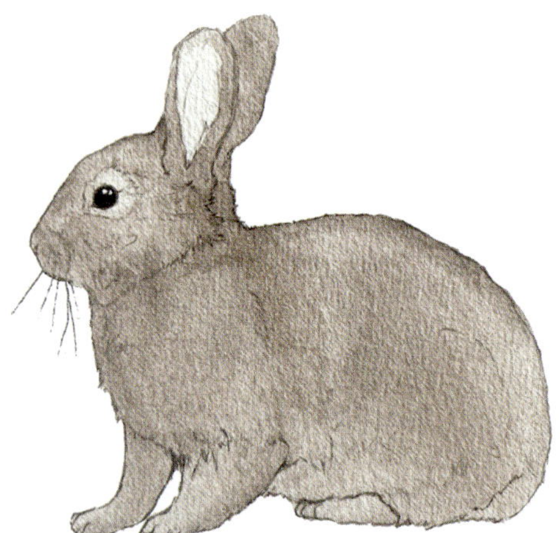



## Step 2: Paint the Base Layer

For the base layer of the rabbit's color, use a size 4 brush to mix a light-tone solution of sepia. We want this color to be a pale, watery cool-tone brown. Glaze this color over the entire rabbit and allow the paint to fully dry. Next, add another layer of the same glaze to the rabbit, but omit color by avoiding the fur around the eye and the inner ear. Allow the paint to fully dry, then finally add one more layer of the same glaze to the fur at the back of the neck and along the curve of the back.

## Step 3: Add Color to the Fur

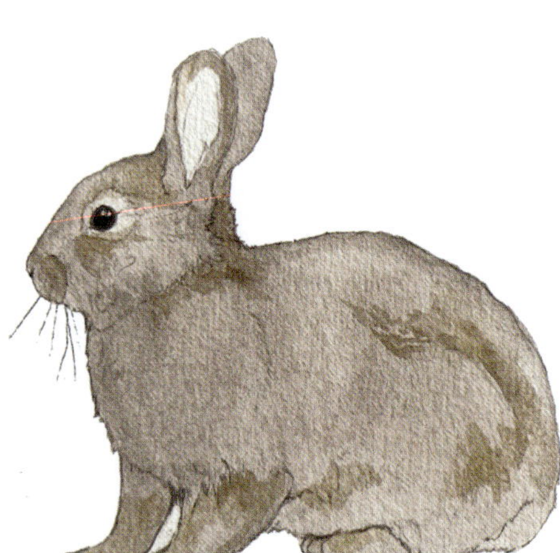

To prepare the color that will be used to create the fur's depth, use a size 1 brush to mix a midtone solution of raw sienna with a dab of Vandyke brown for a warm caramel color. Using short, quick brushstrokes, paint on layers of this color, creating a buildup of a fur texture under and above the eye, on the nose and cheek, along the upper curve of the left ear, on the fur at the back of the neck, along the curve of the leg, on the upper left paw, on the lower-body fur and on the left foot. Allow the paint to fully dry, then add another layer of these short, quick brushstrokes using the tip of the brush along the fur at the back of the neck, the curve of the leg and the fur on the upper left front paw.

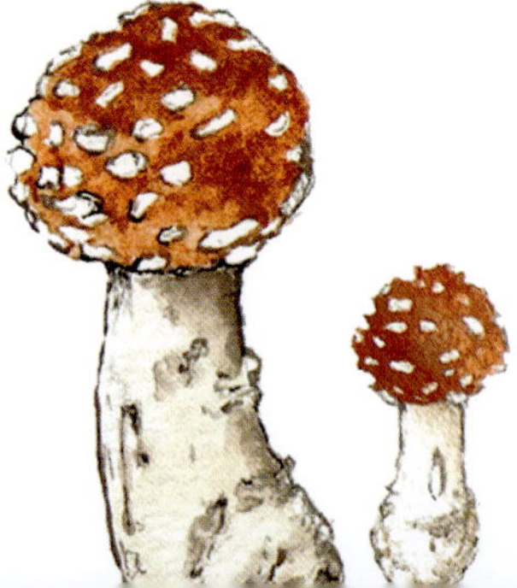

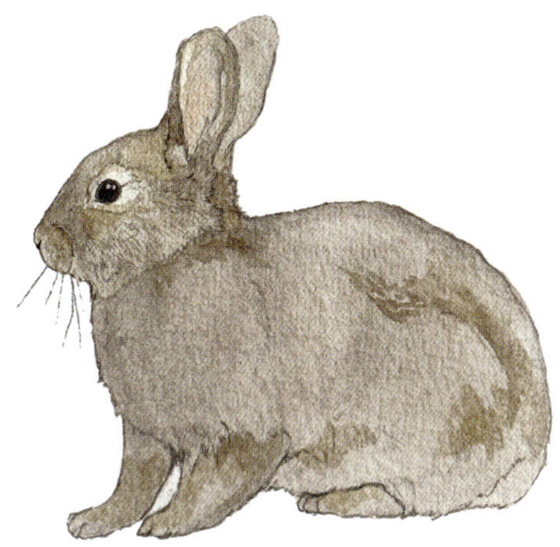

## Step 4: Add Depth to the Face

For the color that will fill the rabbit's inner ear, mix a light-tone solution of light red using a size 3/0 brush to create a watery, pale pink. Glaze this color inside the inner ear of the rabbit, softening the edges of the paint to blend seamlessly with the brown under layer. Allow the paint to fully dry.

To create the fur on the face, use a size 3/0 brush to mix a midtone solution of sepia and load the color onto the bristles. Hold the brush at the ferrule so you can have the most control over your brushstrokes. Beginning at the nose, paint short, delicate brushstrokes that follow the natural growth pattern of the fur on the face. The fur at the front of the face is going to be denser and more compact, so build up layers of brushstrokes that grow from the nose, gradually becoming sparser and more separated as they reach toward the edges of the cheeks. Load another layer of paint onto the brush and glaze this solution onto the left-hand side of the outer ear.

## Step 5: Add Depth to the Body

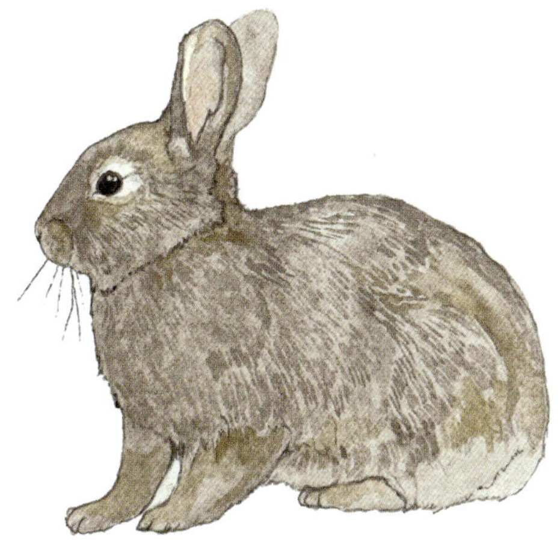

We will use the same size 3/0 brush and method of short, delicate and feathery brushstrokes to create the fur on the body. Load the brush with the midtone sepia mixture and fill in the body with these short hairs, following the curvature of the rabbit's back and growth pattern of fur moving downward to the feet. The density of fur along the back will be thicker, so add another layer of brushstrokes from the fur at the back of the neck flowing downward to the tail. As you will be reloading your brush many times, natural differences in the weight of the color will begin to appear, which will give the fur a very natural gradient.

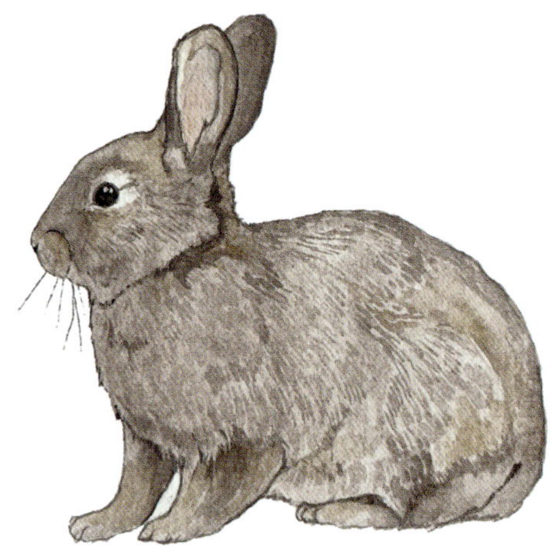

# Step 6: Create Shadows

To create a shadow layer that will give a lot of depth to the rabbit, mix a midtone solution of sepia with a hint of lamp black. We want this hue to be a dark, rich brown and not a matte black, so only a miniscule amount of black is needed. Using a size 1 brush, glaze this color along the outer left and right ears and along the fur at the back of the neck on the left-hand side. Gently fill in the front of the face using short, feathery brushstrokes along the bridge of the nose, around the cheek and above the eye. Paint along the curve of the back to the bottom of the tail and along the fur at the edge of the hind leg. Finally, using the same short brushstroke method, paint along the right-hand side of each foot, softening the brushstrokes as they reach the bottom where the foot flattens.

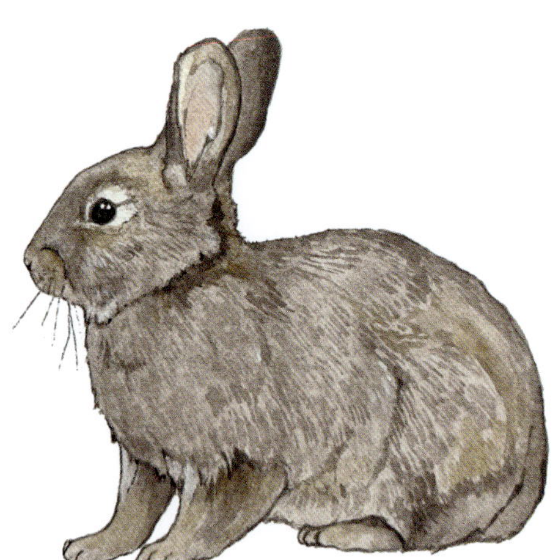

# Step 7: Add the Final Details

Using a clean size 3/0 brush, mix a dark-tone solution of lamp black and load it onto the brush. Use the tip of the brush to fill in the pupil with this thick black color. Use the tip of the brush to trace the lines of the whiskers.

Finally, squeeze a small amount of acrylic white onto your palette, and using a clean size 3/0 brush, paint in two tiny dots on the upper right-hand side of the eye's pupil for a subtle luminous highlight.

Load the tip of the brush again with acrylic white and paint in highlights of fur using short, quick brushstrokes on the left-hand side of the lower cheek, the upper left-hand side of the right and left foot, along the outline of the inner ear and the fur on the lower midsection of the body, where it sits on top of the back foot. The rabbit is now complete, great job!

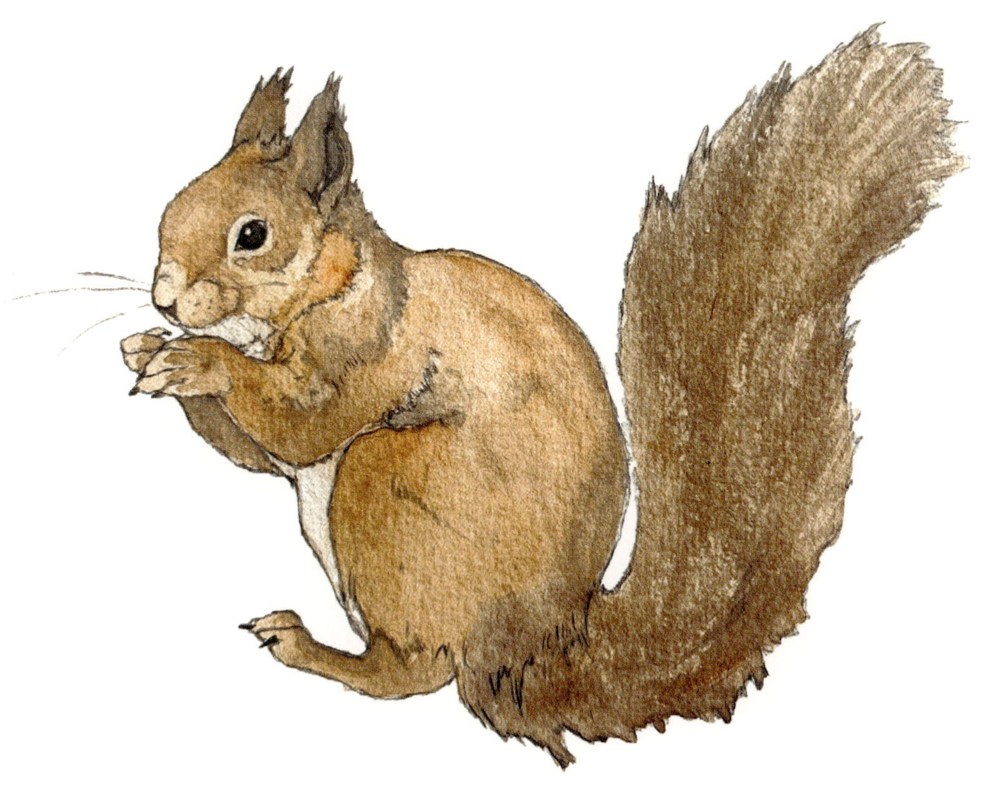

# Red Squirrel

I love squirrels for their playful antics and endearing curiosity. Watching
them dart around with boundless energy, leaping from branch to branch with
agility, never fails to bring a smile to my face! Their bushy tails also give a
wonderful opportunity to practice some dry-on-dry painting techniques.
You'll find that with just a few simple tricks, you will discover how
easy it is to create dense, realistic-looking fur!

# Materials Needed

A sheet of cold-press 140-pound (300-gsm) watercolor paper

HB pencil

A piece of paper towel

Brushes

> Size 4

> Size 0

> Size 3/0

> Size 2/0 Isabey

Watercolor paints

> Burnt sienna

> Burnt umber

> Cadmium orange

> Vandyke brown

> Chinese white

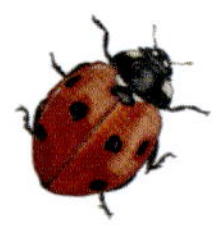

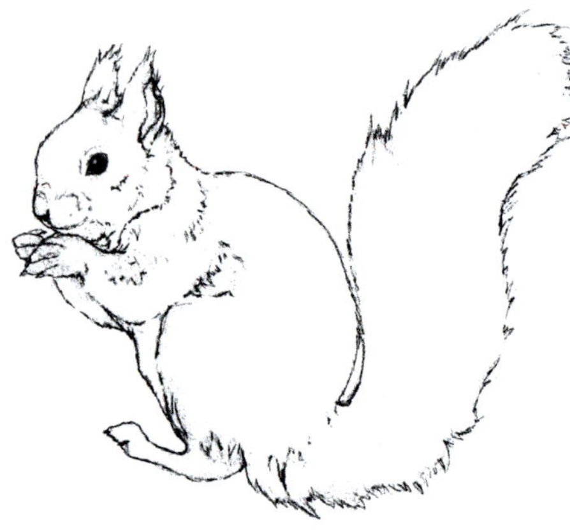

## Step 1: Draw the Outline

Starting on a sheet of cold-press watercolor paper, draw the squirrel's outline and its bushy fur with a sharp **HB** pencil using the corresponding template located in the back of the book (page 167). Do not worry about the fine bushy details of the tail, as these will be painted later on.

## Step 2: Paint the Body

Using a size 4 brush, mix a simple light-tone solution of burnt sienna. We want this to act as a thin glaze that is not too deep in color, so mix enough water so the color is not overly saturated. Paint the squirrel's entire body, head, tail and paws using this mixture. While the glaze is still damp on the paper, get a tiny dab of burnt sienna on your brush and softly paint right at the base of the body where it meets the tail, the cheek and where the arm of the squirrel bends, softening the edges of the paint so there are no hard edges. Once dry, it will blend seamlessly.

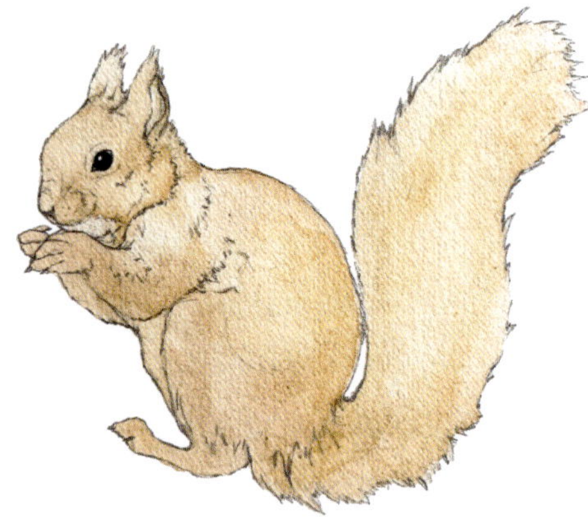

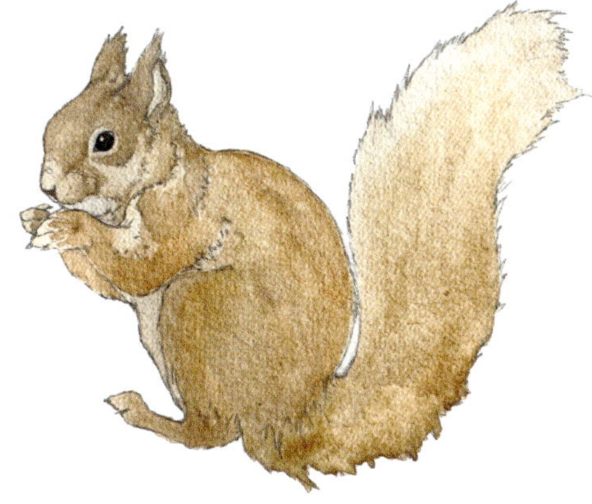

# Step 3: Add Layers to the Body

Using the same size 4 brush, create a midtone solution of burnt sienna, but add a slight dab of burnt umber to deepen the sienna and create a darker tone. We want this mix to act as one to two shades deeper than our initial body layer from step 2, so only a small amount of burnt umber is needed. We want this to be a deep burnt orange rather than a brown. Softly paint this glaze at the top of the head, around the eye, at the front of the paws, down along the bottom side of the arms, along the entire back and left foot and the bottom to midsection of the tail. Leave a slight space between where the neck and body meet and the lower cheek, as we want the base layer to peek through.

Allow the paint to fully dry on the page, and then swirl your brush back into your deep orange mixture. Add another layer to the bent left arm, the bottom of the tail where it is furry at the edges, the top of the back and the top of the head extending up to the points of the ears. Make sure to soften the edges so they blend and leave a seamless depth to these darkened areas.

# Step 4: Add Pops of Color

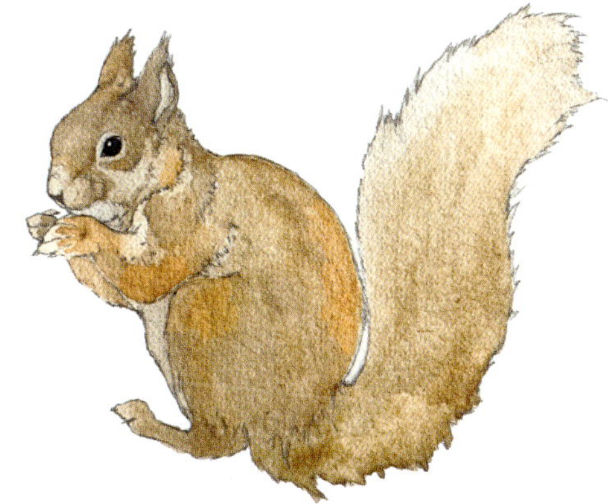

Using a size 0 brush, mix a midtone solution of cadmium orange hue with a touch of burnt sienna. We want this color to be sunny but still belonging to the same family of "burnt"-looking tones. Gently paint a layer of this mixture on the squirrel's right ear, the left paw, along the middle of the snout, the bottom of the cheek where it meets the body, the bottom of the arm, along the top of the back and at the top of the leg where it is bent and meets the arm. While the paint is still damp, clean and dry your brush and run it gently along the edges of the glaze to soften the edges and blend it into the under layers.

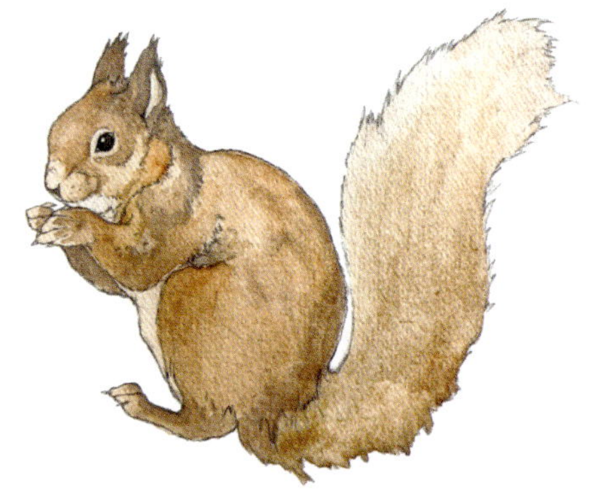

# Step 5: Paint the Shadows

Using a clean size 0 brush, mix a thin solution of Vandyke brown with a hint of burnt sienna. Add slightly more water to create a finer dilution so the mixture will not be too dark and will act as subtle shadows on top of the layers underneath. Paint this mixture on the ears and down the back of the head, along the top of the body where it meets the cheek, the squirrel's lower right arm, the foot and along the lower back, running into the fur at the bottom of the body where it meets the tail.

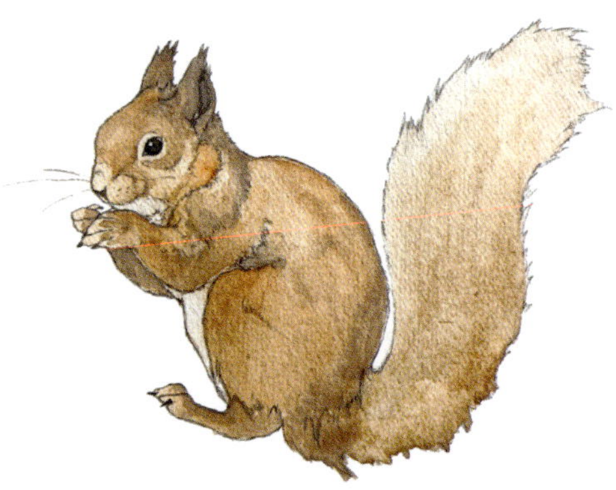

# Step 6: Add the Fine Details

Using a size 3/0 brush, mix a midtone solution of Vandyke brown and use the very tip of the brush to draw in three slightly curved lines outward from each cheek as whiskers. Hold the brush at the top of the handle to create looser, more fluid lines. Paint in the nails on the paws and feet, this time holding the brush at the ferrule for more control and tighter detail. Using a size 0 brush, mix a light solution of Chinese white and a hint of Vandyke brown to create a warm cream. Paint this solution on the chin and along the belly.

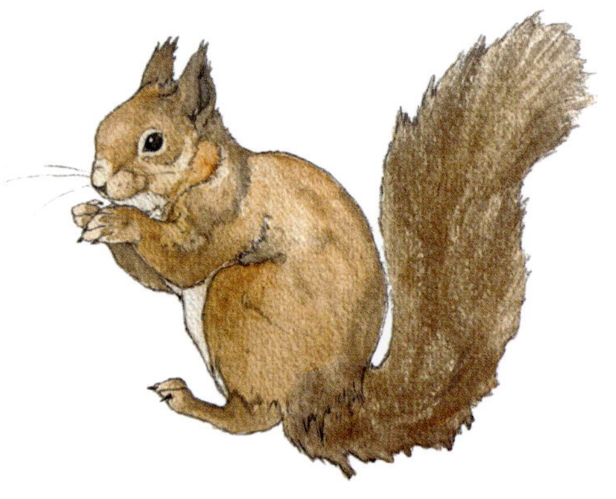

# Step 7: Paint the Tail

Using a size 4 brush, mix a heavily pigmented solution of Vandyke brown and a touch of burnt sienna. Take a dry size 2/0 Isabey brush and swirl the bristles on a piece of dry paper towel. This will separate the bristles outward. Dip the tip of the dry brush into the brown solution and very lightly brush the tips of the bristles along the shape of the tail. As the solution is going to be quite dry, you will need to dip and brush repeatedly to build up texture and color on the paper, but this will give a very dry and coarse "bushy" effect. Build up layers of dry color toward the base of the tail where it meets the body. The squirrel is now complete, well done!

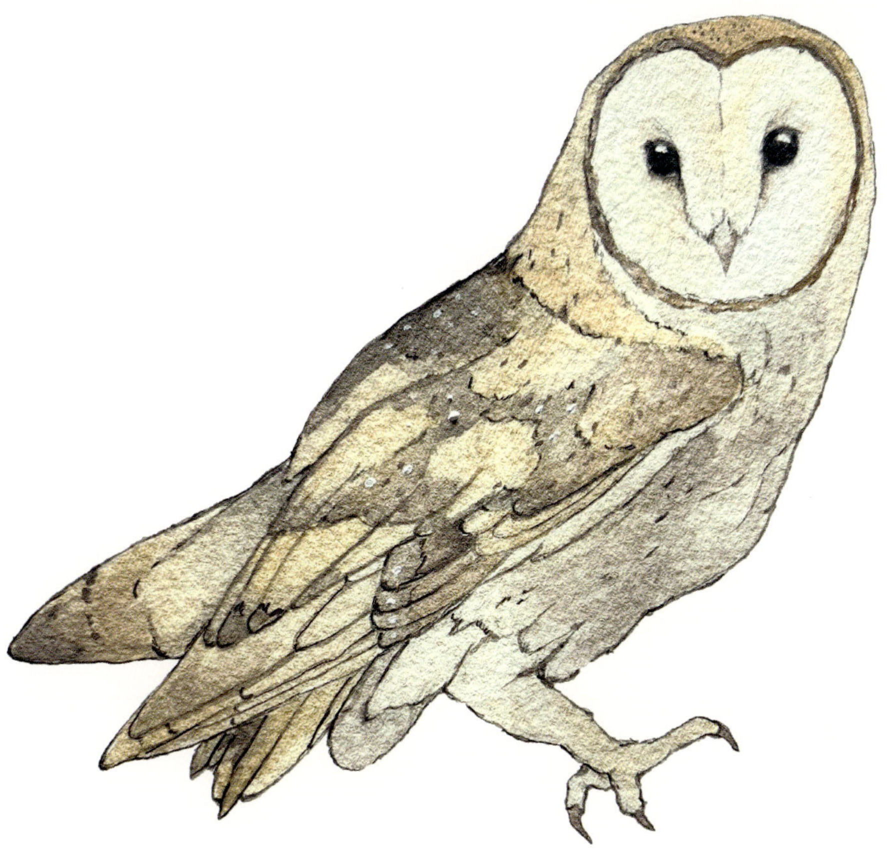

# Barn Owl

The barn owl has long fascinated me, due to it being a rarely spotted nocturnal hunter. I have only been so lucky to come across fewer than ten in the woodland in my lifetime (so far!). Despite scarce sightings, they are easily one of my favorite animals. Their heart-shaped faces, ghostly white appearance, honey-colored wings, front-facing eyes and silent movement when in flight all add to their sense of mystery and allure. It truly is a special, almost dreamlike moment in time if you ever do get to spot one in the wild, an added gift if you get to hear its characteristic rasping shriek!

# Materials Needed

A sheet of cold-press 140-pound (300-gsm) watercolor paper

HB pencil

Brushes

> Size 4

> Size 1

> Size 3/0

Watercolor paints

> Chinese white

> Raw sienna

> Vandyke brown

> Raw umber

> Ivory black

Acrylic white

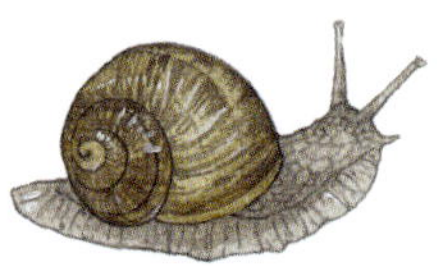

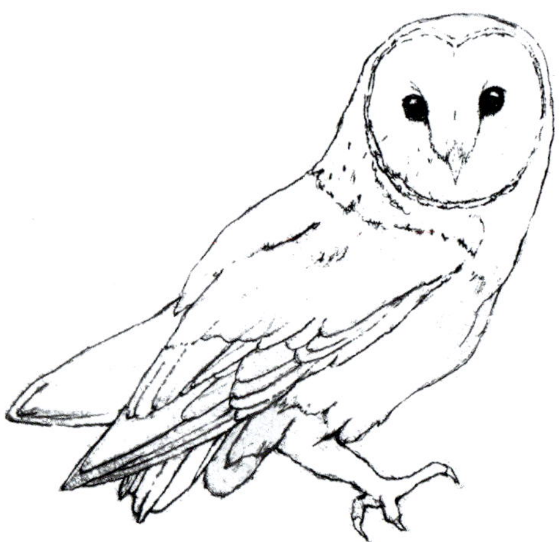

## Step 1: Draw the Outline

Starting on a sheet of cold-press watercolor paper, draw the owl's outline with a sharp **HB** pencil using the corresponding template located in the back of the book (page 169). Note that the feathers on the wing are quite smooth, fluid lines, whereas the feathers on the head that meet the body are lighter and downier. Make sure to shade in the eye, but leave a small dot on the upper left- and right-hand sides for the highlight of the pupils.

## Step 2: Paint the Base Layer of Feathers

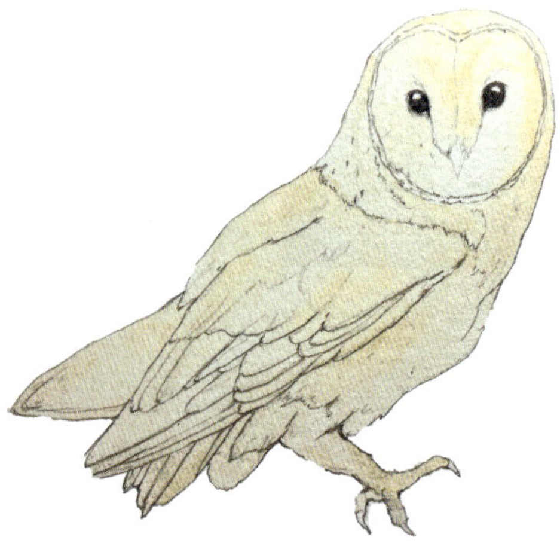

To prepare the color that will fill the owl's entire body as an initial base layer, use a size 4 brush to mix a midtone saturated solution of Chinese white with a dab of raw sienna. We want this color to be a warm cream color. Load the bristles with the mixture and glaze it over the owl's entire head, body, legs and talons.

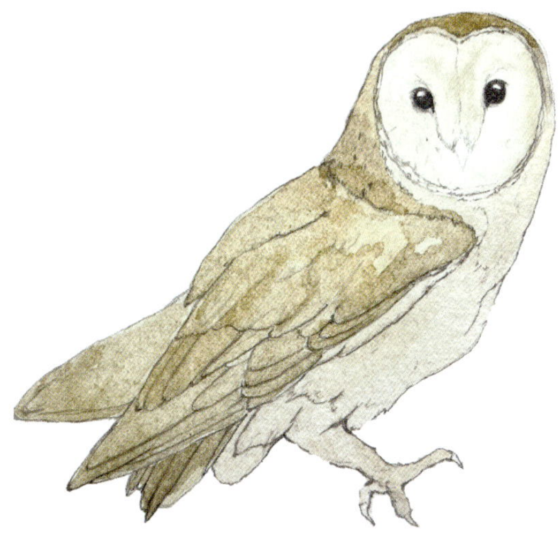

## Step 3: Paint the Upper Head and Wing

Next, to prepare the main color for the upper head and wing, clean your size 4 brush and swirl it into raw sienna with a small dab of Vandyke brown. We want this color to be a warm, honey hue and the consistency to not be too thick. Load the color onto the brush and glaze this wash over the top of the head and the left-hand side of the neck, painting down to cover the entire wing and tail.

While the paint is still damp, switch to a size 1 brush and deepen your mixed honey color on your palette by adding a tiny dab of raw umber to create a richer, more rusty beige. Drop a layer of this color onto the crown of the head and along the outline of the feathers of the neck where they meet the wing. Paint a layer of this color on the right-hand side of the bottom of the upper wing and on the feathers of the underside of the wing at the very bottom. Finally, paint a layer of this rusty beige on the tip of the tail.

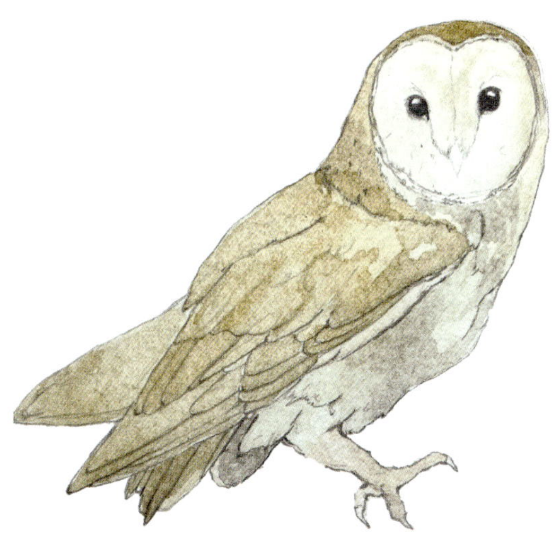

## Step 4: Add Depth to the Plumage

To add darker shadows and depth to the owl's plumage, use a size 1 brush to mix a simple lightly saturated solution of ivory black. The color's hue should be a pale, watery gray. Load the color onto the brush, and using the tip, paint along the right-hand side of the head close to the crown and along the bottom of the head where it meets the neck. Paint a layer of this gray wash over the entire plumage and a layer on the feathers at the bottom of the tail underneath the wing. While the paint is still damp, swirl your brush back into the pale gray mixture and drop the color onto the very center of the plumage and the feathers along the wing, as well as another layer to the bottom of the tail to create a deeper shade of gray.

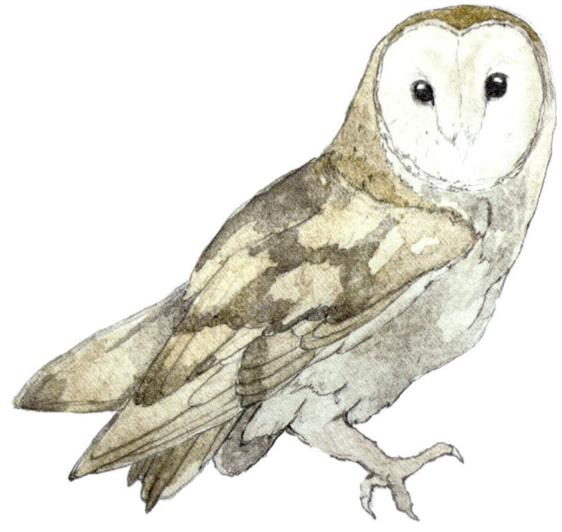

# Step 5: Paint the Patterns on the Wing

To paint the intricate dark patterns on the owl's wing, we will be using the wet-on-wet technique. First, we will observe the wing: The feathers are arranged in a tier, stacked on top of each other. Using a size 1 brush, glaze the tips of the tail and feathers in each individual stacked layer with a thin wash of plain, clean water and allow the paper to absorb it so it is damp, not wet. Add a thin layer of water to the top left-hand side of the wing and to the section of the tail where it meets the wing. While the paper is damp, use your brush to mix a simple midtone solution of ivory black. Then, use the tip of the brush to drop this color into each section that you glazed with water. The tip of each feather, the upper left of the wing and the tip and top of the tail should all have a layer of pale charcoal black.

# Step 6: Define the Face and Speckled Patterns

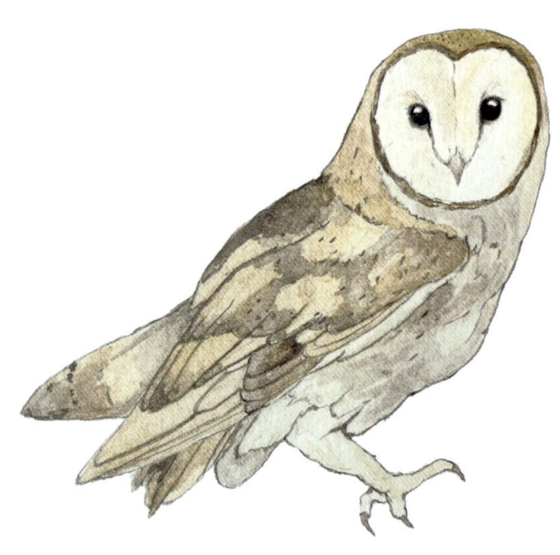

An iconic feature of the barn owl is that it has a speckled pattern on its feathers. To create this, use a size 3/0 brush to create a midtone solution of Vandyke brown and water. This mixture should be fluid but not too watery. Load the color onto the tip of the brush, and using short, flecked brushstrokes, fill the wing with sparse dots, following up along the neck and a small amount on the front plumage. Create a concentrated buildup of flecks at the tip of the tail. The patterns of the speckles do not need to be perfect; embrace the organic, irregular nature to capture the essence of the owl's wing.

We will use the same brush and midtone brown for the feathers on the circular border of the face and the beak. Load the bristles with pigment and fill in the circle of feathers that surround the white of the face. Fill in the talons with the same Vandyke brown solution and glaze the full beak.

Clean and dry the brush, then press the bristles onto the tip of the beak to lift out the brown color in this patch, leaving behind a subtle highlight.

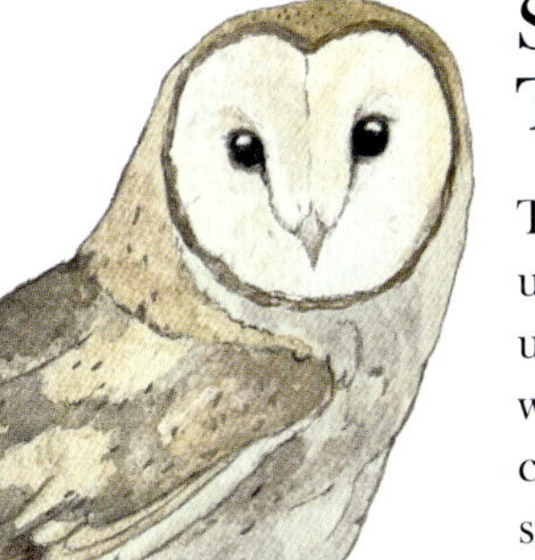

## Step 7: Add Color Depth to the Tail and Wing

To add another layer of color dimension to the owl, use a size 1 brush to mix a light-tone solution of raw umber and water. This should be a warm, rusty hue with a watery consistency. Load the bristles with this color and glaze the wash over the upper right-hand side of the wing, the tip section of the tail and the bottom tips of the wing. Clean and dry the brush, then gently stroke the bristles over this rusty wash.

## Step 8: Add the Final Details

Using a size 3/0 brush, mix a heavily saturated, thick solution of ivory black. Load the bristles with the pigment and carefully trace around the contours of the entire owl. Define the lines of each individual feather, the line of the neck and the outline of the body, head and foot. Use the same brush and thick inky black to fill in both eyes.

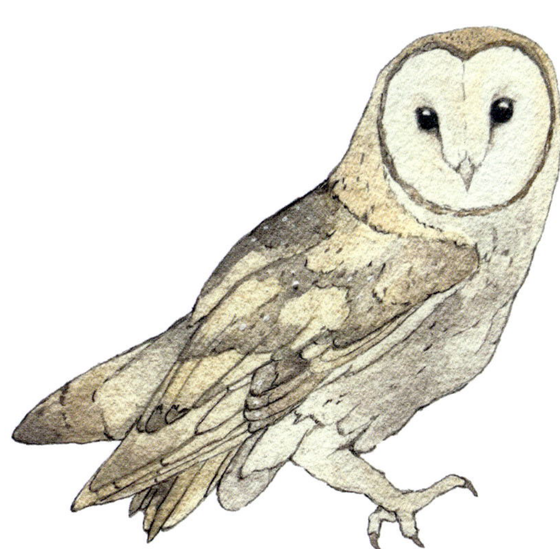

Clean and dry the brush, then squeeze a less than pea-size blob of acrylic white onto your palette. Dip the brush and cover the bristles with paint. To add subtle highlights to the spotted pattern of the feathers, use the tip of the brush to create the same flecked, short brushstrokes as on the owl's wing. These speckles are quite subtle and not densely packed, so a large amount is not needed.

Finally, paint in two dots of acrylic white on the upper left- and right-hand sides of the eyes to create a luminous effect. Allow the paint to fully dry. The owl is now complete, great job!

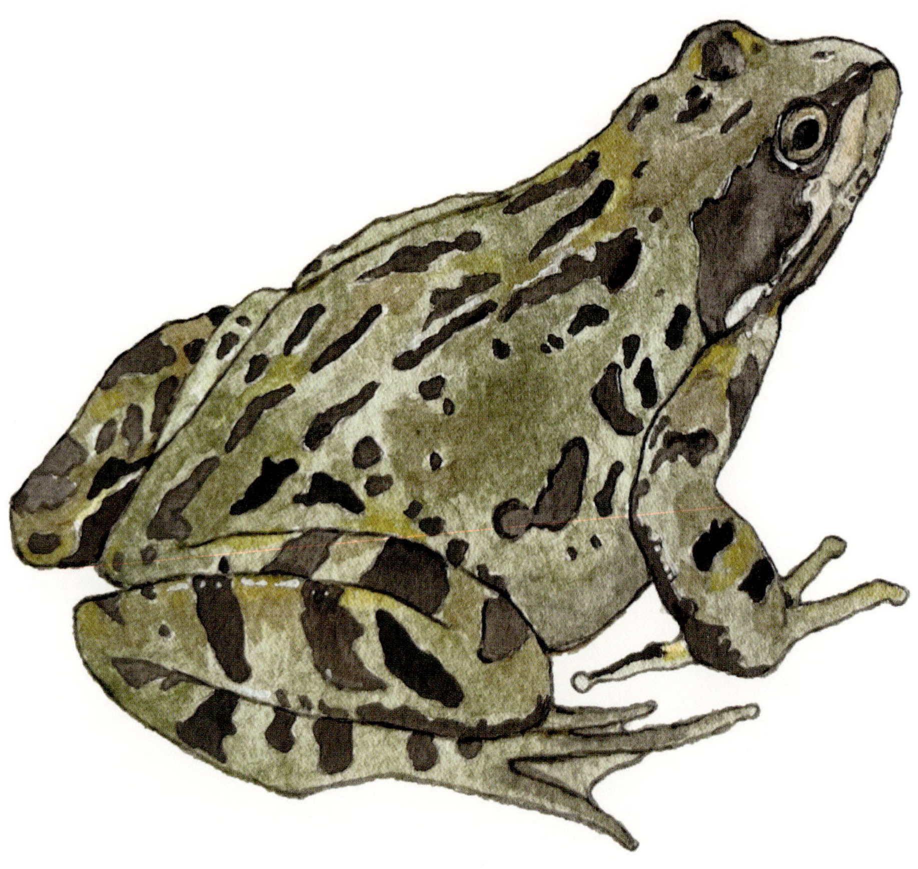

# Frog

A colorful character with a beautifully intricate patterned skin like the common frog can prove a daunting prospect when aiming for a realistic result in watercolor. But don't worry, after you have tackled this palette of earthy browns, vivid greens and vibrant spots, you will have an appreciation for your newfound skills and also for these unique pond dwellers!

# Materials Needed

A sheet of cold-press 140-pound (300-gsm) watercolor paper

HB pencil

Brushes

> Size 1

> Size 3/0

Watercolor paints

> Hooker's green light

> Yellow ochre

> Raw umber

> Burnt sienna

> Sepia

> Ivory black

Acrylic white

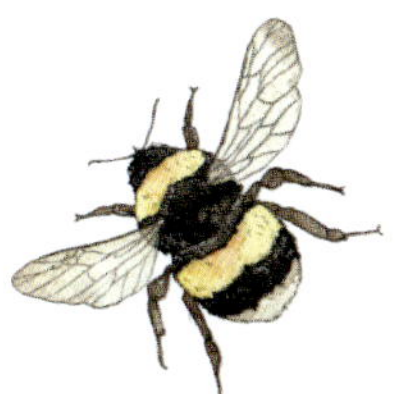

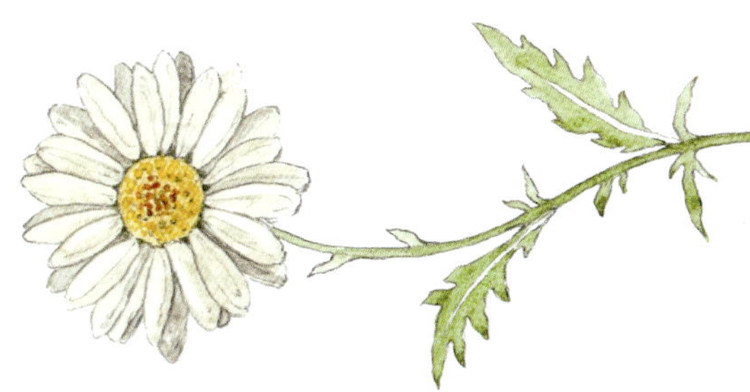

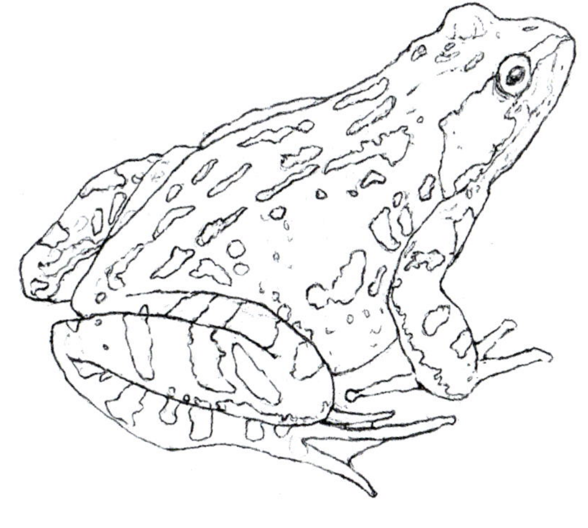

## Step 1: Draw the Outline

Starting on a sheet of cold-press watercolor paper, draw the frog's outline with a sharp **HB** pencil using the corresponding template located in the back of the book (page 169). There are quite a lot of small, intricate details on the frog's pattern, so if you are drawing directly from the image as a reference rather than a template, you do not need to worry about the pattern being completely identical.

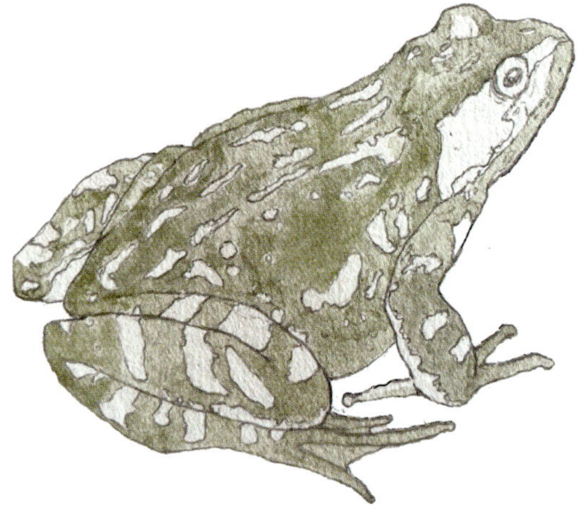

## Step 2: Paint the Base Layer

For the base layer of green on the frog's body, use a size 1 brush to mix a midtone solution of Hooker's green light with a swirl of yellow ochre and a tiny dab of raw umber. We want this color to be a muddy, earthy green. Glaze this wash over the frog's body, leaving the eye and spotted patterns unpainted. My tip on how to paint neatly is to hold the brush at the ferrule, which will give you the most control over the brushstrokes and will keep your work neat and tidy.

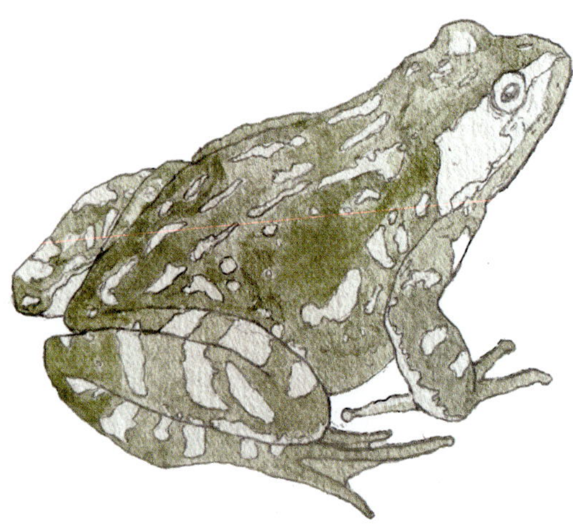

## Step 3: Add the Shadow Tones

Next, we want to deepen sections of the muddy green on the body from step 2. Using a size 1 brush, swirl another dab of raw umber into the earthy green color we mixed earlier to create a richer, deeper hue. Add a layer of this color to the lower left-hand side of the body and center section of the body concentrating on the right-hand side. Add a layer to the tip of the face around the mouth and nose, as well as to the bend of the legs on the frog's most left-hand side.

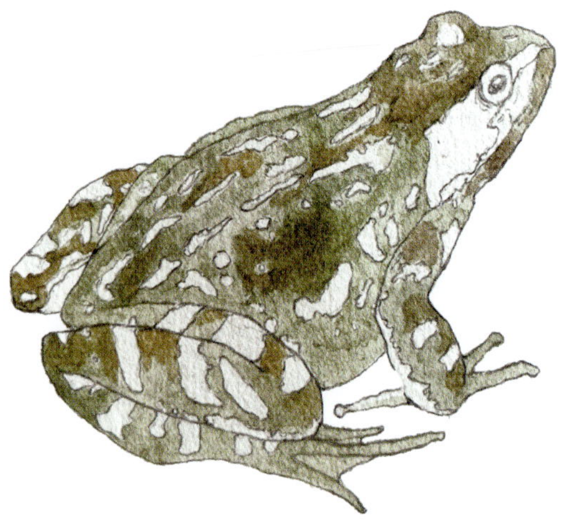

## Step 4: Create Color and Depth

In this step, we want to create further depth to the muddy green shadows on the body and begin to incorporate pops of rust color along the frog's skin.

Using the same size 1 brush, swirl it back into the deep muddy green color from step 3 and glaze this over the central shadow on the body and at the very base of the frog's back, keeping the work neat and tidy around the spots along the skin.

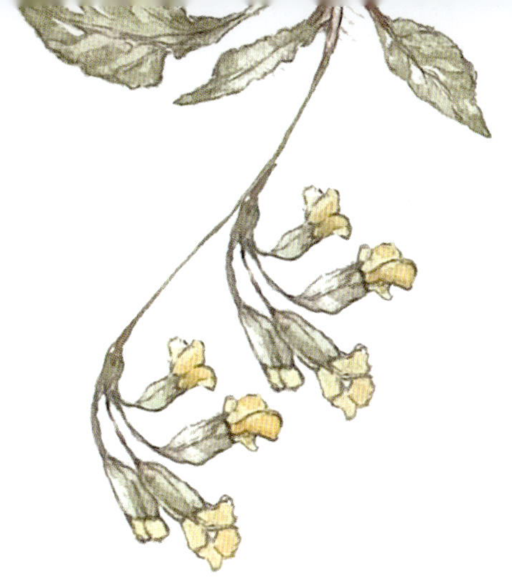

To prepare the rust color that will be dotted along the frog's skin, use a size 3/0 brush to mix a midtone solution of burnt sienna with a dab of yellow ochre. We want this color to be a warm, sunny rust hue. Using the tip of the brush and avoiding painting the frog's spots, glaze a wash of the rust color over the top of the head, leading down to the center of the body and down along the mouth. Dab a layer of the rust color in between the frog's spots on the legs, concentrating the paint on the upper half of the limb and softening the edges as it flows downward. Dab little sections of the color in between the spots on the arms, softening the edges so there is a seamless blend from rust to the under layer of muddy green. Finally, drop in a small section of the rust color on the center of the back toward the left-hand side.

## Step 5: Add the Pops of Yellow

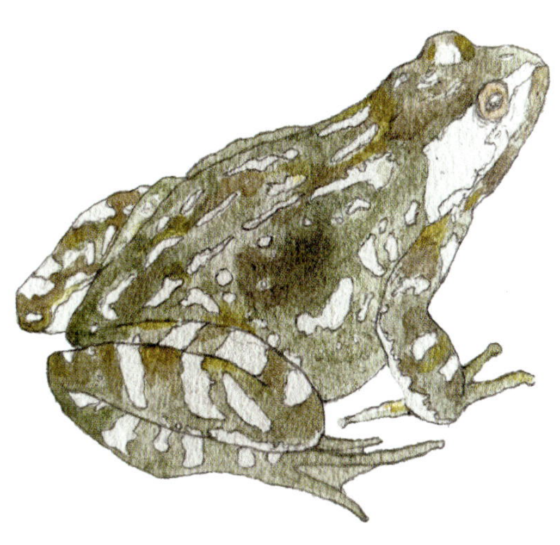

To add pops of yellow to the frog's skin, use a clean size 3/0 brush to mix a simple midtone solution of yellow ochre and water. Dab in little sections of color on the frog's left eyelid, down along the central line of the back and at the tip of the mouth. For the frog's right arm, dab in color at the very top fold of the arm where it meets the mouth and along the outline of the webbed toes. For the legs, dab in little sections of color along the top of the folds of the leg in between the frog's spots.

Finally, dilute this yellow ochre mixture on your palette with water to create a pale, light-tone wash. Use the tip of the brush to fill in the iris of the eye around the pupil.

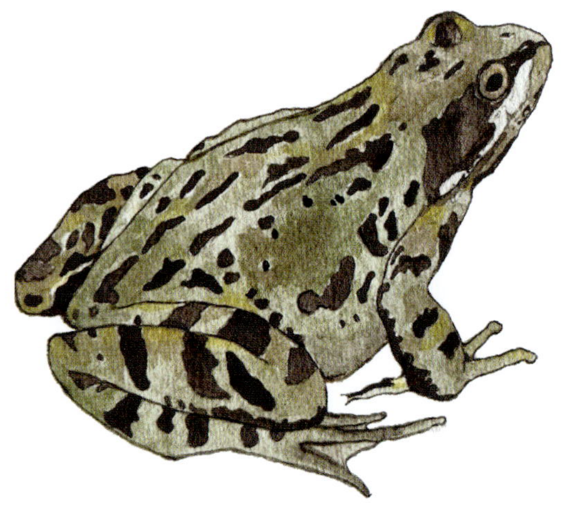

## Step 6: Paint the Spots

To prepare the color that will fill in the frog's spotted pattern, use a clean size 3/0 brush to mix a highly saturated, dark-tone solution of sepia. We want this color to be thick and deep in color, so do not add too much water. Load the pigment on the brush and hold it at the ferrule to ensure that your hand has the most control over the flow of the bristles, which will keep the work neat and tidy. Carefully paint in spots along the legs, back and head. The only spot that is not to be filled in with this dark sepia solution is the lower section just underneath the eye. Once each spot has been filled with dark, matte brown, use the brush's tip and the same mixture to define the outlines of the frog, taking care to outline the lines of the webbed feet and the folds of the limbs, as well as the lines of the head and body.

Clean the brush and load the bristles with a dark-tone solution of ivory black. Fill in the pupil of the eye with this color.

## Step 7: Add the Final Details

To complete the frog, we need to add finishing highlights. Squeeze a less than pea-size amount of acrylic white onto your palette and use your clean size 3/0 brush to create a highlight around the outline of the frog's eye.

Next, add a tiny dab of burnt sienna to the acrylic white and mix until the color turns to a very pale rusty orange hue. Finally, use your brush to carefully paint this color into the spot on the lower face below the eye that we did not fill in with sepia in step 6. The frog is now complete! Good job!

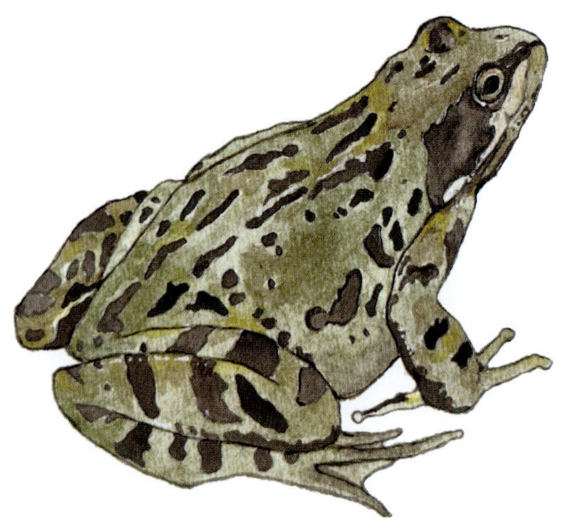

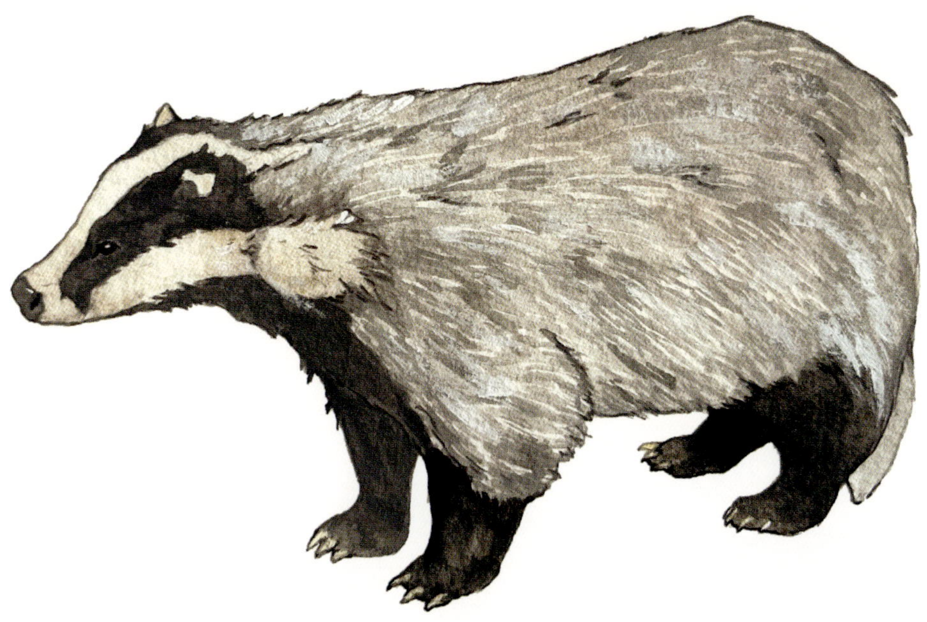

# Badger

Sturdy, shy and nocturnal, badgers, with their simple yet striking features, offer an ideal subject for a watercolor project. Their rugged fur has only two tones and provides a wonderful opportunity to practice both subtle shading and texture through brushstrokes. They are one of my favorite animals to paint as they yield quite a rewarding result through minimal colors and advanced technique!

# Materials Needed

A sheet of cold-press 140-pound (300-gsm) watercolor paper

HB pencil

A piece of paper towel

Brushes

> Size 4

> Size 0

> Size 3/0

Watercolor paints

> Chinese white

> Sepia

> Lamp black

Acrylic white

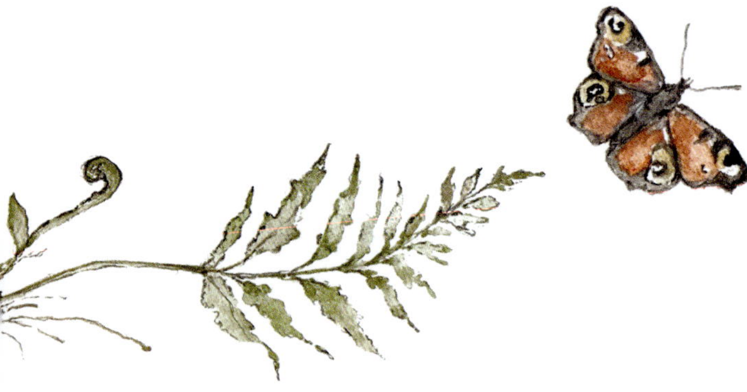

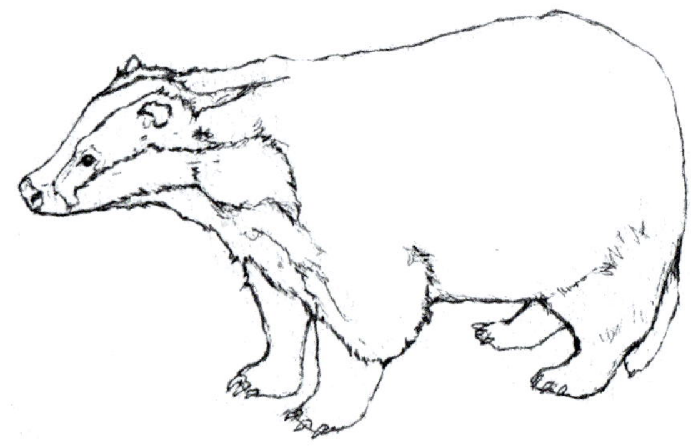

## Step 1: Draw the Outline

Starting on a sheet of cold-press watercolor paper, draw the badger's outline with a sharp **HB** pencil using the corresponding template located in the back of the book (page 169). Don't worry about filling in the texture or fur on the body; we will do this later on with paint.

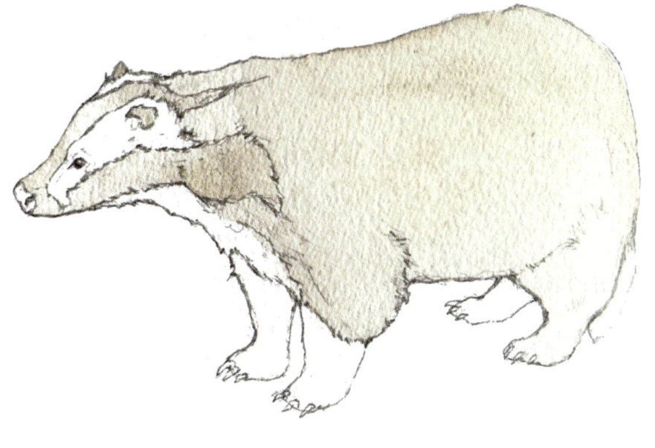

## Step 2: Paint the Body

Using a size 4 brush, mix a blend of Chinese white, a tiny dab of sepia and water until it turns a rich cream color. Glaze this mixture over the badger's entire body and back left paw. While the paint is still wet, add another dab of sepia to your cream mixture until it appears deeper in color using the same brush. Drag your brush along the spine of the badger and the small patches close to, under and over the badger's ear.

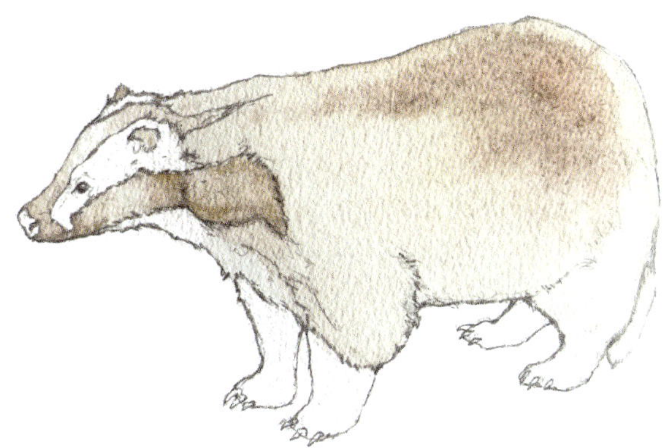

## Step 3: Add the Shadows

Prepare your shadow color by mixing a wet size 0 brush with sepia to create a thin glaze. Follow the curvature of the badger's mouth to the edge of the cheek, immediately softening the edges with a clean, damp size 0 brush. Swirl the same brush back into your sepia mixture and fill in the badger's back upper body, making sure to follow the curves of the body but not painting directly along your line—just inside of it. Spread the paint to cover the upper right-hand side of the body and ensure the edges are softened using a clean damp brush. We do not want the shadows to have hard lined edges but to blend seamlessly into the white base we created in step 2.

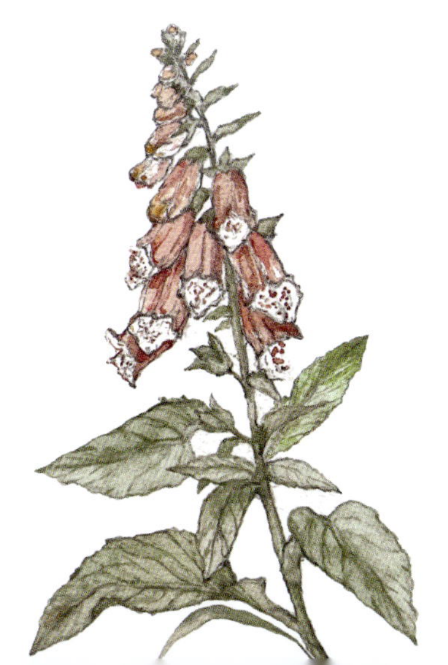

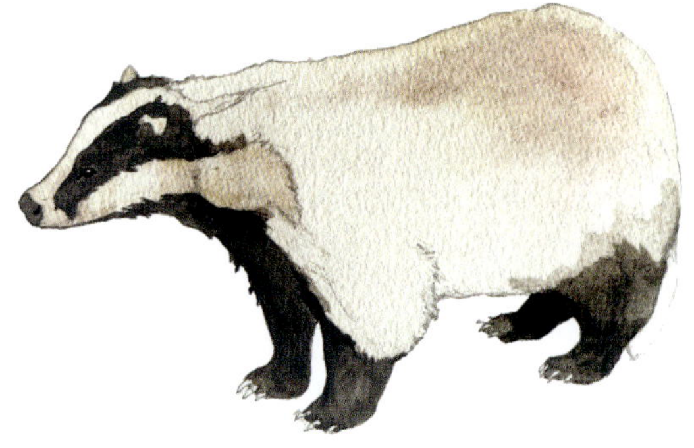

## Step 4: Add the Black

For the badger's iconic black and white fur, the first stage is to prepare our color. Swirl a clean, size 4 brush into lamp black until a thick, glossy mixture is achieved. Fill in the parts of the badger drawing that have not yet been filled with paint: the nose, paws, legs and face except the ear. We want the paint to have a deep, almost matte finish, so ensure that the mixture is not too transparent from adding too much water. We want a higher ratio of pigment in this glaze. Let the paint fully dry and add highlights by applying a wash of water using a size 3/0 brush to the badger's left leg and left back leg. Wriggle the brush until you can see the black base paint lifting from the paper. Press a dry paper towel onto these sections to reveal soft highlights. Using the same 3/0 size brush, use the pigment left on its bristles to paint the lower body on the right-hand side, creating the illusion of a pale gray shadow.

## Step 5: Add the Fur Base

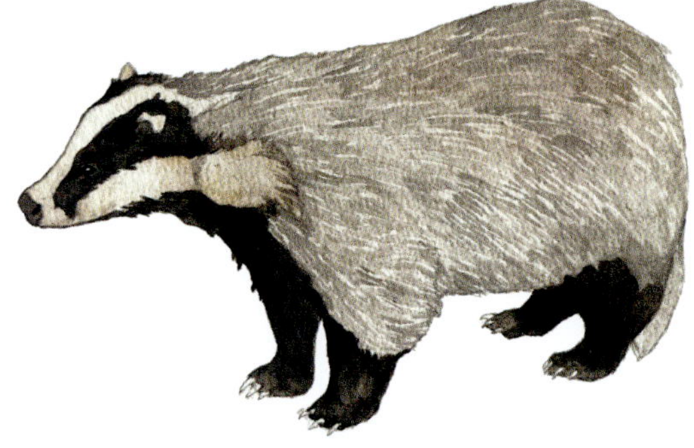

Using a clean size 3/0 brush, make a midtone mix of lamp black with water. We do not want the color to appear black, we want it to be gray, so to achieve this, slightly more water is required. Do not make the mixture so thin that the brushstrokes are too transparent on the paper. To create the fur's texture, accurate work is achieved by simply painting small lines or "drawing" using the brush. I usually hold the brush near the ferrule, which allows maximum control and can result in tight work. Dip the brush into your gray mixture and drag the tip along to create short, outward lines that fill the main body and tail. Only use the tip of the brush, as this will create thinner lines that are more like the badger's coarse and wiry fur.

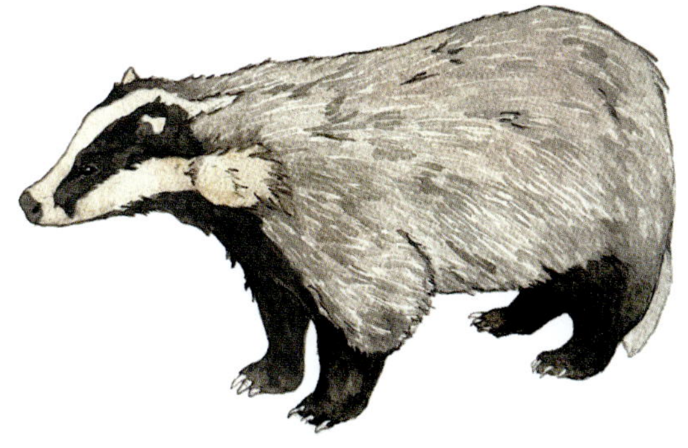

# Step 6: Add the Finer Fur Details

Utilizing the exact same techniques to create fur from step 5, we will now use the same brush to add deeper tones to give the fur depth. Mix a more heavily concentrated solution of lamp black and water. This time we want the color to show as black and not as gray, so less water is required so it will not be as heavily diluted. Use the tip of the brush to create sparsely dispersed strokes. We do not want them to be clustered together but to be small shadows to give a more thick, three-dimensional effect.

# Step 7: Finish the Fur

For this step, we will need acrylic white only. Put a pea-size amount onto your palette, as a little bit goes quite a long way. Dip a clean size 3/0 brush into the paint and paint a layer of short lines on top of the fur just as we did in steps 5 and 6, using the tip of the brush and holding it close to the ferrule for the most control. Focus mostly on the bottom of the belly and at the edges of the fur where it meets the legs. Follow the curvature and shapes of the belly and body itself. Fill in the nails on the badger's paws and the tip of its tail using the same brush and paint. Good job! The badger is now complete!

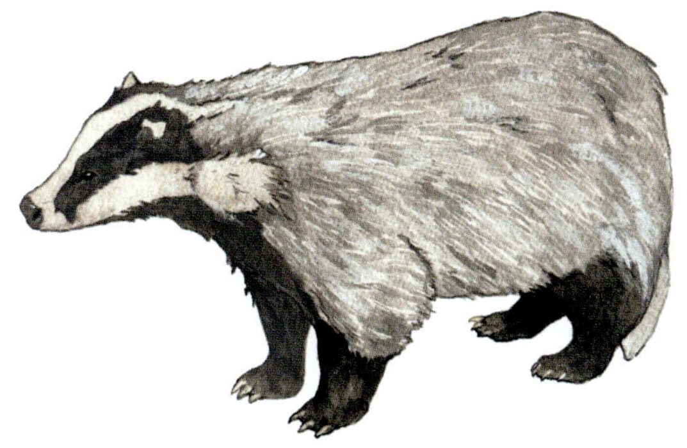

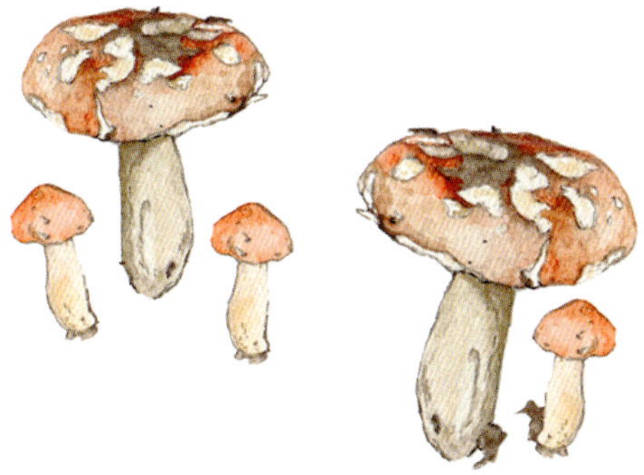

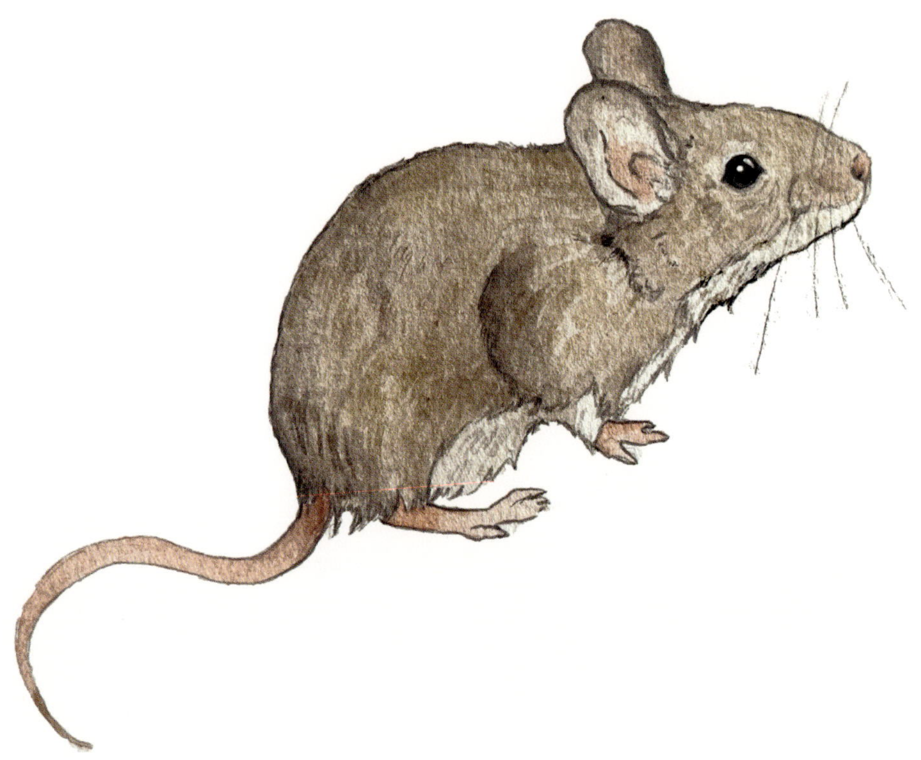

# Wood Mouse

Although not always favored by some, the wood mouse has always held an
endearing charm for me due to its gentle presence, delicate features and playful
antics as it scurries and weaves through the fields. Its soft fur is a joy to paint,
the earthy color palette consists of some of my favorite colors to work with and,
hopefully upon completing this tutorial, you will have a newfound appreciation
for the wood mouse also!

# Materials Needed

A sheet of cold-press 140-pound (300-gsm) watercolor paper

HB pencil

Brushes

> Size 4

> Size 1

> Size 3/0

> Size 0

Watercolor paints

> Raw sienna

> Raw umber

> Chinese white

> Light red

> Sepia

> Lamp black

Acrylic white

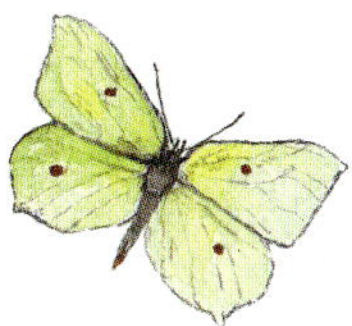

## Step 1: Draw the Outline

Starting on a sheet of cold-press watercolor paper, draw the outline of the mouse's body and its fur with a sharp HB pencil using the corresponding template located in the back of the book (page 169). Fill in the eye (we will deepen this with black paint later) and make sure to leave two dots for a highlight.

## Step 2: Paint the Base Layer

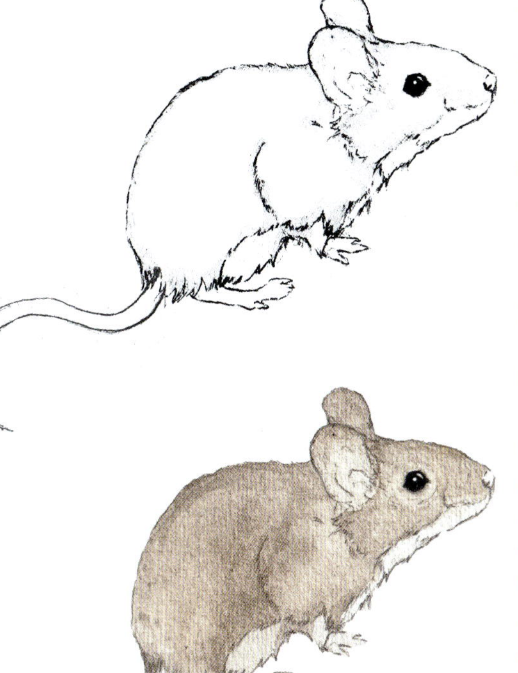

For the base layer of the mouse's color, use a size 4 brush to mix a midtone solution of raw sienna with a dab of raw umber. We want this color to be a pale, caramel-tone brown. Glaze this color over the mouse's entire upper-body fur, and while the paint is still damp, add another layer of the same caramel brown mixture to the top of the ear, along the curve of the face downward to the tip of the nose, along the curve of the back and along the lower belly fur.

(Continued)

To prepare the color that will be the lower-body fur, use a size 1 brush to mix together a midtone solution of Chinese white with a dab of raw sienna. We want this color to be a rich cream. Paint the lower fur on the face, the body and the mouse's paws.

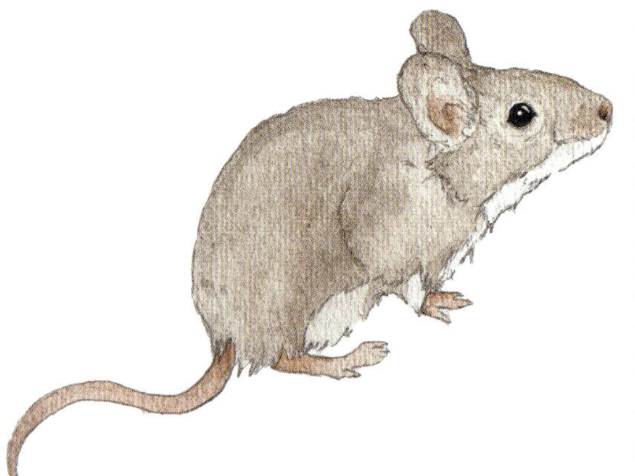

## Step 3: Paint the Pink

Using a size 3/0 brush, mix a light-tone solution of light red and water. We want this mixture to be a pale blush pink. Using the tip of the brush, glaze this color over the paws, the tail, the nose and the inner ear. While the paint is still damp, add another layer of this blush pink to the section of the tail where it meets the lower-body fur, the tip of the tail, the left-hand side of the back foot, the left-hand side of the front paw and the right-hand side of the inner ear, softening the edges of these depth layers to allow them to blend seamlessly into the base layer of pale pink underneath.

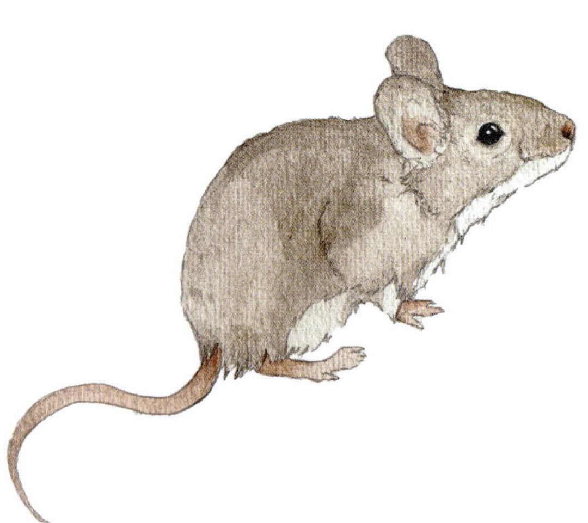

## Step 4: Add the Shadows

Using a size 0 brush, mix a simple light-tone solution of raw umber to create a pale, warm brown. We will use this to create depth and shadow to the fur. Load the bristles with the mixture and gently follow along the curved outline from the ear to the tip of the nose. Paint a larger shadow along the curve of the back from the ear to the center of the body, extending the brown paint downward until it meets the curve of the arm. Paint a final shadow that runs from where the tail meets the fur at the bottom of the body upward to the right, until it meets the bend of the front arm. Keep all of the edges of the shadows soft, as we do not want any harsh lines but for all of the layers of tone to blend seamlessly together.

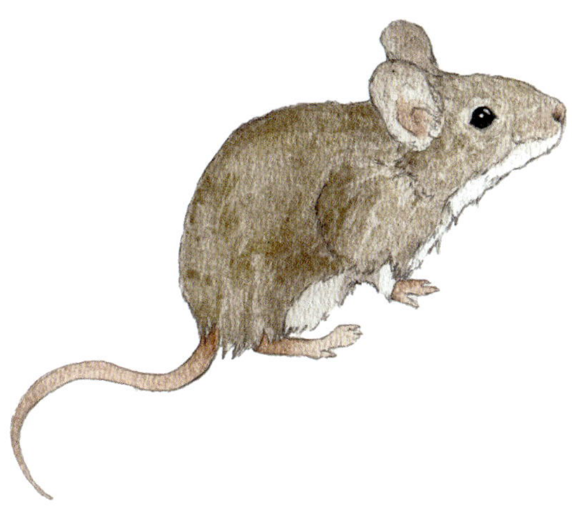

# Step 5: Add the Fur Texture

To create the fur on the face and body, use a clean size 3/0 brush to mix a midtone solution of raw umber and load the color onto the bristles. Hold the brush at the ferrule so you can have the most control over the brushstrokes. Beginning at the nose, paint short, delicate brushstrokes that extend outward, painting from right to left following the natural growth pattern and curvature on the face and body. My tip on how to paint the fur on the body is to follow the curvature shape of the back, sloping the short lines downward to meet the tail. Cover the entire upper-body fur in these short brushstrokes.

Next, we will add more texture and density to the patches of fur where there are shadows and darker tones of color. Load the brush with the same raw umber mixture and add another layer of short brushstrokes to the upper cheek where it meets the ear, along the curve of the back, the left-hand side of the arm, the bottom of the upper-body belly fur and the left-hand side of the body where the fur meets the tail.

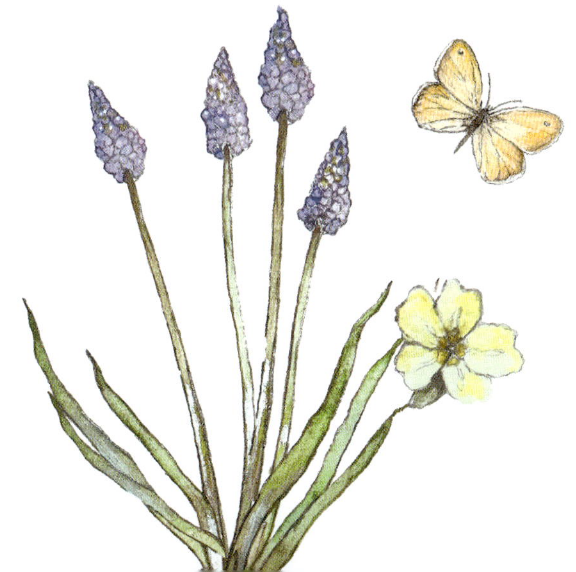

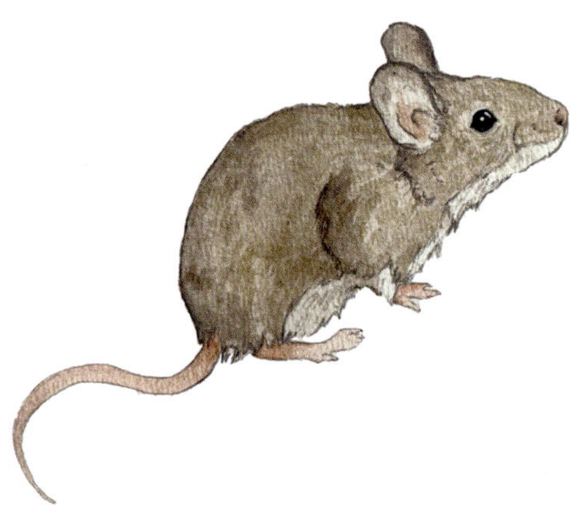

## Step 6: Create Definition

Using a clean size 3/0 brush, mix a light-tone solution of sepia and water. Glaze a small amount of this mixture to create a subtle shadow on the left-hand side of the arm and along the center to lower curve of the back to where the fur meets the tail. Trace carefully along the right-hand side of the mouse's left ear.

Next, we want to define fur on the lower body. Using the tip of the brush, paint the same short, gentle brushstrokes in this light sepia solution over the creamy white fur, sloping them gently downward and following the curves of the back.

Finally, we want to create definition to the mouse. Deepen your light-tone sepia solution by adding in more sepia until it is a more saturated midtone color and not as heavily diluted. Use the tip of the brush to trace around the outlines of the mouse's body, tail, ears, face, cheek and arm. Be mindful of the lines' quality in your brushstrokes: The tail and feet use smooth flowing lines, whereas the fur will use the short, feathery brushstroke technique.

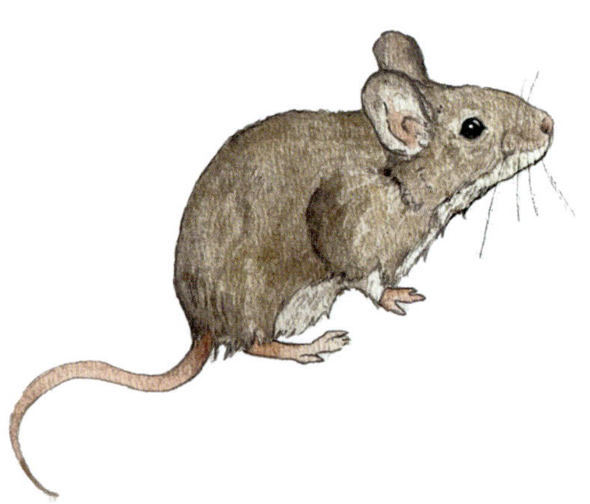

## Step 7: Add the Final Details

Using a clean size 3/0 brush, mix a dark-tone solution of lamp black and load it onto the brush. Use the tip of the brush to fill in the pupil with this thick black color. Use the tip of the brush to trace the lines of the whiskers.

Finally, squeeze a small amount of acrylic white onto your palette, and using a clean size 3/0 brush, paint in two tiny dots on the upper center of the pupil in the eye for a subtle luminous highlight. Well done! The wood mouse is now complete!

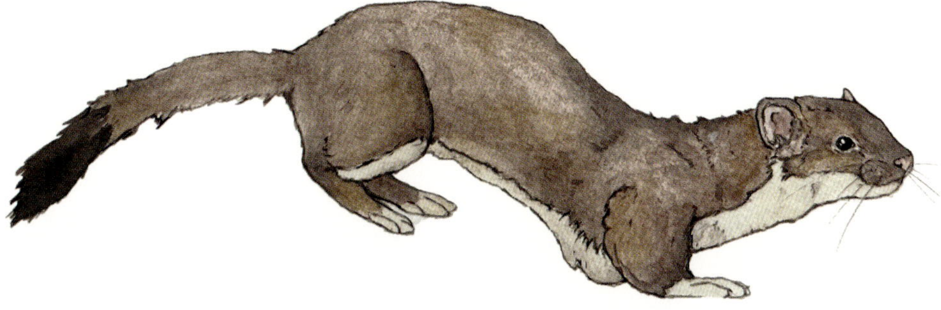

# Stoat

A sighting of a stoat, although rare due to their mysterious and secretive nature,
always makes for an amazing performance. When you are lucky enough to spot
one weaving its way along the rocks and flora with great agility and speed, you
are reminded why they are so mighty for their size. These cunning predators
can twist and bound through a landscape and catch prey up to five times larger
than their own size! Very similar in appearance to a weasel, their dynamic
presence in nature, coupled with their undeniable charm, makes stoats
a captivating subject for any woodland painting project.

# Materials Needed

A sheet of cold-press 140-pound (300-gsm) watercolor paper

HB pencil

Brushes

> Size 1

> Size 3/0

> Size 4

Watercolor paints

> Chinese white

> Yellow ochre

> Light red

> Sepia

> Vandyke brown

> Lamp black

Acrylic white

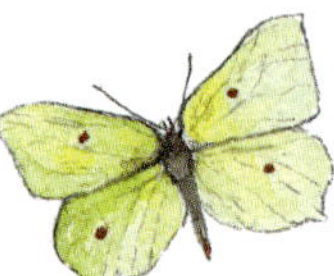

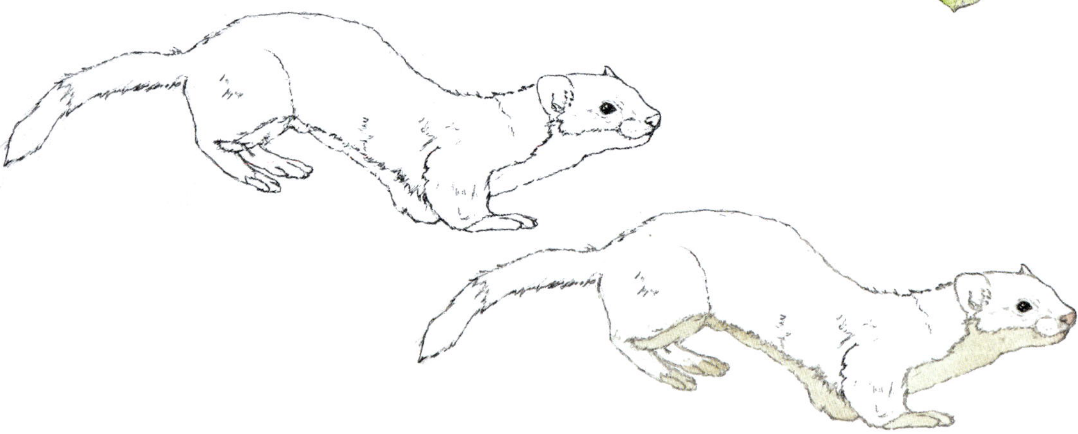

## Step 1: Draw the Outline

Starting on a sheet of cold-press watercolor paper, draw the stoat's outline and the fur of the body with a sharp **HB** pencil using the corresponding template located in the back of the book (page 171). Fill in the eye (we will deepen this with black paint later) and make sure to leave a blank dot for a highlight.

## Step 2: Paint the Lower Fur and Nose

To prepare the color that will fill the lower-body fur, use a size 1 brush to mix a midtone solution of Chinese white with a hint of yellow ochre to create a warm, creamy hue. Glaze the paint onto the lower-body fur and the paws. While the paint is still damp, dip your brush lightly back into the yellow ochre and add this into your mixed cream color, deepening its hue to a soft beige. Drop this color onto the left-hand side of the belly where it meets the bend of the leg and the tip of the back paws.

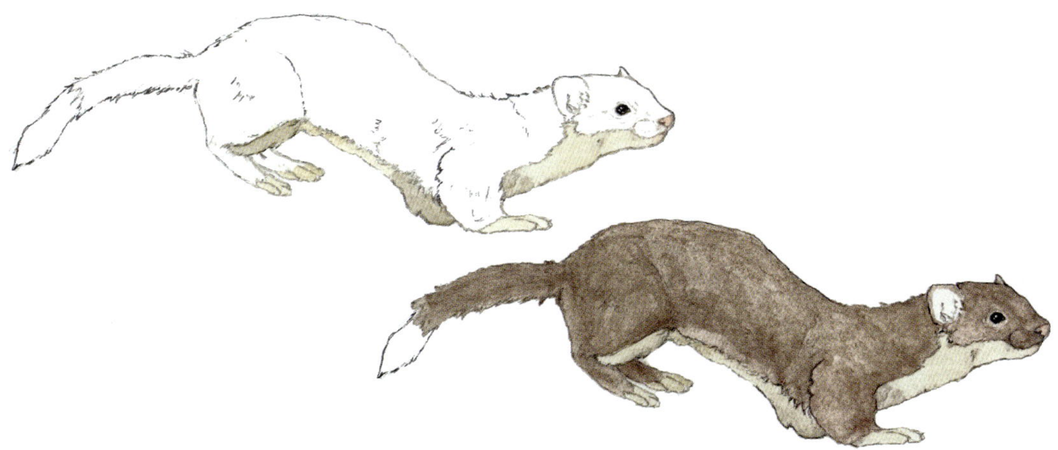

For the pink of the nose, use a size 3/0 brush to mix a light-tone solution of light red to create a pale, watery pink. Load the tip of the brush with color and gently fill in the nose. Allow the paint to fully dry.

## Step 3: Add the Subtle Shadows

For the subtle shadows on the stoat's lower-body fur, use a clean size 1 brush to mix a light-tone solution of sepia to create a watery wash of pale brown. Use the tip of the brush to dab a small amount of this wash on the tip of the chin, the fur on the lower chest, the left leg and the bending joint of the stoat's back right leg. Allow the paint to fully dry.

## Step 4: Paint the Upper-Body Fur

To prepare the color that will be the base layer for the entire upper-body fur, use a size 4 brush to mix a midtone solution of Vandyke brown with a tiny dab of sepia to create an earthy deep brown. Glaze this wash of brown over the stoat's entire upper-body fur and the remaining fur on the paws. Leave the inner ear and the tip of the tail free of paint. While the paint is still damp, load the brush with another layer of color and paint along the outline of the stomach, the back left leg and the right side of the front right paw. Finally, add another layer of brown to the cheek and along the curve of the upper head leading down to the nose to create subtle shadows and depth to the fur.

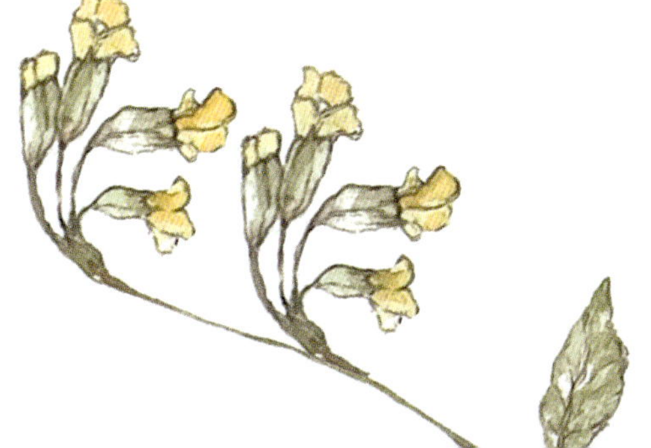

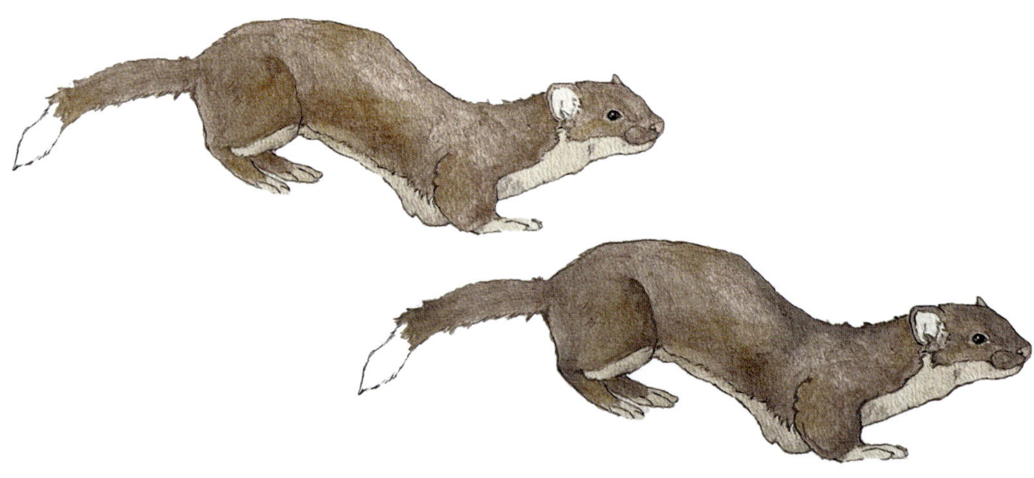

# Step 5: Add Tonal Depth to the Fur

Using the same size 4 brush, clean the bristles with water and mix a midtone solution of Vandyke brown with a tiny dab of yellow ochre to create a warm, sunny chestnut color. Softly glaze this color onto the lower left-hand side of the fur on the stoat's cheek, along the left-hand side of the right paw, the back right paw, the bending joint of the back leg and along the center curve of the back, blending downward to cover the entire lower section of the stoat's brown fur on the lower belly. Finally, add a small dab of this warm chestnut color to the end of the tail where it blends into the tip. Make sure to soften the edges of the layers of paint by cleaning and drying the bristles of the brush and softly stroking over the layers of paint until they fade and blend into the brown layer of fur below.

# Step 6: Create the Shadows

Using a size 1 brush, mix a simple midtone solution of sepia and water. This is the color that will be used to create depth and shadow on the stoat's body. Fill the front of the fur on the stoat's face with this color, gently blending the brushstrokes outward to the left toward the ear. Glaze along the curve of the back, extending the shadow downward slightly when it reaches the center right, and let the paint flow and blend downward where it meets the bend of the front paws. Paint a layer of shadow on the right-hand side of the front paw and along the bend of the back leg along the right-hand side, blending into the brown fur of the back paws. Finally, add a layer of brown shadow to the end of the tail where it blends with the tip. Allow the paint to fully dry.

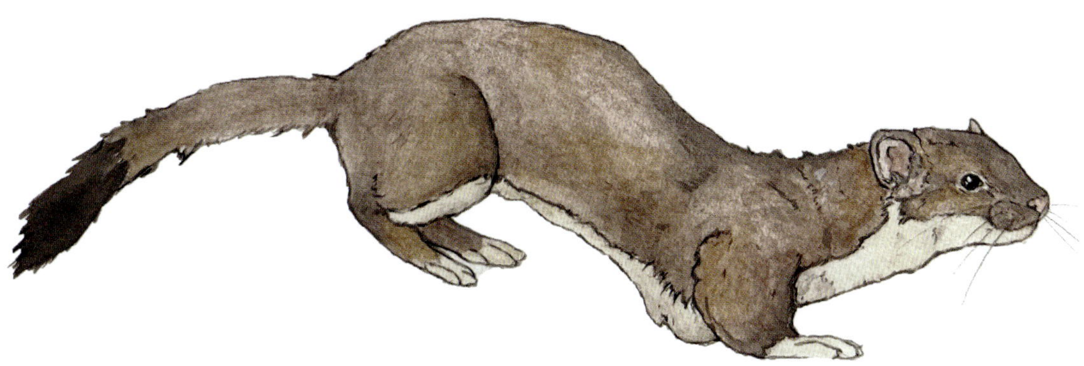

## Step 7: Add the Final Details

Using a size 3/0 brush, mix a dark-tone solution of lamp black and load it onto the brush. Use the tip of the brush to fill in the pupil with this thick black color. Use the tip of the brush to trace the lines of the whiskers.

For the tip of the tail, use a size 1 brush to mix a dark-tone solution of sepia so that the color is thick and matte. Fill in the tip of the tail with this dark brown mixture, using the tip of the brush to create long, quick brushstrokes to emulate the texture of the bushy fur.

Finally, squeeze a small amount of acrylic white onto your palette, and using a clean size 3/0 brush, paint in a tiny dot on the upper left-hand side of the pupil in the eye for a subtle luminous highlight. The stoat is now complete, well done!

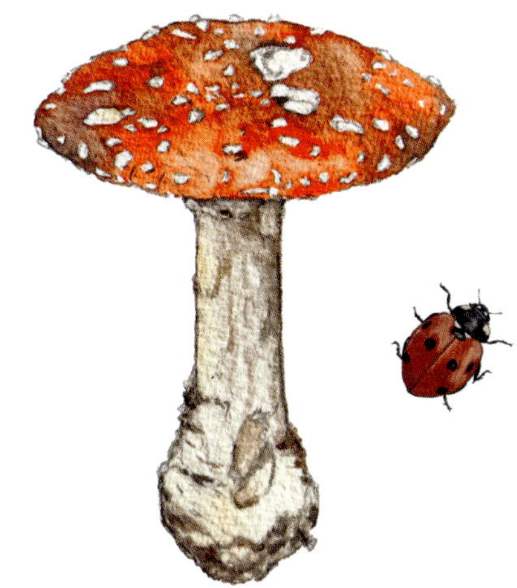

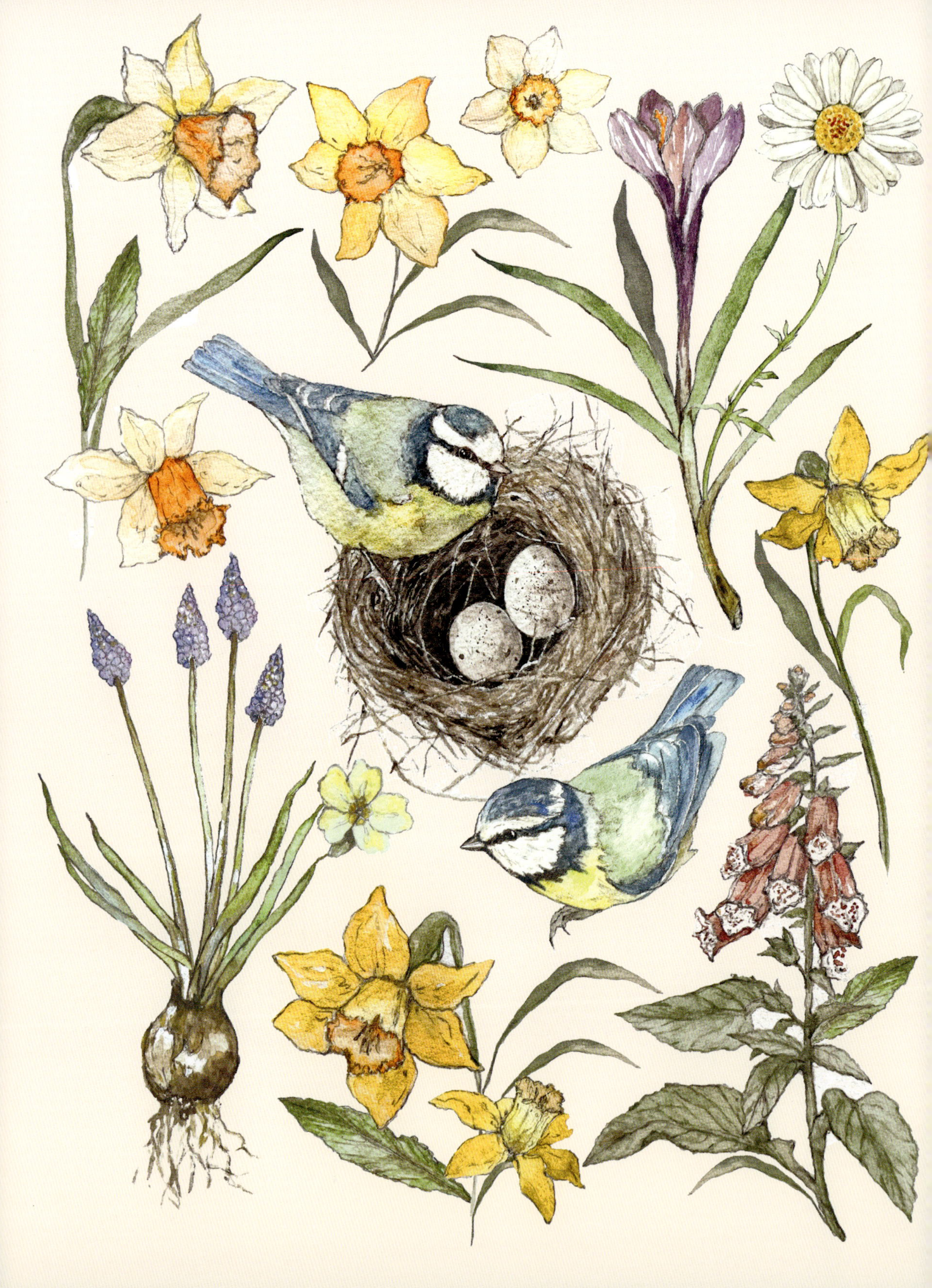

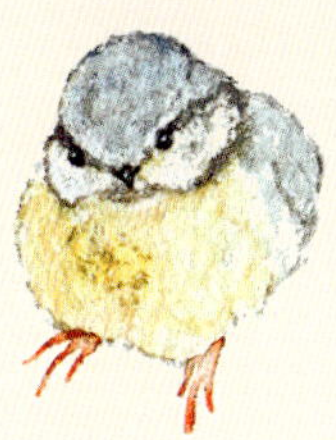

# In the Air

Take a look upward at the clouds and branches as we take flight along-side some of nature's avian companions, from the cheerful chirp of the goldfinch (page 66) to the vibrant plumage of the robin (page 70) and the playful antics of the blue tit (page 85). These charming birds, each with their own unique beauty and character, offer perfect subjects to explore.

In this chapter, you will learn how to paint birds such as chaffinches (page 75); their striking combination of pink, blue and green feathers are a delight to behold. We will focus on capturing the vibrant colors and intricate patterns of their plumage, the delicate balance of light and shadow and the sense of movement that defines their lively nature.

Also included are wrens (page 80). These small but mighty birds are full of personality, with their perky tails and bold, curious expressions. We will learn to portray the subtle variations in their brown and beige feathers, the intricate details of their tiny forms and the dynamic poses that reflect their energetic behavior.

These projects will challenge your skills, but soon you will find yourself soaring as you infuse your paintings with the spirit of flight, mastering the intricate details and lively personalities of each feathered friend.

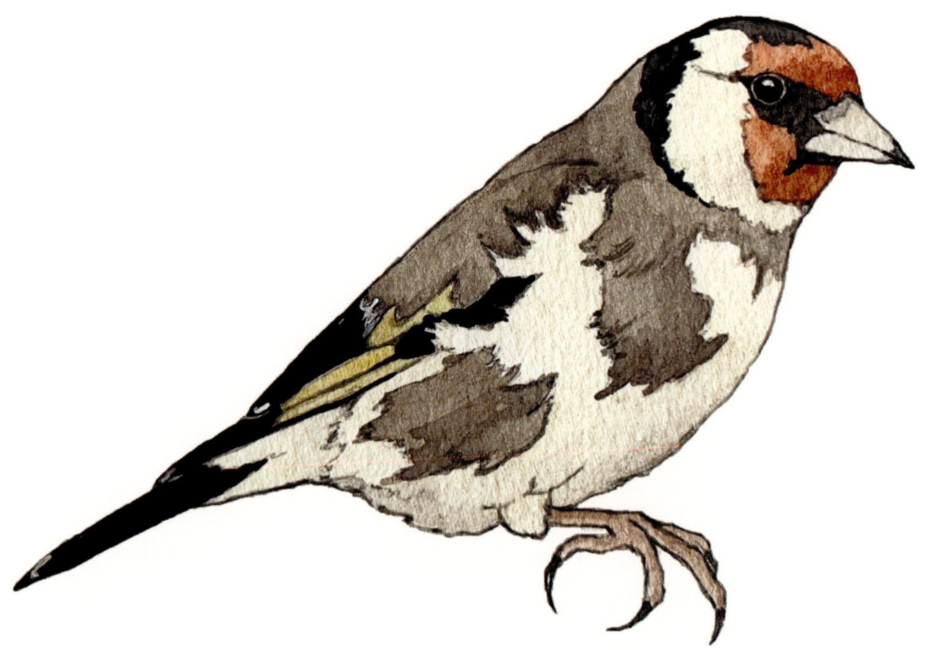

# Goldfinch

I find that the playful and lively nature of the European goldfinch lends itself well to the fluid and expressive qualities of watercolor. Not only do they have a charming demeanor, but the striking contrasts of color on their wings provide an amazing palette to explore mixing and painting wings, which can prove invaluable if you are a bird enthusiast!

# Materials Needed

A sheet of cold-press 140-pound (300-gsm) watercolor paper

HB pencil

Brushes

> Size 4

> Size 1

> Size 3/0

Watercolor paints

> Chinese white

> Sepia

> Light red

> Yellow ochre

> Lamp black

Acrylic white

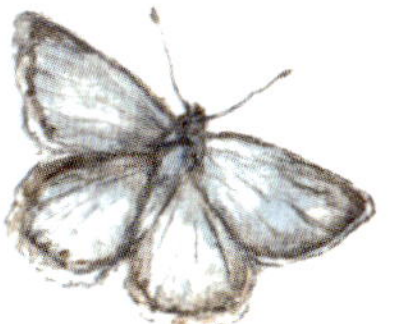

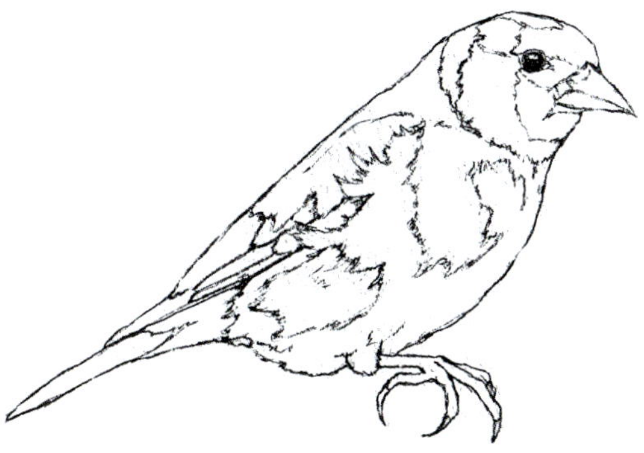

## Step 1: Draw the Outline

Starting on a sheet of cold-press watercolor paper, draw the goldfinch's outline with a sharp **HB** pencil using the corresponding template located in the back of the book (page 171). Note that there will be variation in the line of the feathers. For example, the feathers of the tail are fluid and require a steady hand, whereas the feathers on the head are fluffier and require a lighter touch. Make sure to fill in the eye, but leave a small dot on the upper left-hand side for our highlight.

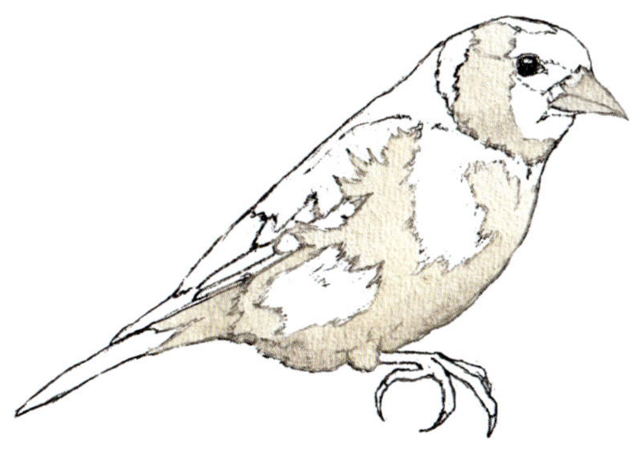

## Step 2: Paint the Body and Beak

To prepare the color that will fill the main mass of the body's feathers, use a size 4 brush to mix together a midtone solution of Chinese white with a tiny dab of sepia to create a warm, creamy hue. Glaze this mixture over the front plumage, the feathers on the lower head and the beak. While the paint is still wet, add another layer of this cream-tone color to the lower-body feathers where the plumage meets the foot of the bird.

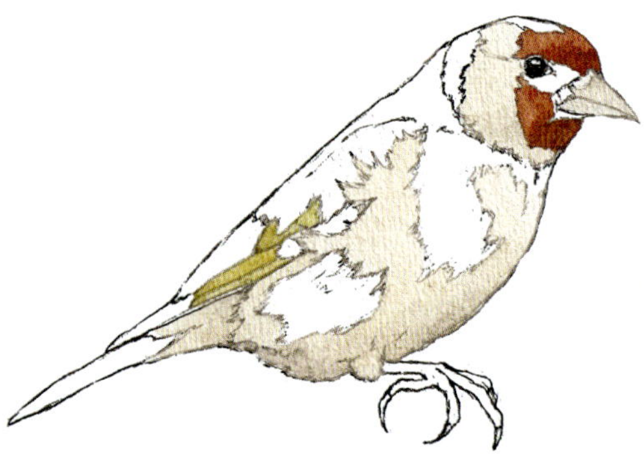

# Step 3: Add Red and Yellow to the Feathers

For the vibrant red feathers on the goldfinch's head, use a size 1 brush to mix a simple dark-tone solution of light red. Concentrating the color on the right-hand side of the head nearest the beak, drag the color across gently. This will soften the gradient of color and naturally let it flow from a darker, more saturated hue on the right to gradually lighter as it moves to the left of the face.

For the pop of yellow feathers on the goldfinch's wing, use a size 1 brush to mix a midtone solution of yellow ochre and glaze this mix carefully over the three feathers on the lower wing. Allow the paint to fully dry.

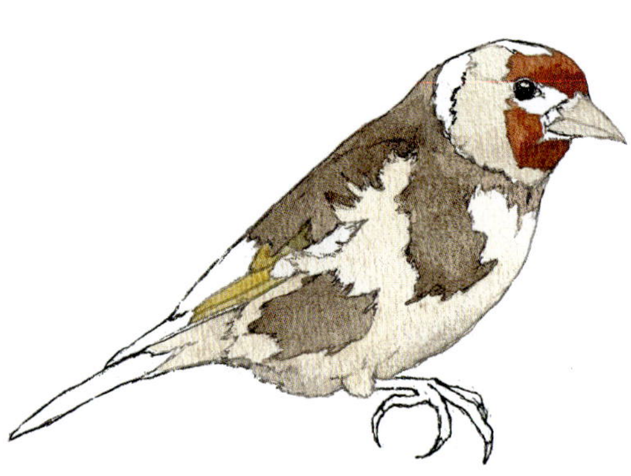

# Step 4: Add Brown to the Feathers

To prepare the color that will fill the brown feathers, use a size 4 brush to mix a midtone solution of sepia and water. Glaze this color over the upper feathers close to the head and the lower feather patch close to the yellow wing. While the paint is still damp, swirl a size 3/0 brush into the midtone solution of sepia and use the tip of the brush to paint along the inner outline of the brown feathers on the back and extending downward onto the front body of plumage. Fill in the small patch of feathers underneath the wing with this sepia solution also.



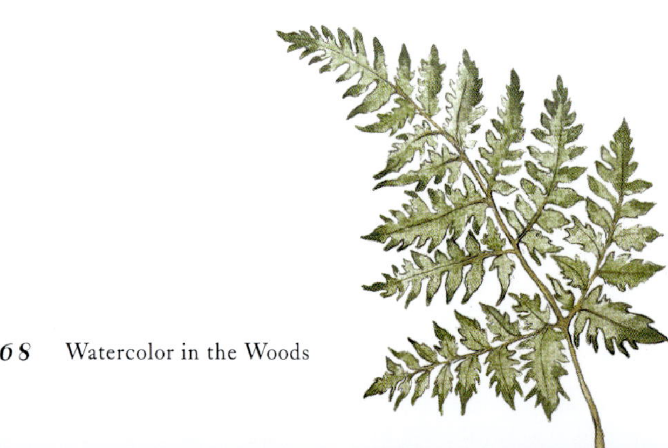

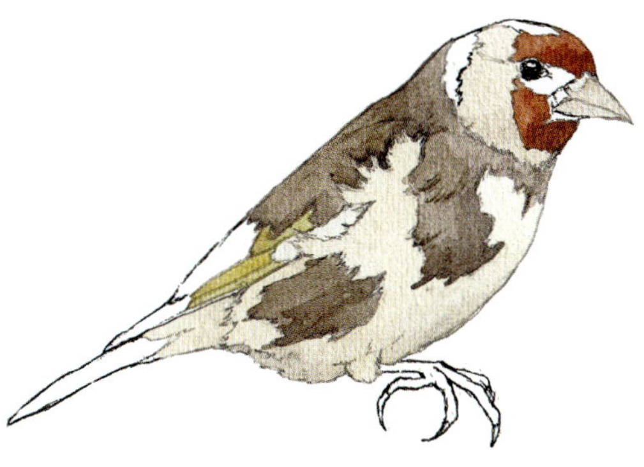

# Step 5: Add the Shadows

Using a size 3/0 brush, mix a dark-tone solution of sepia. We want the color to be a rich brown and highly saturated with color. Load the paint onto the tip of the brush, and using short, wispy brushstrokes, fill in some small feather details that swoop to the left on the plumage, and outline in wispy brushstrokes the parts where the brown and cream feathers intersect along the wing. Thin the dark-tone sepia mix on your palette with water until it is slightly more diluted to a midtone solution. Load this onto the same 3/0 brush and paint shadow layers along the right-hand side of the plumage and along the right-hand side of the lower patch of brown feathers underneath the wing.

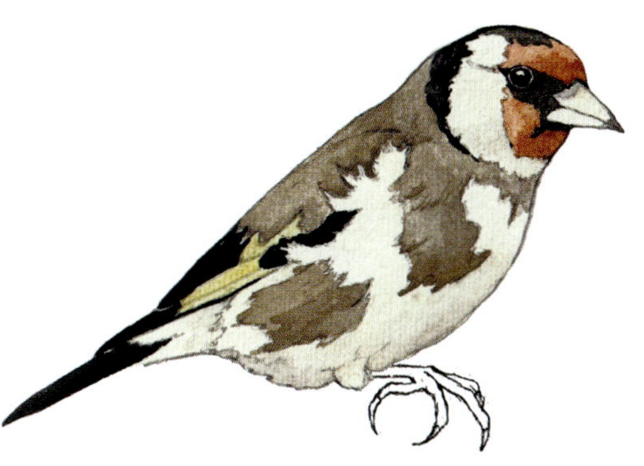

# Step 6: Add the Black

Using a size 1 brush, mix a dark-tone solution of lamp black and water. Paint this color along the lower feathers of the wing, on the feathers on the outer section of the head, along the eye and on the tip of the beak.

# Step 7: Add the Final Details

Using a size 3/0 brush, mix a light-tone solution of light red and fill in the foot with this light glaze. Clean the brush and dip it into the same dark-tone mix of lamp black we used in step 6. Using the tip of the brush, fill in the pupil and the talons.

Finally, clean the brush and dip it into a small amount of acrylic white. Use the very tip of the brush to create a tiny highlight on the goldfinch's pupil and an outline of white around the pupil. The goldfinch is now complete, well done!

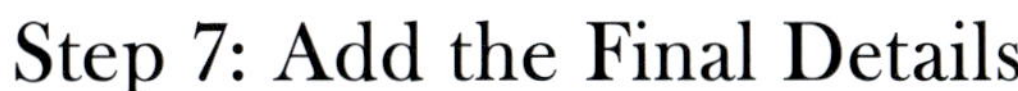

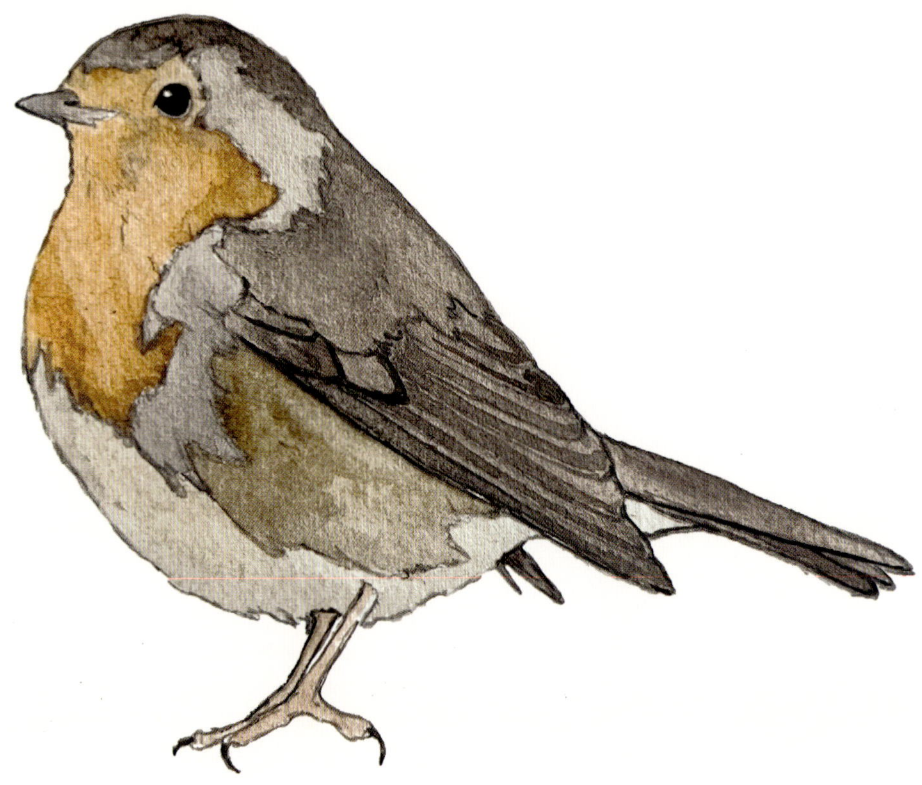

# Robin

Every winter, I look forward to having a robin as my close companion in the garden. The presence of not only its song but also the striking burst of color from its red breast is a welcome reminder that the heralds of spring are soon to come after a colder season of reflection and hibernation. The bird's color palette of earthy red and brown tones also makes for a wonderful painting project. Not only are robins a symbol of the festive season but also of renewal and hope for brighter seasons to come.

# Materials Needed

A sheet of cold-press 140-pound (300-gsm) watercolor paper

HB pencil

Brushes

> Size 1

> Size 3/0

> Size 4

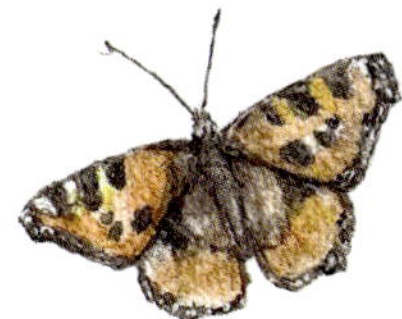

Watercolor paints

> Burnt sienna

> Cadmium orange

> Ivory black

> Chinese white

> Yellow ochre

> Raw umber

> Sepia

> Light red

Acrylic white

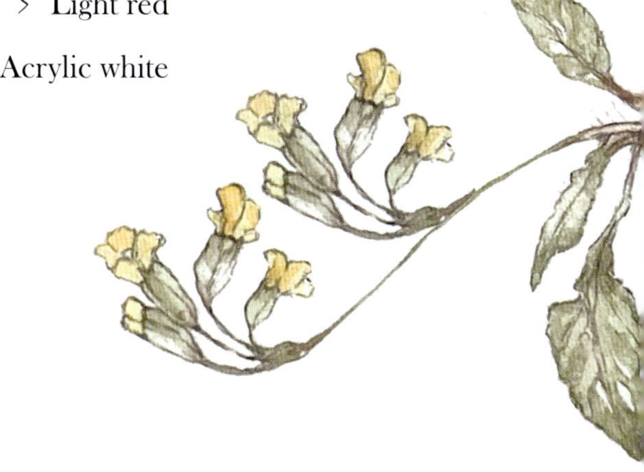

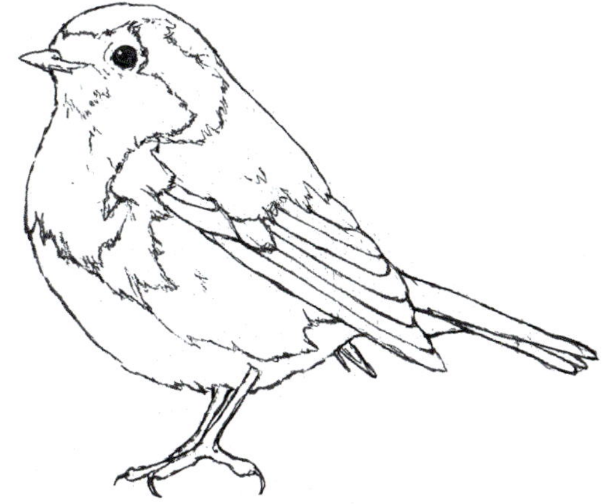

## Step 1: Draw the Outline

Starting on a sheet of cold-press watercolor paper, draw the robin's outline with a sharp HB pencil using the corresponding template located in the back of the book (page 171). Note that there will be variation in the line of the feathers. For example, the feathers of the tail are fluid and require a steady hand, whereas the feathers on the head are fluffier and require a lighter touch. Make sure to fill in the eye, but leave a small dot on the upper left-hand side for the highlight of the pupil.

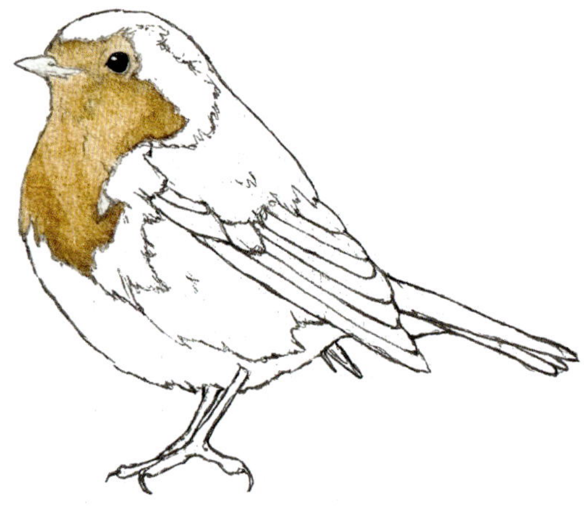

## Step 2: Paint the Head

To prepare the color that we will use for the robin's head, use a size 1 brush to mix a midtone solution of burnt sienna with a tiny dab of cadmium orange hue. We want this color to be a burnt rusty orange hue, so make sure not to swirl in too much cadmium orange hue as this will make the color appear too bright and sunny. Fill in the feathers of the head. While the paint is still damp, deepen the tones of the lower feathers by adding another layer of the rusty paint to the plumage's lower bottom section and along the upper right-hand side. Soften the edges by gently dragging the paint so it blends seamlessly into the bottom layer of paint.

## Step 3: Paint the Lower Plumage and Beak

For the color of the beak, use a size 3/0 brush to mix a light-tone dilution of ivory black. We want this color to be a very light gray. Using the tip of the brush, glaze this solution, concentrating on the left-hand side where the tip of the beak is and softening the edges toward the right-hand side so there is a natural gradient that goes from dark to lighter shades of gray. While the paint is damp, drop another layer of the mixed gray color at the tip of the beak on the left-hand side, creating a deeper saturation of color at that point. Allow the paint to fully dry.

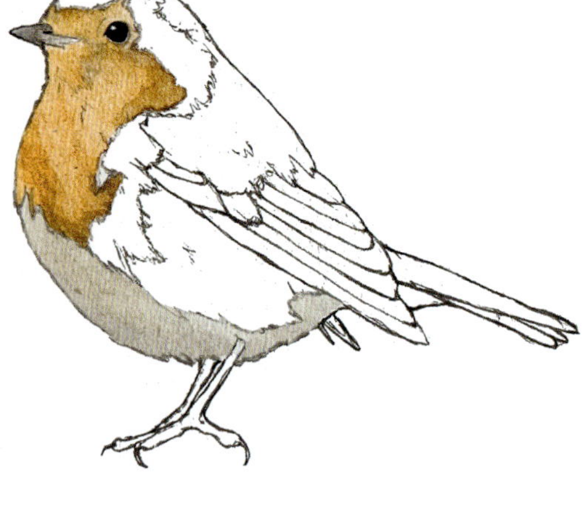

For the robin's lower plumage feathers, use a size 4 brush to create a midtone solution of Chinese white with a dab of yellow ochre. We want this color to be a warm cream. On the dry down of this cream color, Chinese white can sometimes give a matte "gray" hue, so do not worry if your watercolor mixture does give off a cooler tone in certain light. Glaze this solution over the entire lower plumage. Allow the paint to fully dry.

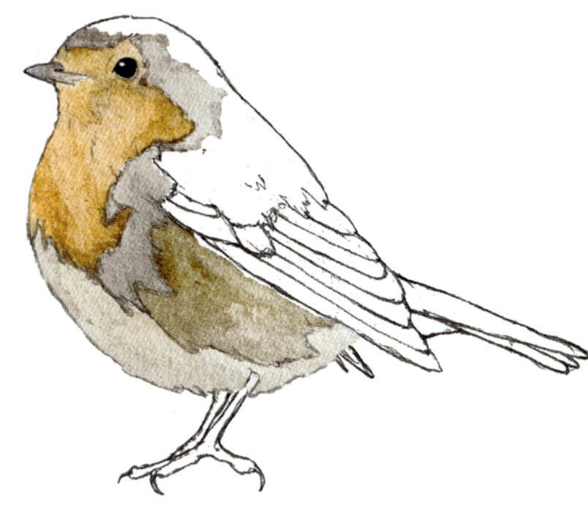

# Step 4: Paint the Midsection

To prepare the color that will fill the gray-tone feathers of the robin, use a size 1 brush to mix a light-tone solution of ivory black. This will be a similar gray-tone glaze that we used in step 3. Fill the feathers that sit beside the head and stretch down along the lower body. While the paint is still damp, deepen your light gray mixture slightly by adding a small dab of ivory. We do not want this to appear as black but as a deeper gray that is still diluted. Use the tip of the brush to drop this color along the gray feathers at the very top of the head, where they meet the red feathers, and along the lower section on the right-hand side where they will meet the beige-tone feathers.

For the feathers that will sit below the wing, use a size 1 brush to mix a midtone solution of raw umber and yellow ochre. We want this color to have an earthy beige hue, so add slightly more yellow ochre to warm up the cooler tones of the raw umber. Glaze this mixture over the entire section of feathers that sit just below the wing. While the paint is still damp, swirl the brush back into the warm beige mixture and use the tip to create a glaze on the left-hand side where the feathers meet the upper gray section. Soften the edges by gently dragging the paint along the natural downward curves to the right.

# Step 5: Paint the Upper Body, Wings and Tail

For the remaining feathers, use a size 4 brush to mix a midtone solution of sepia. Fill in the remaining feathers on the head, wing and tail with this mixture. While the paint is still damp, swirl the brush back into this brown color and use the tip of the brush to paint another layer of color along the feathers of the tail, the upper head, the right wing and the lower feathers on the wing where they meet the beige feathers of the body.

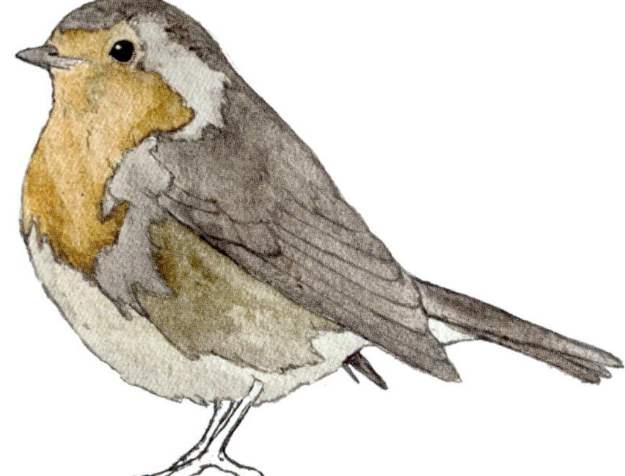

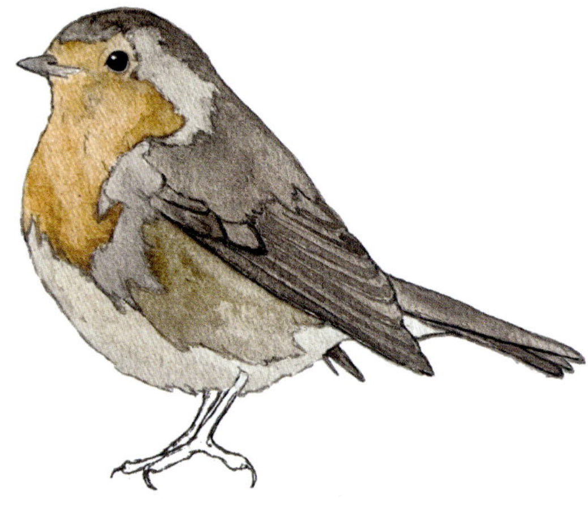

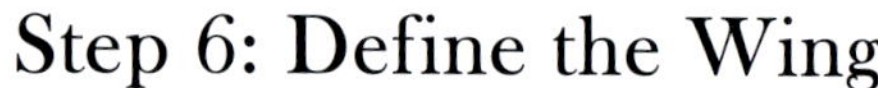

# Step 6: Define the Wing

To define the feathers on the robin's wing, use a size 3/0 brush to mix a midtone solution of sepia and ivory black on your palette. We want this color to be a deeper hue of sepia, a very dark brown but not black. Using the tip of the brush, paint along the lower outline of each individual feather as they sit in a stack-like arrangement on the wing. I would recommend painting from top to bottom, as this will avoid smudging. Using the same dark brown mixture, paint the lower feathers on the tail and a tiny section of the robin's left wing to create a sense of depth and shadow. Finally, glaze the brown feathers on the upper section of the robin's head with a layer of the dark brown mixture. Allow the paint to fully dry.

# Step 7: Add the Final Details

For the robin's feet, use a clean size 3/0 brush to mix a light solution of light red to create a pale pink hue. Fill in both of the feet with this mixture.

Using the same size 3/0 brush, clean the bristles with water and mix a dark-tone solution of ivory black and load it onto the brush. Use the tip of the brush to fill in the pupil with this thick black color. Trace the talons of the feet using the tip of the same brush and dark black.

Finally, squeeze a small amount of acrylic white onto your palette, and, using a clean size 3/0 brush, paint in a tiny dot on the left-hand side of the pupil in the eye for a subtle luminous highlight. Good job, the robin is now complete!

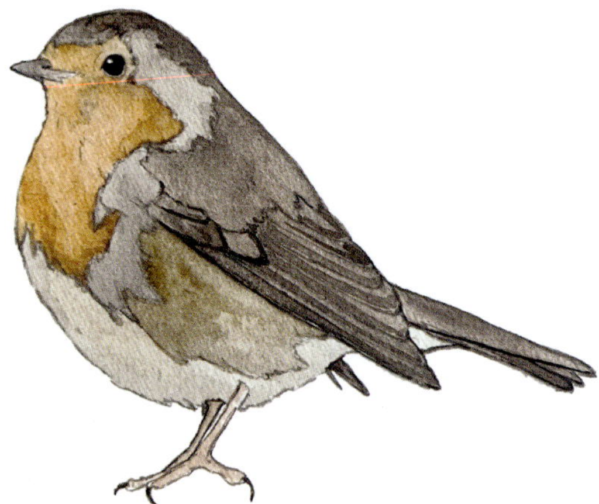

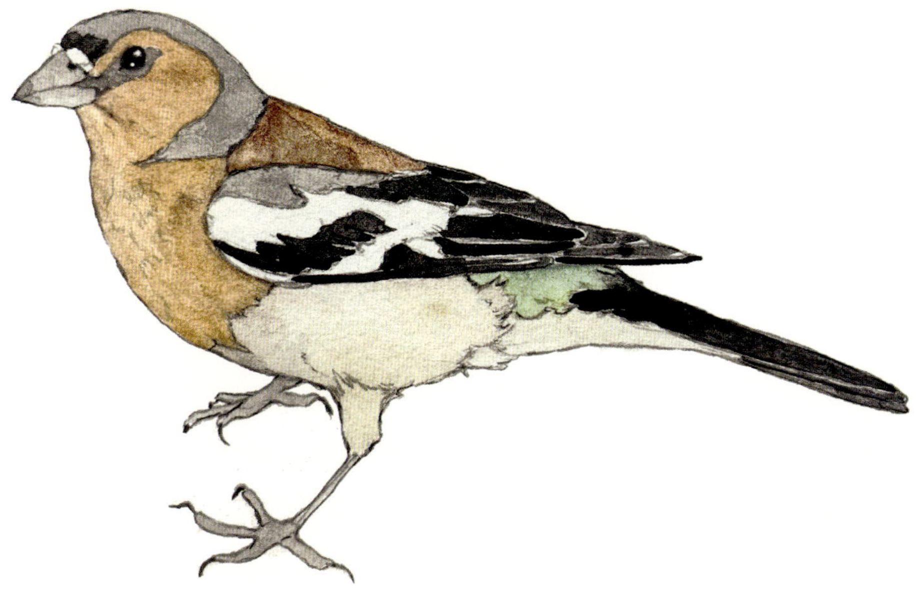

# Chaffinch

One of my favorite hobbies is bird-watching, and in my observation, the male chaffinch possesses a timeless and understated beauty that makes it an ideal subject for watercolor painting. With their distinctive plumage with soft hues of pink, aqua blues and rust in intricate patterns, chaffinches hold a rich tapestry of colors and textures, all while simply perched on a branch!

# Materials Needed

A sheet of cold-press 140-pound (300-gsm) watercolor paper

HB pencil

Brushes

> Size 1

> Size 4

> Size 3/0

Watercolor paints

> Burnt sienna

> Yellow ochre

> Burnt umber

> Chinese white

> Ivory black

> Emerald

> Prussian blue

Acrylic white

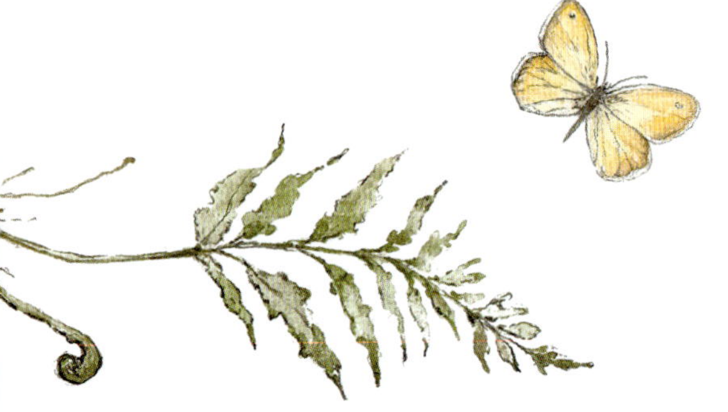

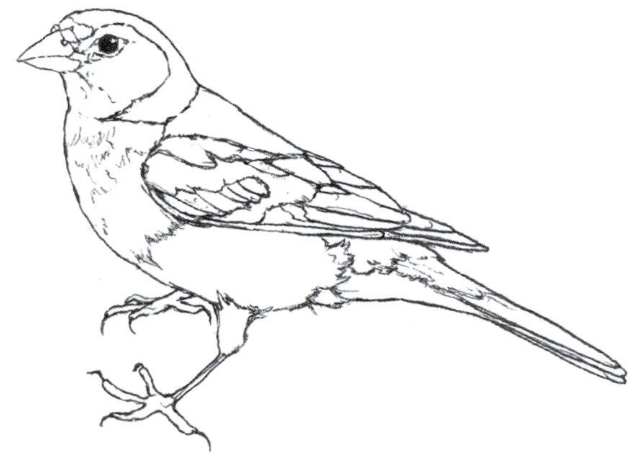

# Step 1: Draw the Outline

Starting on a sheet of cold-press watercolor paper, draw the chaffinch's outline with a sharp **HB** pencil using the corresponding template located in the back of the book (page 171). Note that the feathers on the chaffinch's chest plumage are quite light and downy, whereas the feathers on the tail will require a more fluid, confident line. Make sure to fill in the eye, but leave a small dot on the upper right-hand side for our highlight.

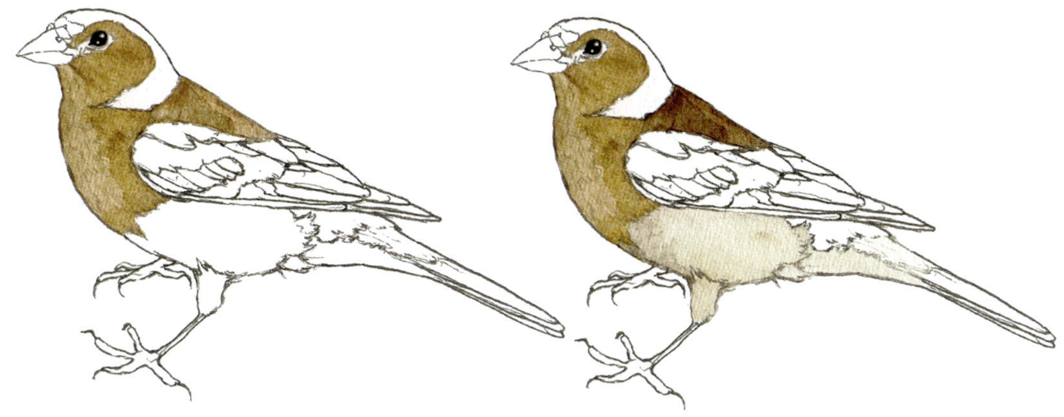

## Step 2: Paint the Upper Body and Head

To prepare the color that we will use for the upper part of the body and head, use a size 1 brush to mix a midtone solution of burnt sienna with a swirl of yellow ochre. We want this color to be a warm, burnt orange. Glaze this mixture over the part of the head surrounding the eye, blending downward onto the upper feathers of the wing, to the midsection of the plumage. Allow this layer to dry, then add a second layer of the burnt orange color around the eye and the feathers nearest the wing and on the upper body. Allow this to fully dry, then add a final layer to the upper-body feathers where they meet the head and extend downward above the wing.

## Step 3: Paint the Lower Body and Tail

Prepare the paint that will deepen the tones of the upper-body feathers by using a size 1 brush to mix a midtone solution of burnt umber with a hint of burnt sienna. We want this color to be a deep rusty tone. Glaze this wash over the upper-body feathers that sit above the wing, concentrating the paint where they meet the lower head, and gently and softly extend the wash down the curve of the body to soften the gradient.

To mix the creamy pink color that will fill in the lower body and the upper tail, use a size 4 brush to mix a midtone solution of Chinese white with a subtle dab of burnt sienna to make a dusky pink–tone cream. Paint this over the entire lower body, gently blending the cream into the burnt orange where it meets the upper body and causing a subtle transition of color between the two. Fill in the upper tail with this dusky pink cream and allow the paint to fully dry.

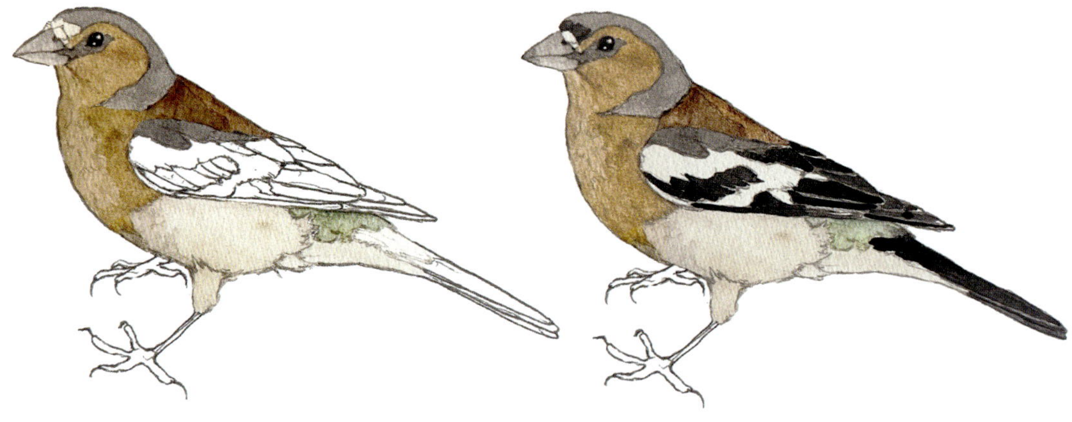

# Step 4: Add Subtle Pops of Color

For the color that we will use for the head and beak, use a size 1 brush to mix a light-tone solution of ivory black with a swirl of Chinese white. We want this color to have a muted hue and a dusky gray tone. Fill in the upper head, the beak and the feathers around the eye and at the top of the wing with this gray tone. Allow the paint to fully dry. Then, add another layer of this gray to the feathers around the eye and the top of the wing, and while the paint is still damp, load one more layer of this color onto your brush and drop the color onto the feathers that sit at the top of the wing.

To add the iconic pop of green to the underside of the chaffinch's wing, use a size 1 brush to mix a midtone solution of emerald and glaze this onto the entire section of feathers that sits at the top of the tail. While the paint is still damp, drop in a tiny dab of Prussian blue into your emerald color mixture and trace the underside of the wing to deepen the tone and create subtle shadows of where the wing's feathers overlay the body.

# Step 5: Paint the Wing and Tail

Using a size 1 brush, mix a light-tone solution of ivory black. Switch to a size 3/0 brush, load the fine tip with the thin glaze and fill in the very tip of the beak. Next, switch back to your size 1 brush and create a midtone solution of ivory black by swirling in more pigment to your initial light glaze solution. Use the tip of the brush to paint in the very tip of the head where it almost meets the beak, leaving space for a small segment of white feathers, then paint a layer on the tail's feathers. Finally, create a dark-tone solution by adding more ivory black to your midtone mixture to deepen the color further and paint in each individual feather one by one. Note that more of the feathers on the right-hand side are black and more of the feathers on the left-hand side are white, so take your time in following this picture reference. Glaze the tail feathers and switch to a size 3/0 brush to fill in the main body of the eye with this dark inky black.

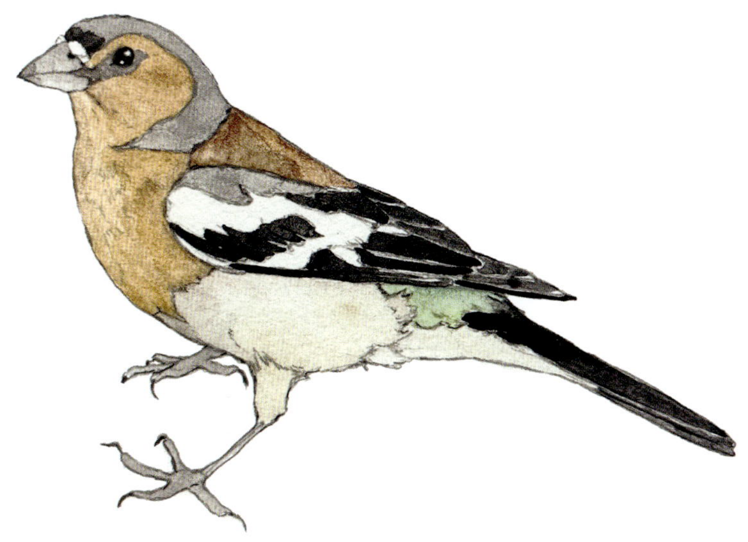

## Step 6: Add the Final Details

Squeeze a small amount of acrylic white onto your palette, and using a clean size 3/0 brush, paint in two tiny dots in the eye for highlights. Switch to a size 1 brush and load the acrylic white onto the bristles. Fill in the feathers on the upper left side of the wing and the top of the beak.

Use a clean size 3/0 brush to mix a light-tone solution of ivory black and water and fill in both of the chaffinch's feet with a light gray color. Next, mix in some more ivory paint to create a midtone solution. Finally, using the same size 3/0 brush, load this midtone solution onto the bristles and carefully trace over the outlines of each color section and individual feathers on the wing to create sharp definition. Great job, the chaffinch is now complete!

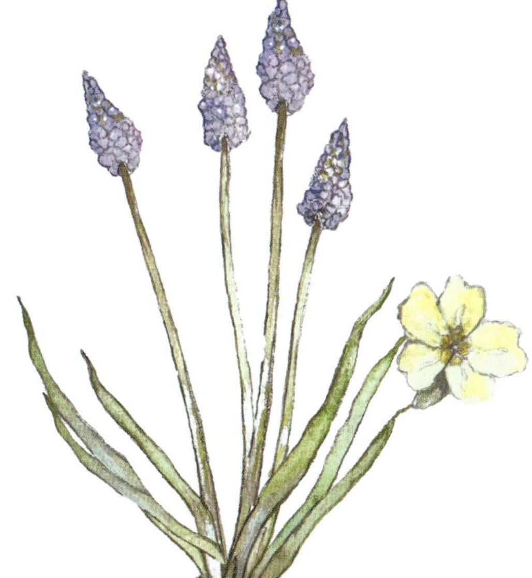

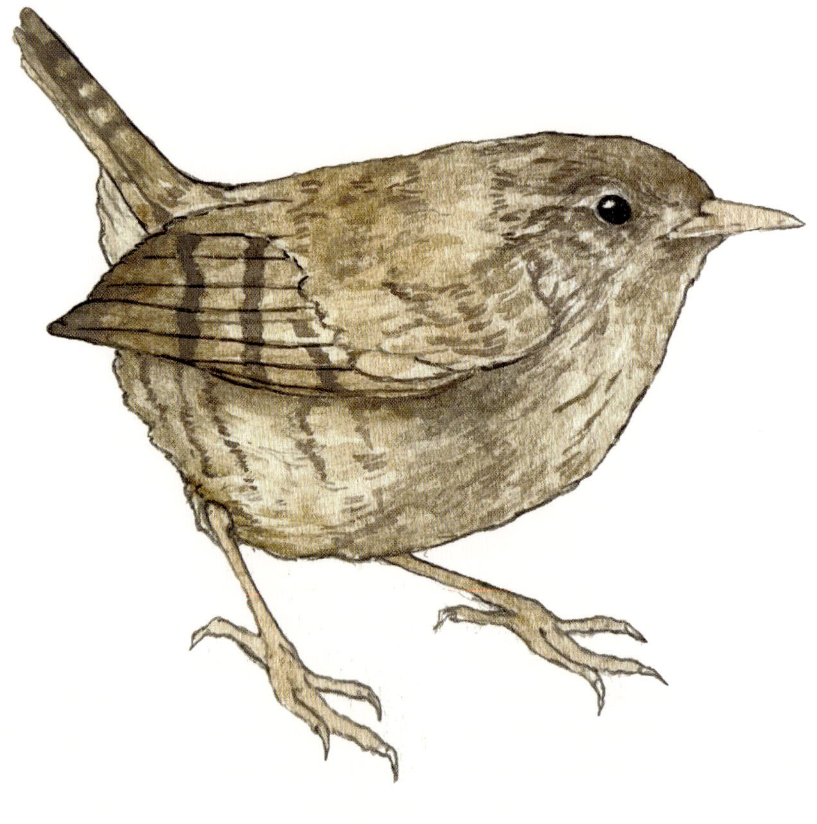

# Wren

The wren is a wonderfully tiny bird, which I am proud to say is one of my
favorite animals. I am so glad that they are dotted throughout the countryside
here in Ireland. A reason for my admiration is that although tiny in stature and
shy in nature, the wren makes a stunningly loud song for such a small
creature. As they are so secretive, painting a wren in this project may be the
closest encounter some may ever get to have with one! The melody of their
tune is a cherished companion while out on a walk, and if I am lucky, I will
get the chance to spot one hidden among the leaves—an adorable
round ball of feathers!

# Materials Needed

A sheet of cold-press 140-pound (300-gsm) watercolor paper

HB pencil

Brushes

> Size 1

> Size 3/0

Watercolor paints

> Raw umber

> Raw sienna

> Vandyke brown

> Sepia

> Burnt sienna

> Lamp black

Acrylic white

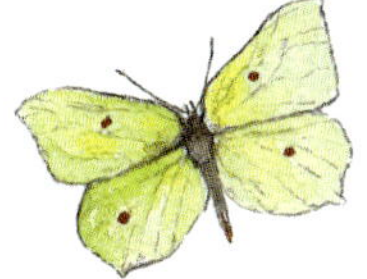

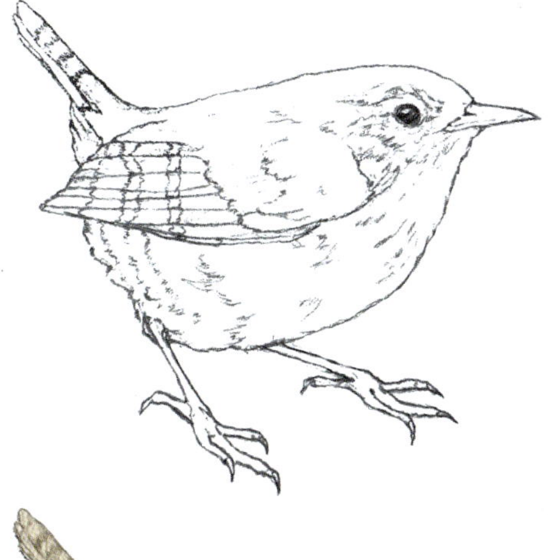

## Step 1: Draw the Outline

Starting on a sheet of cold-press watercolor paper, draw the wren's outline with a sharp HB pencil using the corresponding template located in the back of the book (page 173). Lightly fill in the feather details using fluffy strokes, as the wren has quite a lot of short, downy feathers which give it a soft, fuzzy appearance. Make sure to fill in the eye, but leave a small dot on the upper left-hand side for the highlight of the pupil.

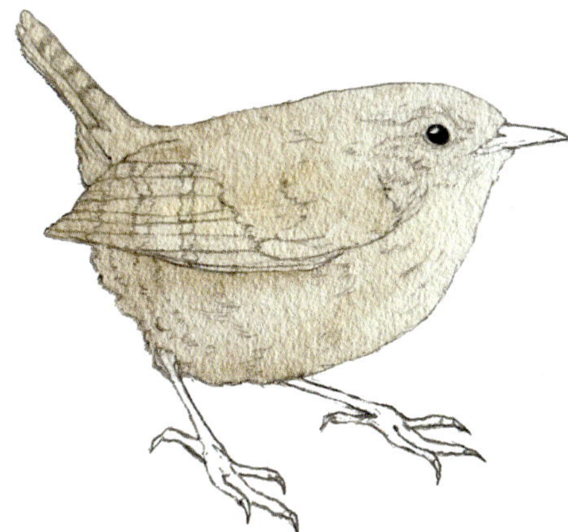

## Step 2: Paint the Body

To prepare the color that will fill the body's base layer, use a size 1 brush to mix a mid- to light-tone solution of raw umber with a dab of raw sienna. We want this color to be a rich, earthy yellow–tone brown. Glaze this solution over the entire feathered body, except for the beak and the feet. While the paint is still damp, swirl the brush back into this earthy brown color and drop the color along the left-hand side of the wing at the tip of the feathers and another layer on the underside of the wing to create a subtle shadow.

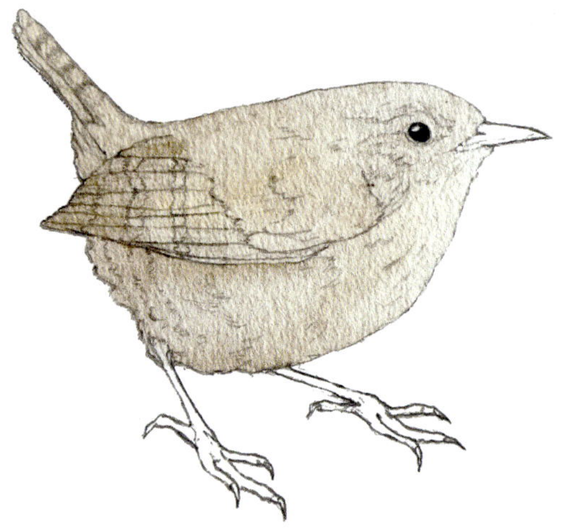

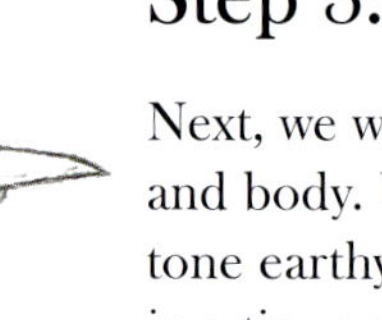

## Step 3: Create the Shadow Layer

Next, we will add depth and shadows to the wing and body. Using the same size 1 brush and light-tone earthy brown color we mixed in step 2, swirl in a tiny amount of raw umber to the mixture to deepen its hue to a darker brown. Lightly paint a layer of this color to the tip of the wing on the left-hand side, softening the edges by gently blending the color into the base layer below it. This will create a subtle gradient of darker to lighter as it blends to the right-hand side of the feathers on the wing.

## Step 4: Paint the Fluffy Feathers

To paint the wren's fluffy feathers, use a size 3/0 brush to mix a light-tone solution of Vandyke brown. With the fine tip of the brush, use short, quick strokes to start layering the diluted Vandyke brown onto the body, wings and head. Follow the natural curvature of the bird's rounded body. We want to create a sense of volume and texture, so once the first layer of short, rounded brushstrokes is dry, repeat the step and add another layer of this soft fluffy texture to the top of the head around the eye, the feathers underneath the wing and the edge of the lower body where the feathers meet the wren's leg.

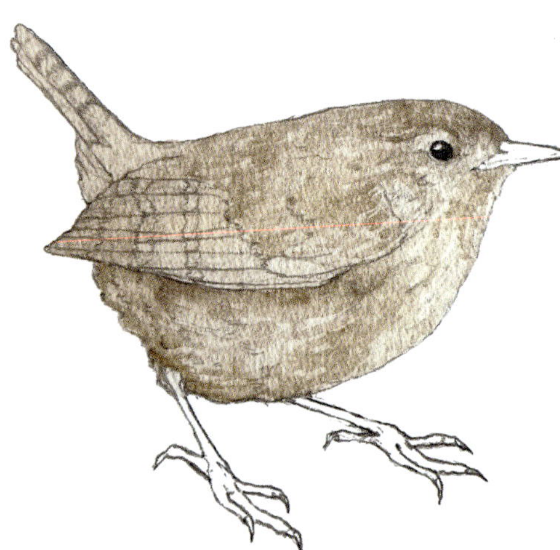

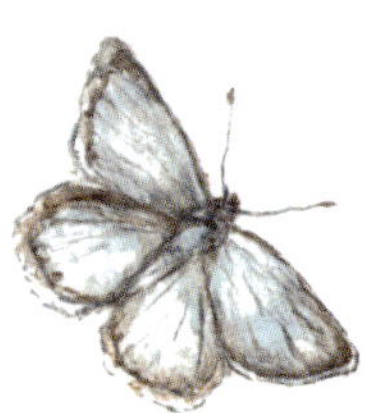

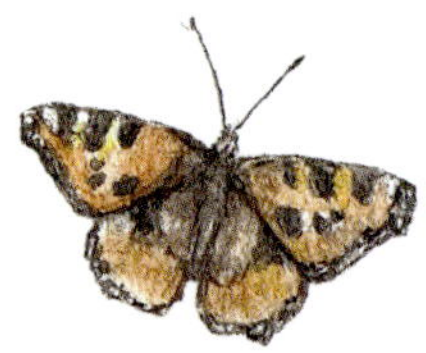

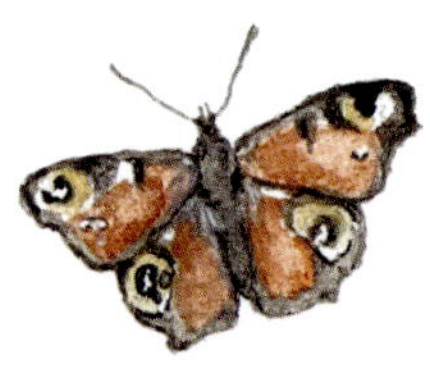

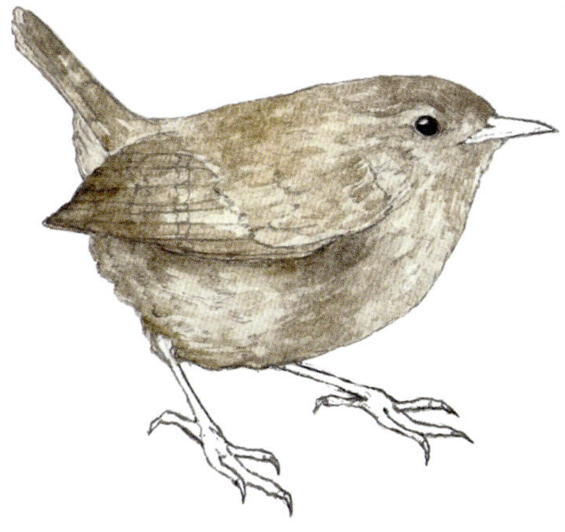

# Step 5: Add the Layers of Color

Next, we want to add depth and color to the wren's fluffy body and wing. Begin by using a size 1 brush to mix a midtone solution of raw sienna with a dab of raw umber to create a warm burnt beige color. Using the tip of the brush, use the same short, quick layered brushstroke technique to create a fluffy feather layer on the midsection of the upper body.

To create a sense of depth to the wren's brown feathers, use a size 1 brush to mix a light-tone solution of sepia. Using the tip of the brush, gently use the short, quick brushstroke technique to add a layer of color to the top of the head above the eye, the tips of the feathers on the wing, dabbing upward along the tail and the underside of the wing.

Paint a layer of short, gentle brushstrokes on the lower right-hand side of the body, following downward and along the outline of where the feathers meet the feet. Allow the paint to fully dry, then add one more layer of this sepia solution to the tips of the wing on the left-hand side and where the feathers meet the beak to add further depth and tone.

# Step 6: Define the Feathers

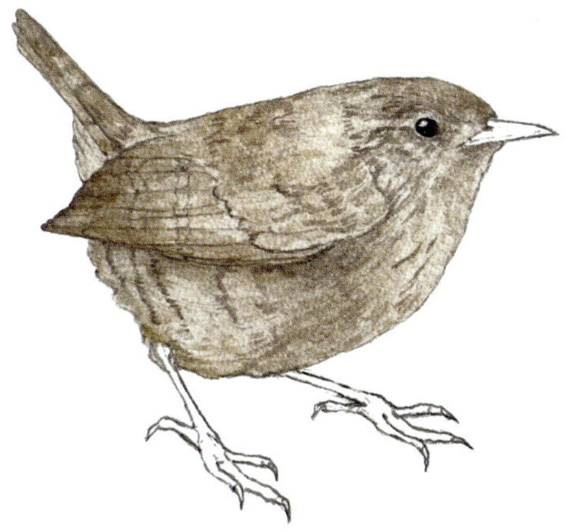

Using a size 3/0 brush, mix a dark-tone solution of sepia. Using the tip of the brush and holding it at the ferrule so your hand has the most control to do tight and neat work, paint short, quick layered brushstrokes around the eye, creating a fluffy texture. Paint in more lines along the bottom right-hand side of the wing, following the curvature of the feathers and traveling down and curving along the lower body. As you go, vary the weight of brushstrokes with your hand, keeping some movements gentle and others heavier to emulate the natural arrangements of the wren's soft feathers.

(Continued)

Create more defined outlines on the lower body and left-hand side by loading the tip of the brush with color and painting three downward lines consisting of tiny short strokes to keep the texture looking fluffy. Follow the same technique for the tail by creating defined line patterns by painting in four lines traveling up the tail consisting of short, quick brushstrokes.

## Step 7: Paint the Feather Patterns

Using the same 3/0 brush and high-concentrated solution of sepia, carefully outline the shape of the wren's wing and individual feathers, ensuring smooth, flowing lines that follow the bird's natural contours from our template drawing. Using the tip of the brush, fill in the three downward line patterns on the feathers with this same matte brown color. Fill in the similar line patterns that travel upward on the tail's feathers. Finally, drop some of this concentrated sepia color on the tips of the wing, gently softening the edges to let the color blend seamlessly.

## Step 8: Add the Final Details

Using a size 1 brush, mix a light-tone solution of burnt sienna to create a pale rust color. Use the tip of the brush to fill in the wren's beak and the feet.

Using a 3/0 brush, mix a dark-tone solution of lamp black and load it onto the brush. Use the tip of the brush to fill in the pupil with this thick black color.

Finally, squeeze a small amount of acrylic white onto your palette, and using a clean size 3/0 brush, paint in a tiny dot on the left-hand side of the pupil in the eye for a subtle luminous highlight. The wren is now complete, well done!

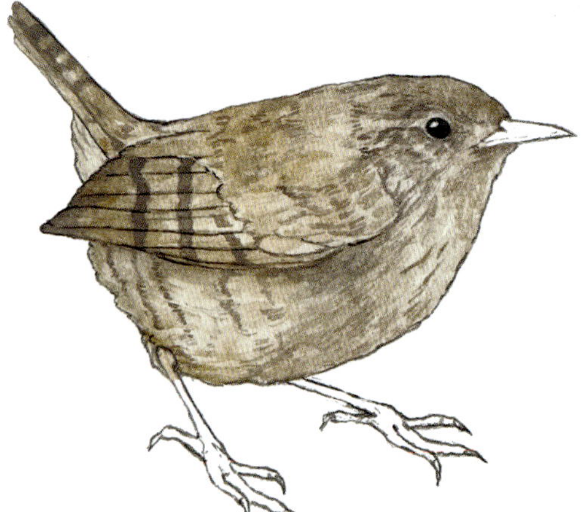

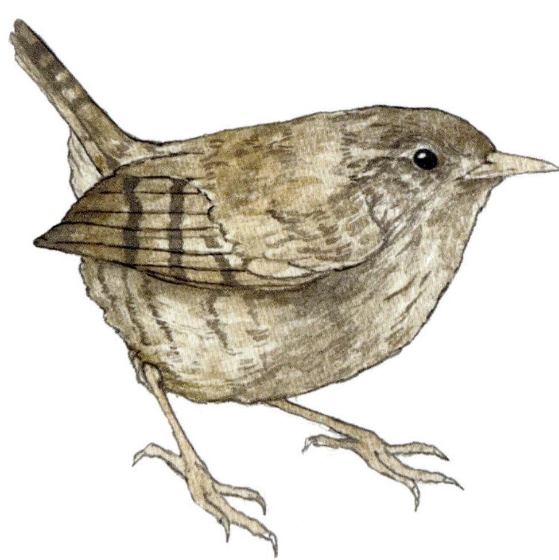

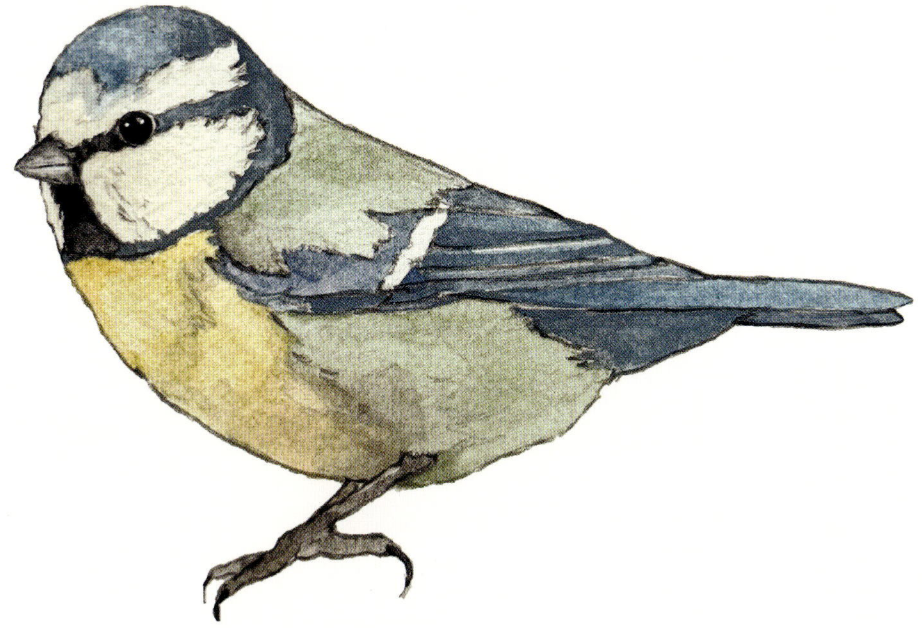

# Blue Tit

Blue tits, although so small in size and agile in their movements, bring so much natural color and vibrance to any setting as they flit among the branches. Naturally, their plumage and adorable faces make a stunning subject to paint due to the contrast of jewel colors, which will fly right off the page!

# Materials Needed

A sheet of cold-press 140-pound (300-gsm) watercolor paper

HB pencil

Brushes

> Size 1

> Size 4

> Size 3/0

> Size 0

Watercolor paints

> Chinese white

> Raw umber

> Cadmium yellow

> Hooker's green light

> Sap green

> Lamp black

> Cobalt blue

> Prussian blue

Acrylic white

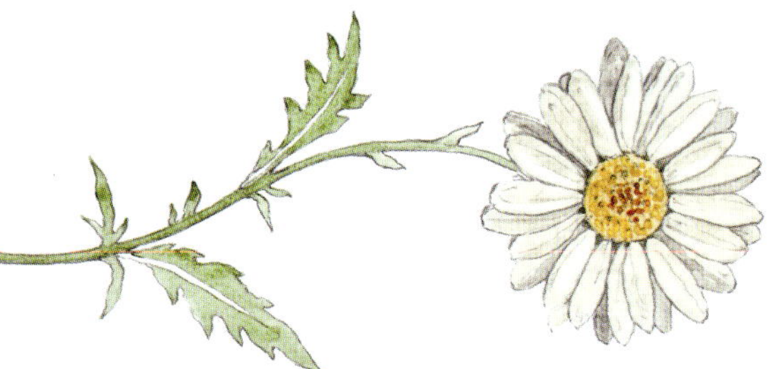

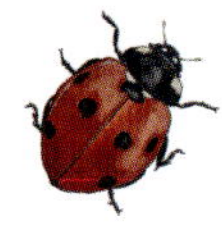

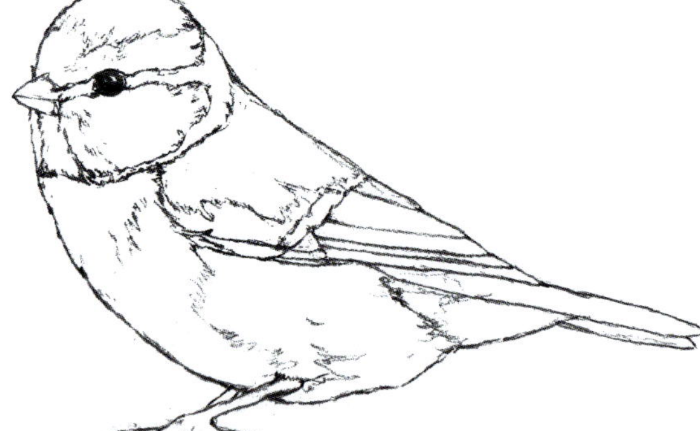

# Step 1: Draw the Outline

Starting on a sheet of cold-press watercolor paper, draw the blue tit's outline with a sharp **HB** pencil using the corresponding template located in the back of the book (page 173). Note that there will be variation in the line of the feathers. For example, the feathers of the tail are fluid and require a steady hand, whereas the feathers on the head are fluffier and require a lighter touch. Make sure to fill in the eye, but leave a small dot on the upper right-hand side for our highlight.

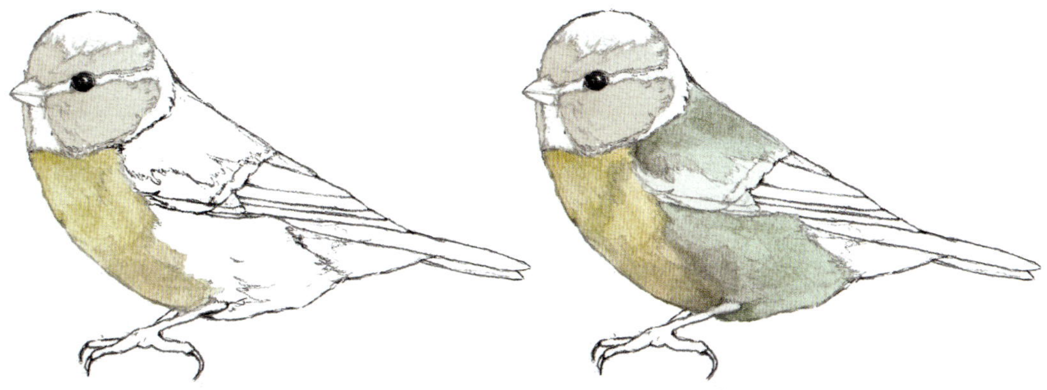

# Step 2: Paint the White and Yellow

To prepare the creamy white that will fill in the bird's head, use a size 1 brush to mix together a midtone solution of Chinese white with a tiny hint of raw umber to turn the white into a warm cream tone. On the dry down of this cream color, Chinese white can sometimes give a matte "grayish" hue, so do not worry if your watercolor mixture does give off a cooler tone in certain light. Glaze this color over the three sections of the head: above the eye and to the bottom left and bottom right of the beak.

For the yellow of the body, use a size 4 brush to mix a midtone solution of cadmium yellow hue and glaze this over the entire front of the plumage. While the paint is still wet, swirl a tiny amount of raw umber into your midtone yellow on your palette to create a deeper and slightly darker tone of yellow. Load this onto your brush, and using the tip, trace along the top of the plumage closest to the head and along the very bottom where it meets the foot. The paint will disperse naturally onto the damp paper and create a subtle shadow tone once fully dry.

# Step 3: Add the Green

For the green section of the plumage and wing, use a clean size 4 brush to mix together a midtone solution of Hooker's green light with a hint of sap green to create a bright, grassy tone.

Glaze this wash along the top of the wing and over the entire middle section of the body underneath the wing, gently painting and blending the color into the yellow section of the plumage that we painted in step 2. Allow the paint to fully dry, then go back with the same brush and grassy green color to add a further layer of paint along the top section where it meets the head. Trace along the bottom middle where it meets the wing, softening the edges so there are no hard edges.

Next, we want to mix the transition color that will sit at the bottom of the plumage between the yellow and green. Using a size 3/0 brush, mix a light-tone wash of raw umber with a tiny hint of lamp black to deepen its tone. Gently glaze this thin mix along the line at the bottom of the body where the yellow and green meet, using gentle strokes to blend the three colors together seamlessly.

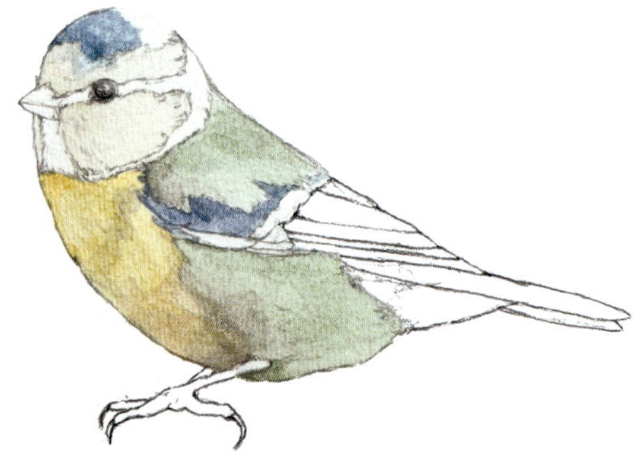

# Step 4: Paint the Blue

Using a size 0 brush, mix a simple midtone wash of cobalt blue and gently glaze this color on the top section of the head from the eye back until you reach the halfway point. Paint the same color on the wing's upper section, using the tip of the brush to gently blend the color into the green section. Dip the tip of the brush back into the blue solution and drop this color at the very front of the head and along the outline of where the blue and green of the wing meet to deepen the tones.

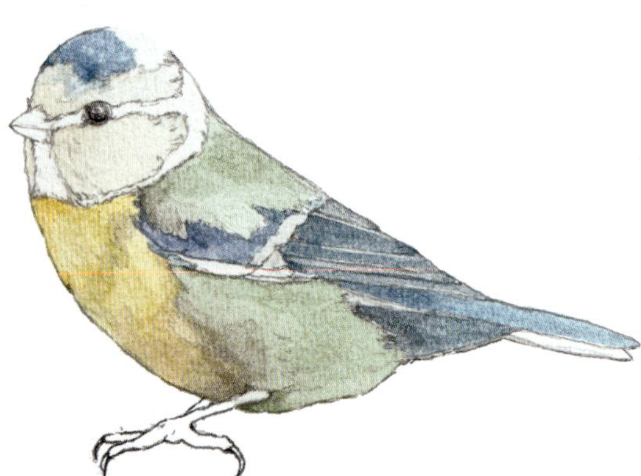

# Step 5: Paint the Wing

For the wings, use a clean size 0 brush to mix a midtone solution of cobalt blue and glaze a layer of this color over each individual feather on the wing and the underside of the body where it runs into the tail. While the paint is still damp, switch to a size 3/0 brush and load the cobalt blue solution onto the bristles. Using the tip, trace the outline of each individual feather and the underside of the wing where the tail begins and meets the green of the body. Allow this to fully dry. Then, using the same size 3/0 brush, clean the bristles and add one more layer of the cobalt blue mixture on the top left-hand side of the feathers and the underside of the body where it meets the green section.

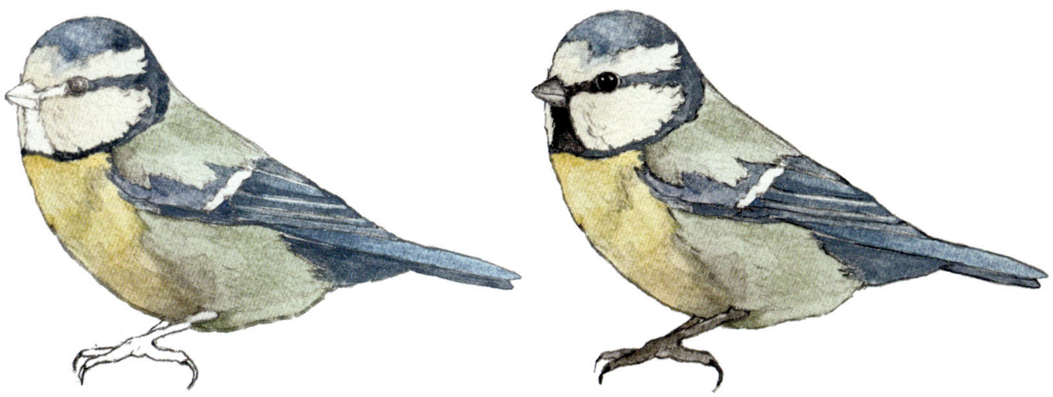

## Step 6: Add Tonal Depth

Using a clean size 3/0 brush, mix a midtone solution of Prussian blue with a tiny hint of lamp black. We want this color to be a rich, inky blue but not too dark, so only a tiny hint of black will be very effective. Using just the tip of the brush, paint along the lower sections of each feather on the wings and the remaining feathers of the upper head, the stripe that leads toward the eye, then following the feathers downward and painting along the feathers that connect the head and green of the wing. Paint the lower right-hand side of the body that runs into the tail.

## Step 7: Add the Final Details

For the final details of the face, beak and eye, we will be using lamp black but to varying degrees of saturation. To prepare the first layer, use a size 3/0 brush to mix a light-tone solution of lamp black and water. Glaze this color over the beak and use the very tips of the brush to paint tiny downy feathers on the white part of the lower face to the left hand side, creating definition. While the paint is still wet, add more lamp black to your light-tone solution to create a midtone mix. Using the same brush, trace the bottom and top of the beak so there is a natural gradient that runs from dark to light toward the center of the beak. Use this same midtone solution to paint the feathers that run down the lower center of the head and toward the eye. While the paint is drying, add more lamp black to the midtone solution to create a thick, dark saturation of black. Using the tip of the brush, fill in the eye and the nails of the bird's foot.

For the leg, use a size 0 brush to mix a simple midtone solution of raw umber with a hint of lamp black and glaze this wash over the entire foot.

Finally, squeeze a small amount of acrylic white onto your palette and load the color onto a clean size 3/0 brush. Using the very tip, paint in two tiny dots on the upper pupil and fill in the midsection of the wing where it splits into layered feathers. The blue tit is now complete, great job!

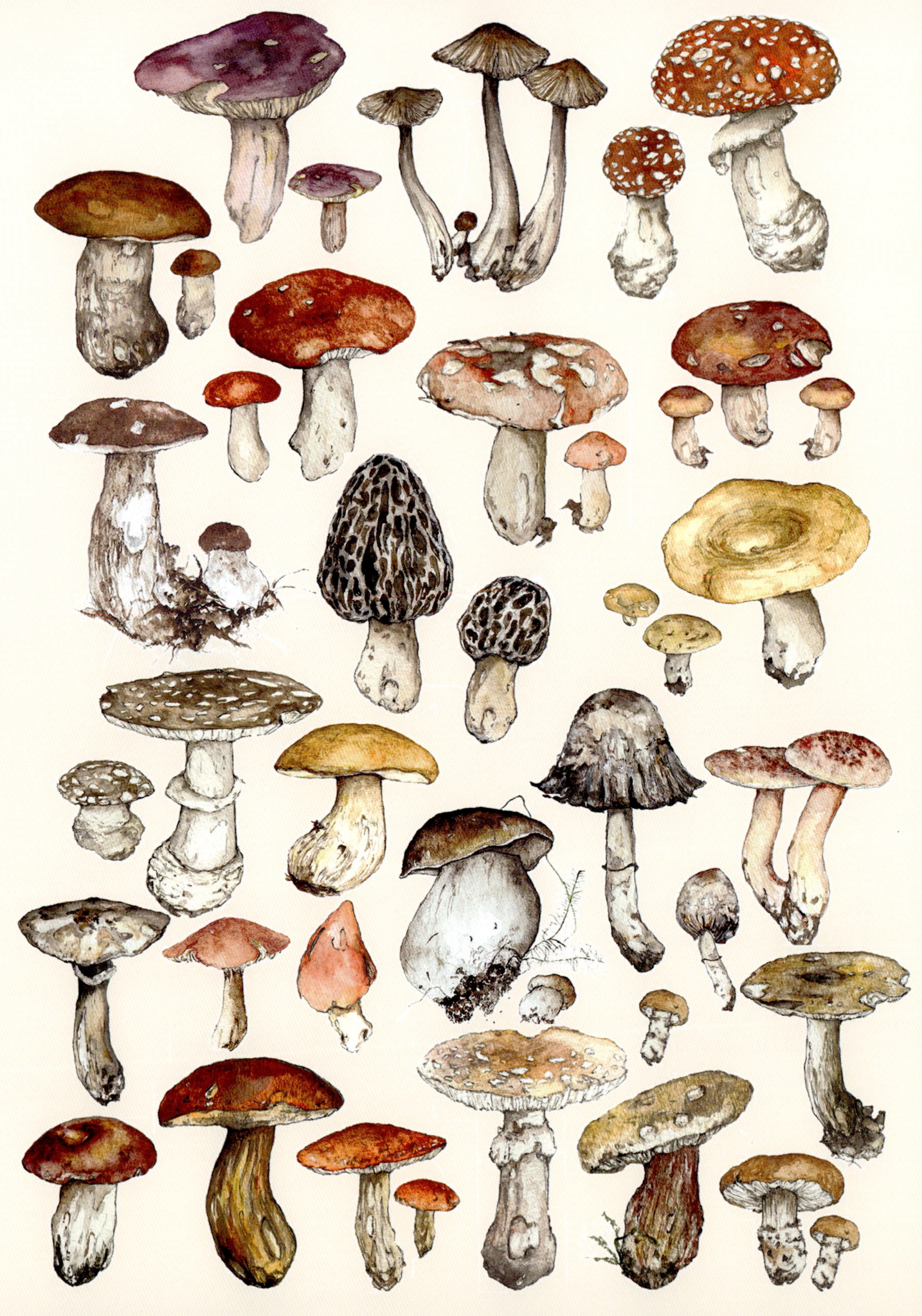

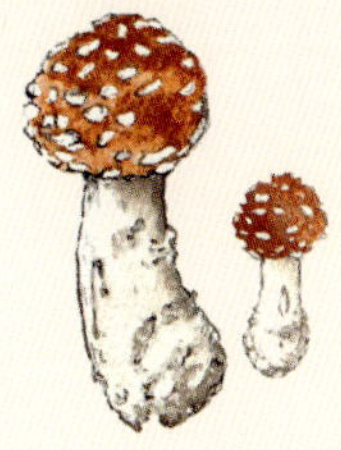

# Foraged Finds

Embark on a journey and discover the hidden treasures of nature, capturing the wonders of untamed beauty in the woodland that may often go unnoticed. With a paintbrush, capture the vibrant hues of berries and the graceful curves of enchanting toadstools and discover the intricate details of freshly picked acorns from the woodland floor.

One of my favorite subjects to paint are toadstools, in particular the fly agaric and its fantastic spotted cap with a blood red hue (page 92). The fantastical colors and amazing forms give you an amazing opportunity to explore various explosions of color, as well as indulge in a really magical subject matter. Often, I have to remind myself that these are in fact found in nature and not lifted directly from a storybook!

Included also are acorns (page 105). These symbols of autumn and growth present a unique challenge with their smooth, shiny nuts and rough textured cups. Learn to depict their form and detail, emphasizing the contrast between the two elements.

And, finally, you'll paint wild berries (page 96). Whether nestled in the shadows or illuminated by sunlight, berries add a pop of color and life to your compositions. We will explore different types of berries—from the deep purples of blackberries to the bright reds of strawberries—and how to create their plump, juicy appearances.

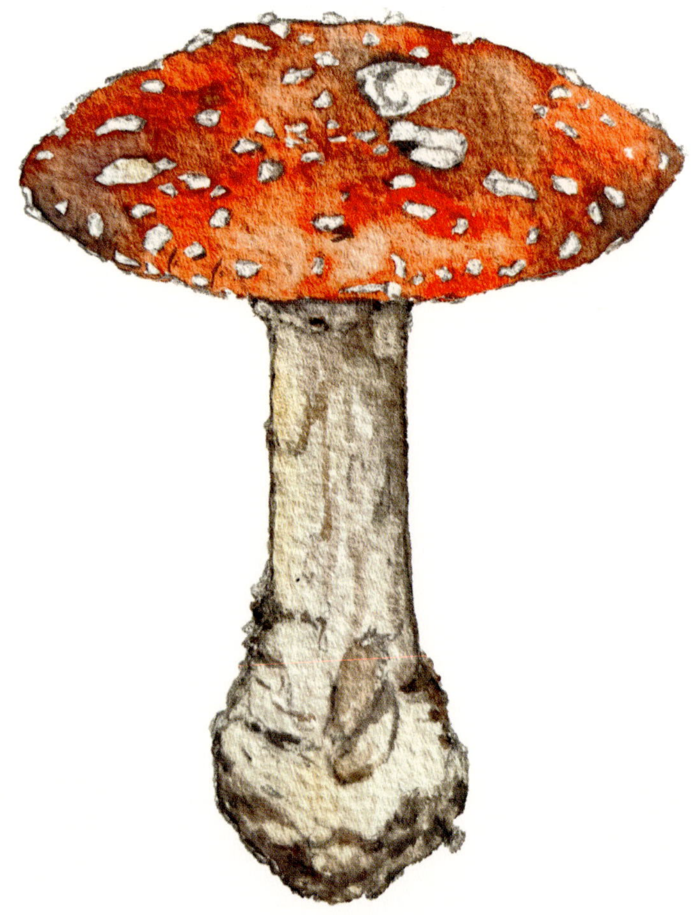

# Fly Agaric Toadstool

Fly agaric toadstools are one of my favorite features in not only fairy stories but in the woodland itself. Even just seeing a still image of them is like finding a magical prize—spotting their little red and white caps on the woodland floor holds something so whimsical! They are such a joy to paint in watercolor, they hold such a simple yet striking color combination. This is a project that will not require a lot of color mixing but will give such a playful result!

# Materials Needed

A sheet of cold-press 140-pound (300-gsm) watercolor paper

HB pencil

A piece of paper towel

Brushes

> Size 0

> Size 1

> Size 2/0

> Size 000

Watercolor paints

> Cadmium red light

> Yellow ochre

> Sepia

> Chinese white

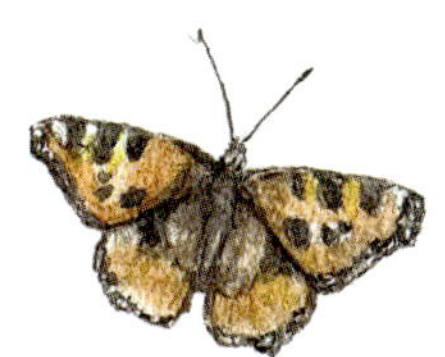

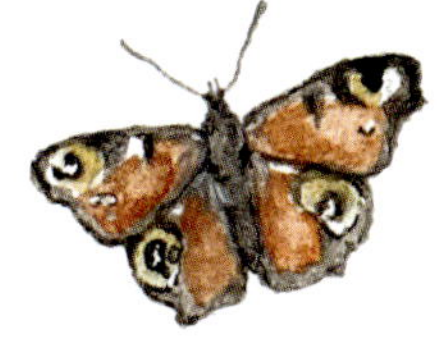

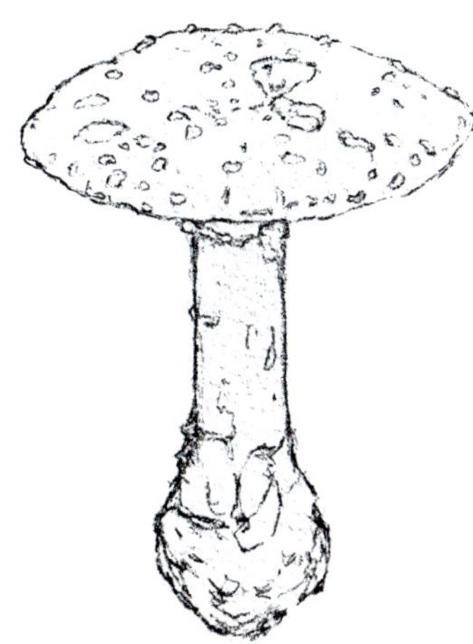

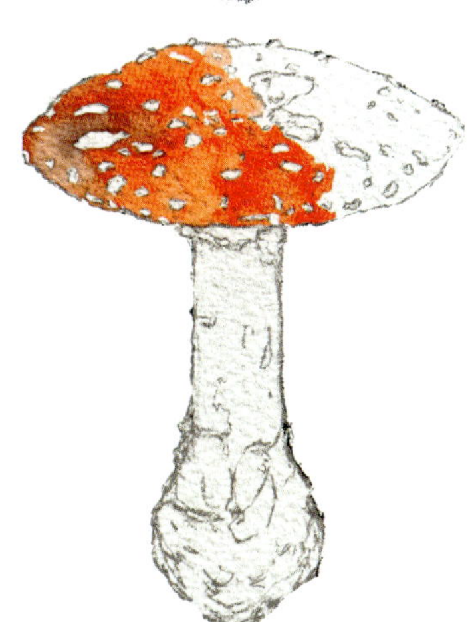

## Step 1: Draw the Outline

Starting on a sheet of cold-press watercolor paper, draw the toadstool's outline with a sharp HB pencil using the corresponding template located in the back of the book (page 173). Lightly sketch in finer details using your pencil to emphasize the soft, fluffy, organic outlines on the flesh of the stem. Include soft, "imperfect" circular and oval shapes to create the white spots that sit on the toadstool's cap.

## Step 2: Paint the Cap

Using a size 0 brush, prepare your color that will fill the toadstool's cap by mixing a rich concentration of cadmium red light with a hint of yellow ochre to create a high saturation of the color. We want the red tones of the toadstool cap to be rich, so less dilution of water is needed. We are aiming for a thicker mixture rather than pale and watery. Flood the toadstool's cap with your bright red mixture, being careful to avoid the circle and oval shapes we created earlier that will become the white spots on the toadstool.

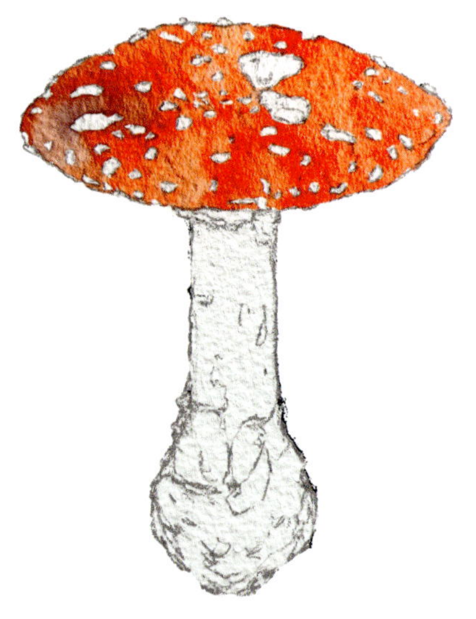

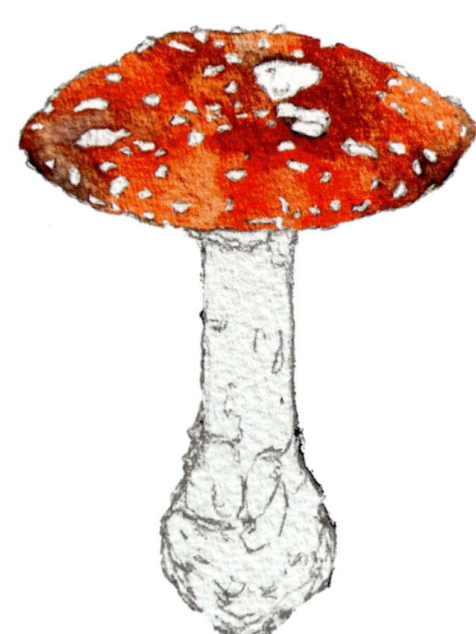

## Step 3: Add the Highlights

Before the paint dries, use a clean, damp size 1 brush to lift out the paint in several patches along the top of the toadstool's cap. Place an emphasis on the right-hand side, which will create lighter tones and give the impression of light. Alternatively, "wiggle" a wet brush onto the sections where you want light to be and press down a piece of paper towel firmly until the paint has been absorbed.

## Step 4: Add the Shadows

We now want to create the appearance of shadows, but we do not want to make them too dark and overbearing, so a higher concentration of water can be used when mixing to make it more diluted and, thereby, less saturated. Prepare your shadow color by using a wet size 0 brush to mix sepia to create a glaze. Follow the curvature of the rim at the bottom of the toadstool's cap and the very center of the toad-stool, immediately softening the edges with a clean, damp size 0 brush. Leave to dry and repeat the layers of shadow, softening the edges upon each application. Build higher layers of shadow right along the very edge of the rim to create more depth of shadow that softens as it reaches outward.

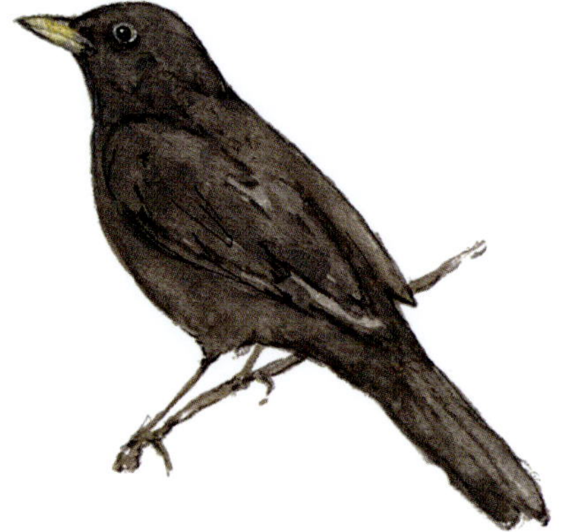

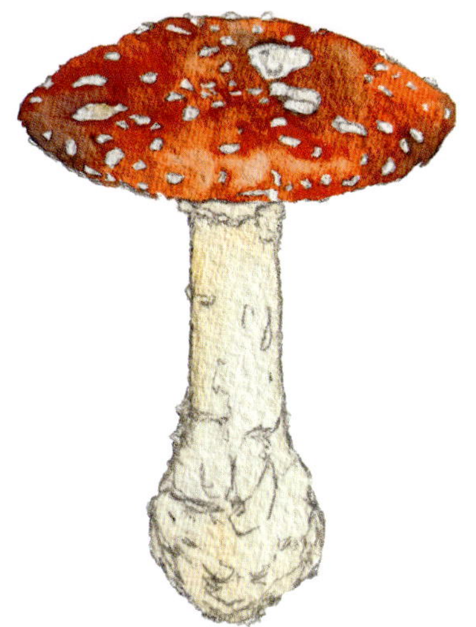

# Step 5: Paint the Stem and Spots

Use a size 1 brush to mix a blend of Chinese white, a dab of yellow ochre and water until it turns a rich cream color. Glaze this mixture over the entire stem, using this same cream mixed color for the spots but applied with the tip of a size 2/0 brush.

While the paint is still wet, drag a higher saturation of the color along the left and underside of the cap to create greater depth. Use your brush to dab this higher concentration along the base and into the spots, softening all edges so all the layers blend seamlessly.

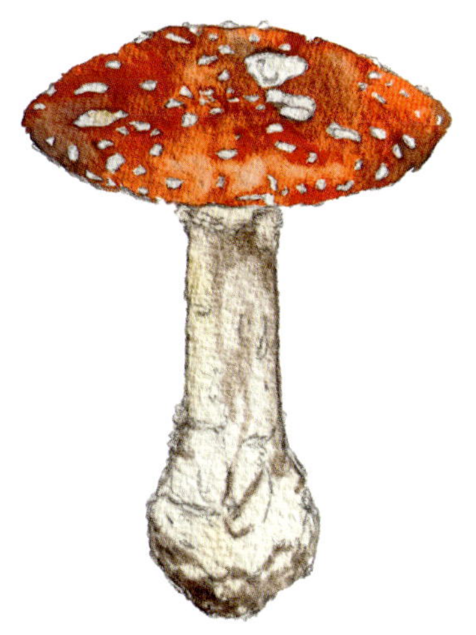

# Step 6: Add the Stem Shadows

On the tip of a clean size 2/0 brush using the same earthy brown we mixed for our previous cap shadows, apply a very pale, even wash of details over the darker areas of the stem. When this initial wash is fully dry, repeat the process, building up layers of color along the bottom of the stem to create the appearance of soil and along the right-hand side of the stem to create the appearance of feathery flesh that is slightly peeling. Ensure that you darken the places on the stem closest to the cap, as this is where the least amount of light would fall.

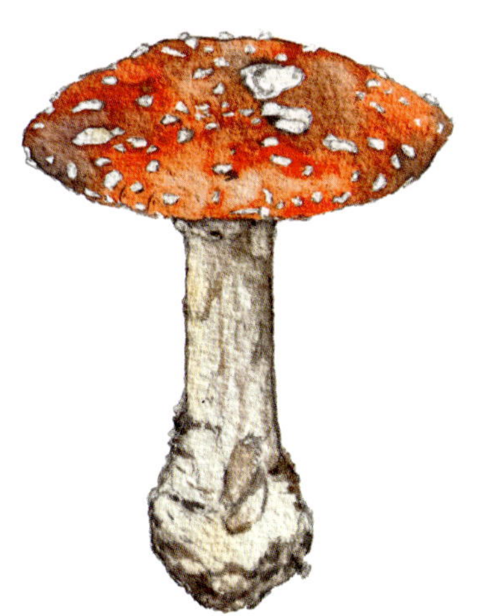

# Step 7: Add the Surface Details

Using a saturated mix of sepia, add the illustrative outlines of the stem, cap and white dots using the very tip of a size 000 brush. As the tip of this brush is very slight, it can be used like a pencil and max-imized in terms of mark-making ability to create illustrative shapes and detail while still using paint. Well done, the toadstool is now complete!

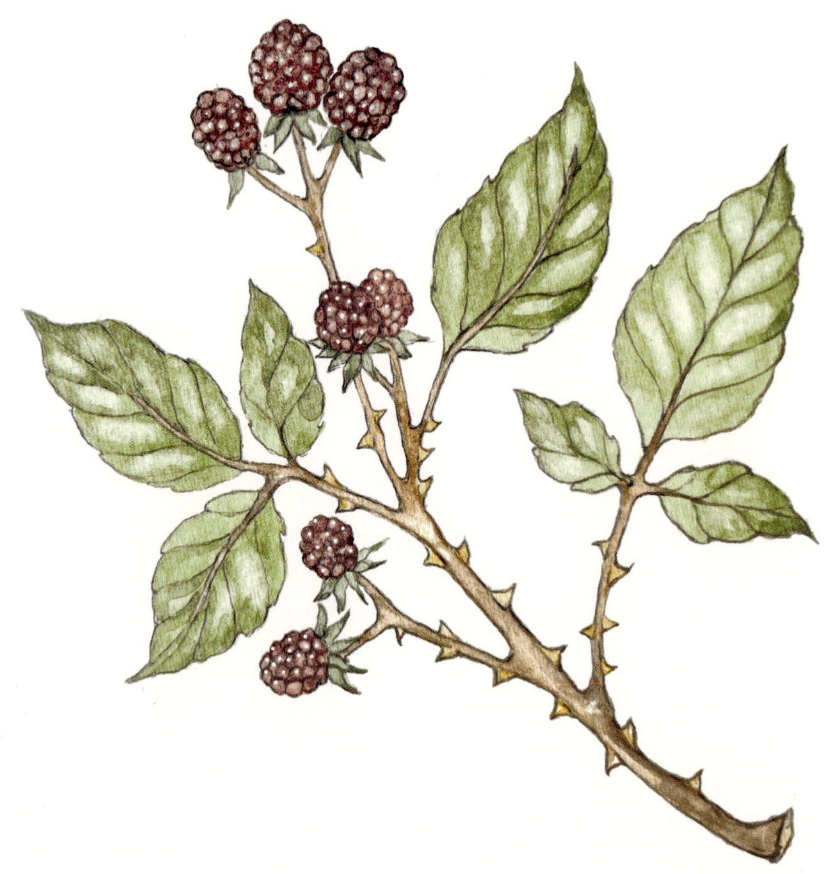

# Wild Berries

The memories of picking wild berries from my childhood linger vividly in
my mind, each plump fruit bursting with the warmth of late summer. Those
carefree days spent in the embrace of nature left an indelible mark on my
soul, which, of course, lives through my work today. Painting these wild berries
alongside their brambly leaves provides a really rewarding outcome. The
organic shapes and rich hues provide an excellent opportunity for practicing
basic techniques such as washes, layering, blending and leaf-painting
that I use in almost every painting of my own!

# Materials Needed

A sheet of cold-press 140-pound (300-gsm) watercolor paper

HB pencil

A piece of paper towel

Brushes

> Size 0

> Size 3/0

Watercolor paints

> Alizarin crimson

> Prussian blue

> Hooker's green light

> Yellow ochre

> Vandyke brown

Acrylic white

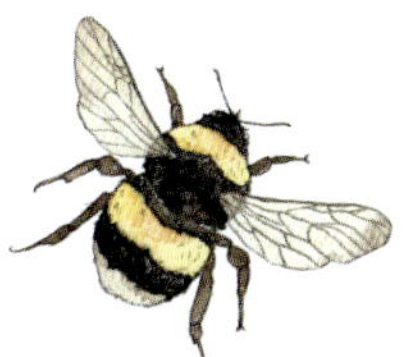

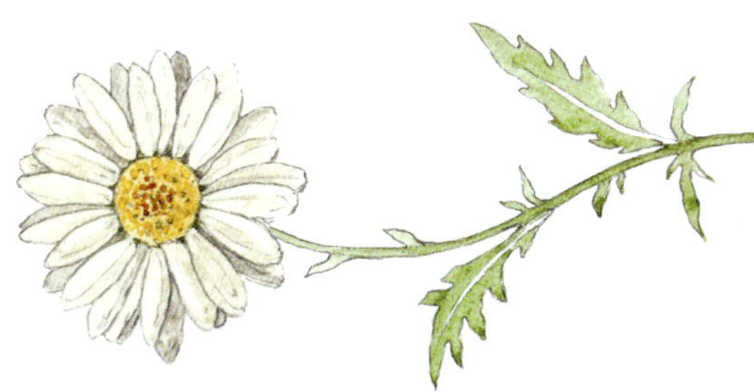

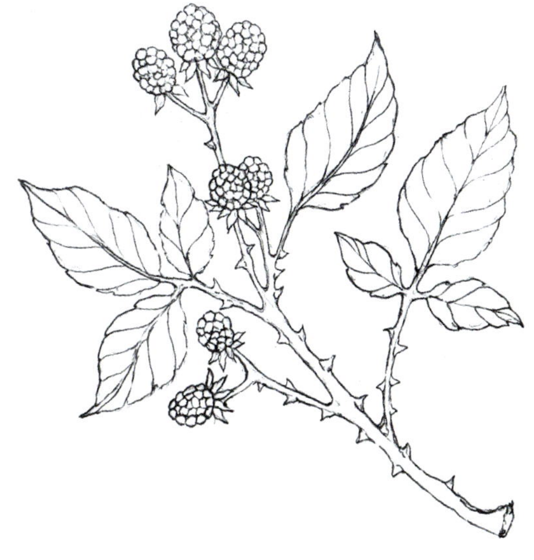

## Step 1: Draw the Outline

Starting on a sheet of cold-press watercolor paper, draw the berries' outline, the leaves and the thorns with a sharp **HB** pencil using the corresponding template located in the back of the book (page 173).

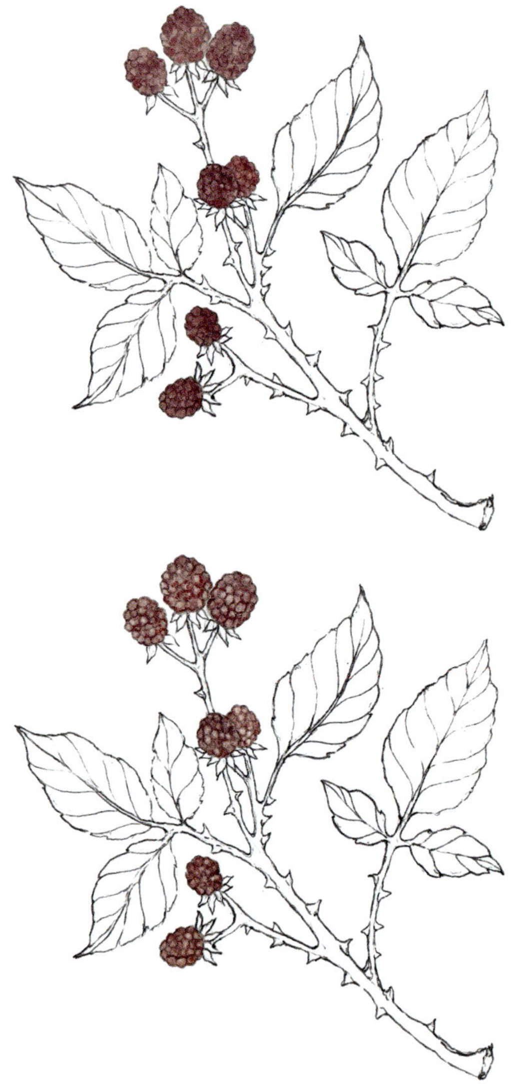

# Step 2: Paint the Berries

To prepare the rich wine color that will be the berries' base layer, use a size 0 brush to mix together a rich solution of alizarin crimson hue with a swirl of Prussian blue. We want the color to be a cool-tone wine that has a very faint purple hue. We also want the consistency of the paint to be thick and not too watery. Carefully paint the color into each berry and allow the paint to fully dry.

# Step 3: Create the Highlights

Dip a clean size 3/0 brush into water and carefully wriggle just the tip of the brush into the center of each little seed of the individual berries. This is going to be very delicate work, so I recommend holding the brush right at the top of the ferrule where your hand will have the most control over the movement of the bristles and working on one individual berry at a time. The wriggling of the bristles will cause the base layer of paint to lift up. Using a clean, dry paper towel, press firmly onto the damp patches where you worked your brush. The lifted paint will absorb onto the towel and leave behind tiny circular highlights.

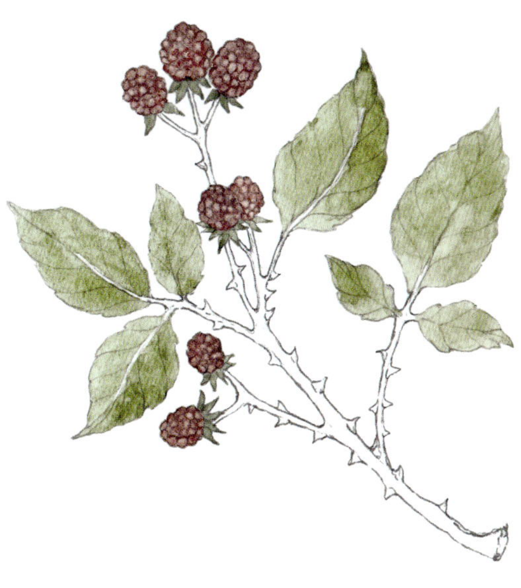

# Step 4: Paint the Leaves

Using a size 0 brush, mix a midtone solution of Hooker's green light with a small dab of yellow ochre. We want this color to be warm and sunny but still earthy, so ensure you do not add too much yellow! A small hint will lift the cooler tone of the Hooker's green light effectively. Glaze this solution over the leaves that grow from the stem, taking care not to paint the center rib. While the paint is still damp, mix in a tiny dab of Vandyke brown to your earthy green color, which will deepen its tone. Drop this color onto the very tip of each leaf and allow the damp paper to absorb and carry the paint downward naturally.

For the leaves which form the berries, use a size 3/0 brush to mix together a midtone solution of Hooker's green light with a tiny dab of Prussian blue. This will result in a cool-tone green. Carefully paint each individual leaf on the underneath of each berry, working from where they meet the fruit outward.

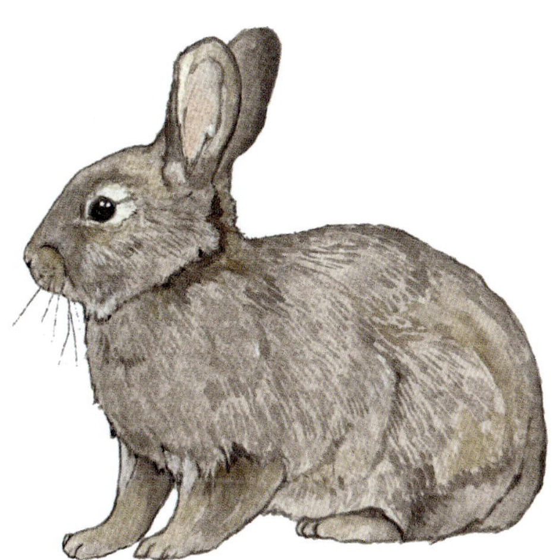

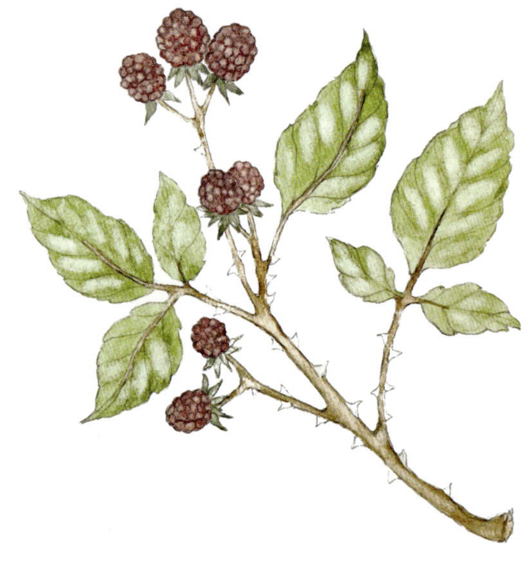

# Step 5: Create the Highlights and Paint the Stem

To create the highlights on the leaves, we will use the same dry paper towel method we learned in step 3. I recommend starting and finishing one leaf at a time, which will ensure that the paint stays damp and you do not have to work quickly. You can take your time, which will always give the best detail. Dip a size 0 brush into water and wriggle the bristles along the center of each section of the leaves that are divided by its veins. The paint will lift up into the water and onto the brush, so keep cleaning your brush as you go. Press a clean, dry paper towel firmly onto the damp pieces of paper, and upon lifting up, there will be subtle oval highlights on each leaf section.

To paint the stem, use a size 3/0 brush to prepare a simple light wash of Vandyke brown. Glaze this mixture over the entire stem and center rib of each leaf. While the paint is still wet, swirl your brush back into the Vandyke brown paint on your palette and use just the tip of the brush to trace along the outline of the stem and the ribs which extend outwardly left and right on each leaf.

# Step 6: Complete the Thorns

To paint the thorns, mix a simple light wash of yellow ochre and gently fill each thorn using the tip of a clean size 3/0 brush.

Clean the bristles fully. Squeeze a less than pea-size amount of acrylic white paint onto your palette and dip in just the tip of the brush. Carefully dot each individual seed with a tiny amount of the white, giving a juicy, highly reflective appearance to each little orb. Allow the paint to fully dry. The berries are now complete, good job!

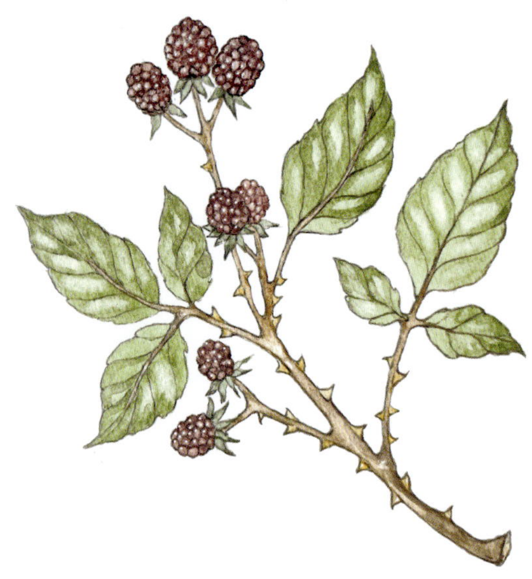

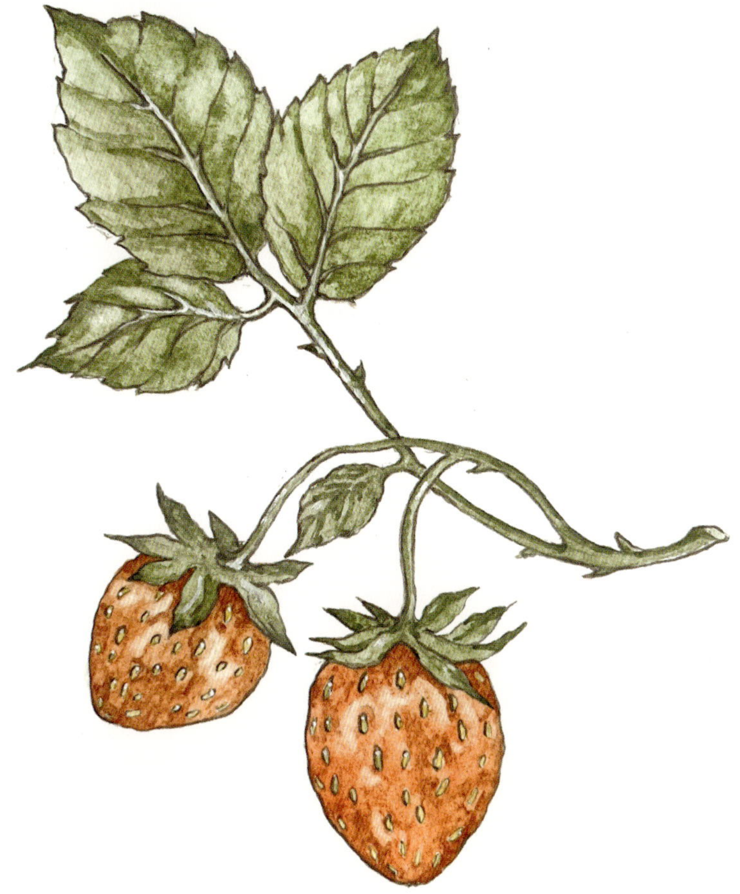

# Hedgerow Strawberries

One of my favorite things to paint (and eat!), strawberries remind me of lazy summer days spent picking ripe berries from the garden in childhood and indulging in my haul! The luscious texture and glossy sheen of the fruit present an opportunity to really understand the importance of creating highlights, and when paired with very vibrant base tones, they can be so effective and really give an amazingly realistic three-dimensional effect!

# Materials Needed

A sheet of cold-press 140-pound (300-gsm) watercolor paper

HB pencil

A piece of paper towel

Brushes

> Size 0

> Size 3/0

Watercolor paints

> Light red

> Hooker's green light

> Vandyke brown

> Yellow ochre

> Lamp black

Acrylic white

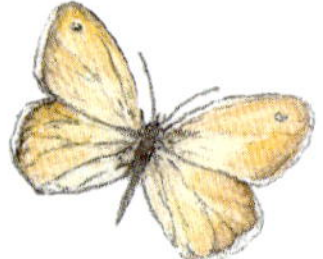

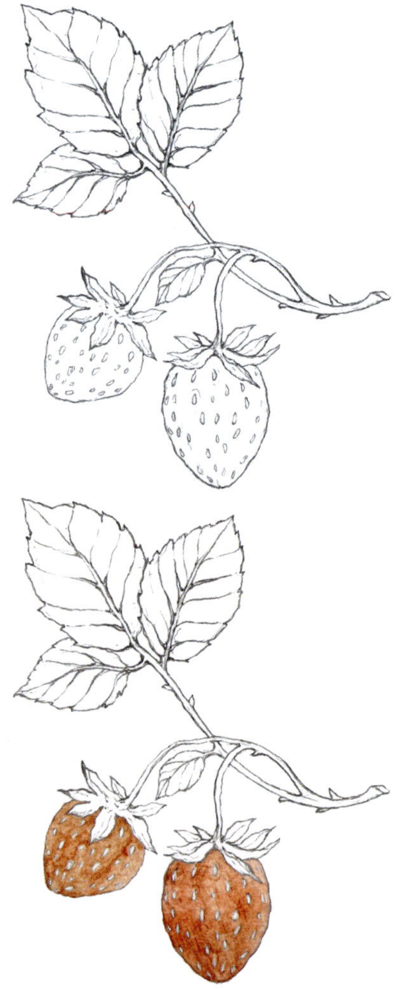

## Step 1: Draw the Outline

Starting on a sheet of cold-press watercolor paper, draw the strawberries' outline, the veins of the leaves, the stem and the seeds of the fruit with a sharp **HB** pencil using the corresponding template located in the back of the book (page 175).

## Step 2: Paint the Strawberries

Prepare the color that will be the base for the strawberries by using a size 0 brush to mix a midtone color of light red and water. Glaze this mixture over the entire strawberry fruit, but take care not to bleed the paint into the seeds. You can switch to a size 3/0 brush around the more delicate parts if you feel you need more control over the paint, holding it close to the ferrule to ensure tight, detailed work. Allow this first layer to fully dry, then dip back into the mixture and add another layer with softened edges to the very bottom of each strawberry and to the right-hand side to create subtle shadows and deeper tones of the same light red.

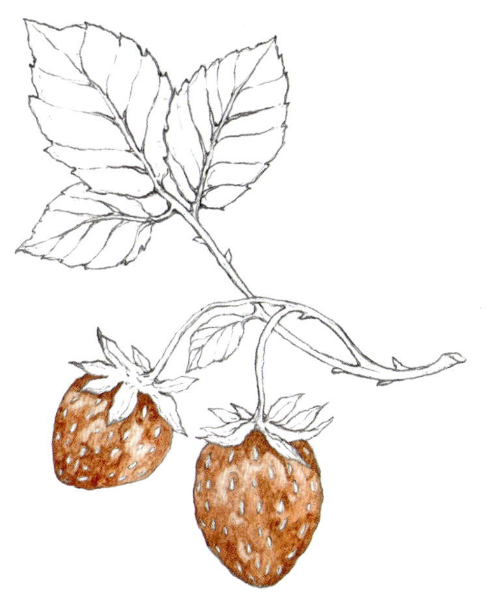

## Step 3: Add the Highlights

Using the tip of a clean, wet 3/0 size brush, lift the red base of the strawberry by wriggling the brush around each individual seed, focusing on the center of each strawberry. Clean your brush repeatedly, if necessary, as there is quite a lot of paint to lift and we want the surface of the strawberry to appear very reflective and shiny. Using a clean, dry paper towel, press onto the dampened surface of each strawberry, which will absorb the paint and leave behind a lighter surface and the appearance of bright highlights.

## Step 4: Paint the Stem and Leaves

Using a size 0 brush, create a midtone glaze of Hooker's green light and paint the entire stem and leaves. While the paint is still damp, swirl your brush back into the green and gently dab along the outer tips of the leaves and also where the leaves meet the stem, allowing the darker pigment to softly disperse inward to create a natural layered shadow.

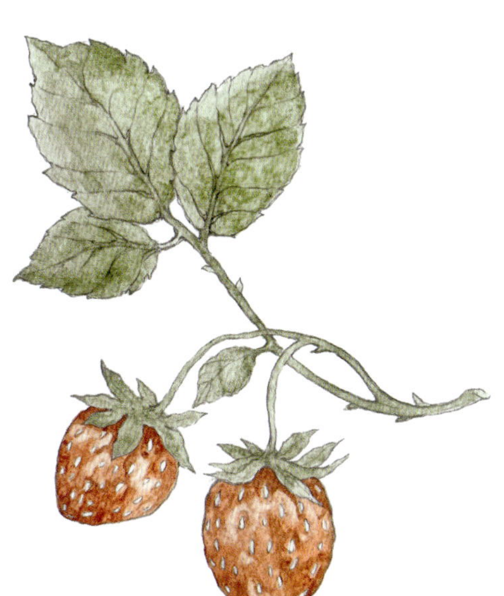

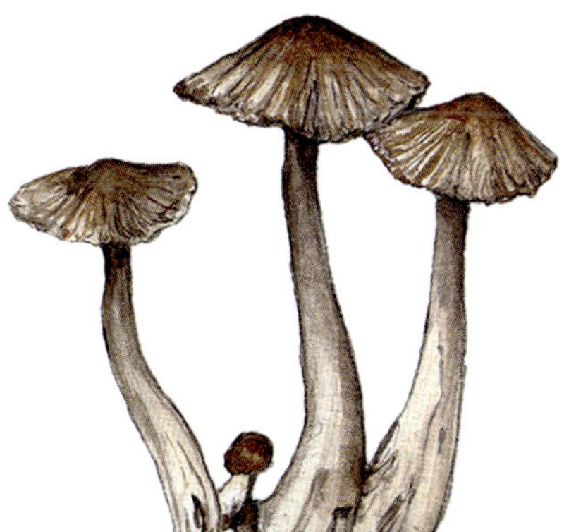

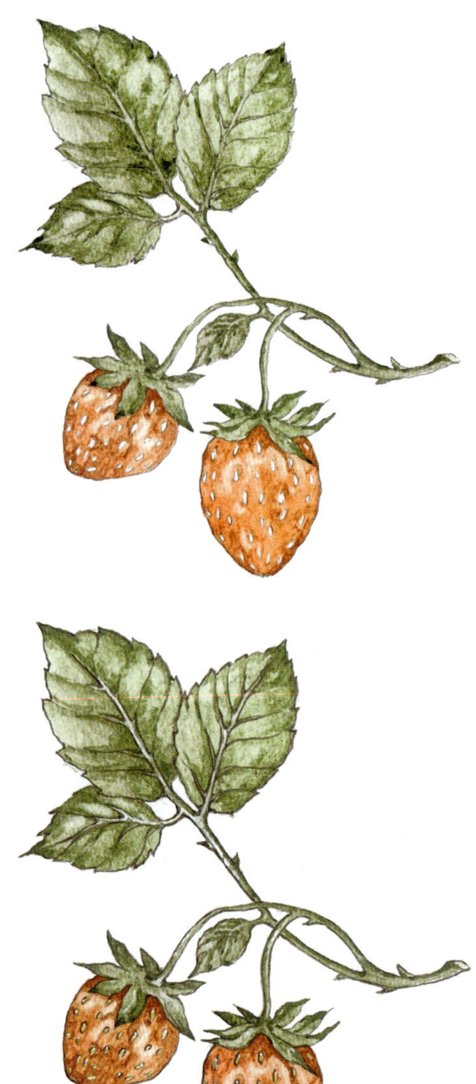

## Step 5: Add the Stem and Leaf Shadows

Using a clean size 0 brush, create a light mix of Hooker's green light with a tiny dab of Vandyke brown to make it a deeper tone of green. Paint the tips of the leaves, the central rib shooting upward along the veins, along the right-hand side of the stem and where the stem meets the leaves at the head of the strawberries. We want the shadows to be soft, so gently push the paint along and blend it into the base to avoid creating harsh outlines. As this is a light mix, allow the paint layers to dry, then dip back into your green mixture and repeat the steps, softening each time.

## Step 6: Add the Final Details

For the seeds, use a size 3/0 brush to mix a light wash of yellow ochre and fill in each individual seed with this thin glaze. Allow the paint to fully dry, clean the brush and swirl it into lamp black. Using the very tip of the brush, outline the outer left-hand side of each seed to create a shadow effect. Clean the brush. Squeeze out a pea-size amount of acrylic white onto your palette, dipping in just the tip of the bristles. Paint along the left-hand side of the stem, from the middle up toward the top, and extend outward into the midway point of each of the leaf veins. Dip back into the acrylic white and lightly paint the right-hand side of the point where the stem meets the fruit leaves. The strawberries are now complete, good job!

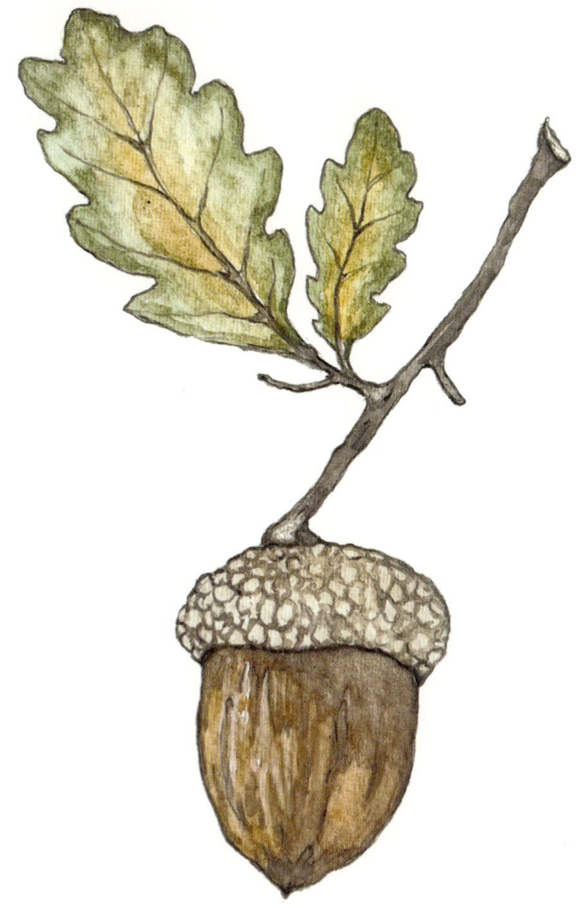

# Acorn

Symbols of strength, potential and the changing seasons, the oak tree and its fruit can provide endless inspiration for watercolor painting. Painting acorns in particular provides a wonderful opportunity to explore texture and to learn the importance of subtle layering of color to create a true three-dimensional effect. As acorns are also deeply rooted in folklore and storytelling, I think you will find the end result holds quite a magical feeling!

# Materials Needed

A sheet of cold-press 140-pound (300-gsm) watercolor paper

HB pencil

Brushes

> Size 1

> Size 4

> Size 0

> Size 3/0

Watercolor paints

> Sepia

> Vandyke brown

> Burnt sienna

> Yellow ochre

> Raw sienna

> Hooker's green light

Acrylic white

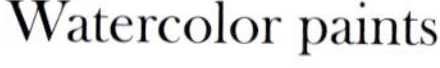

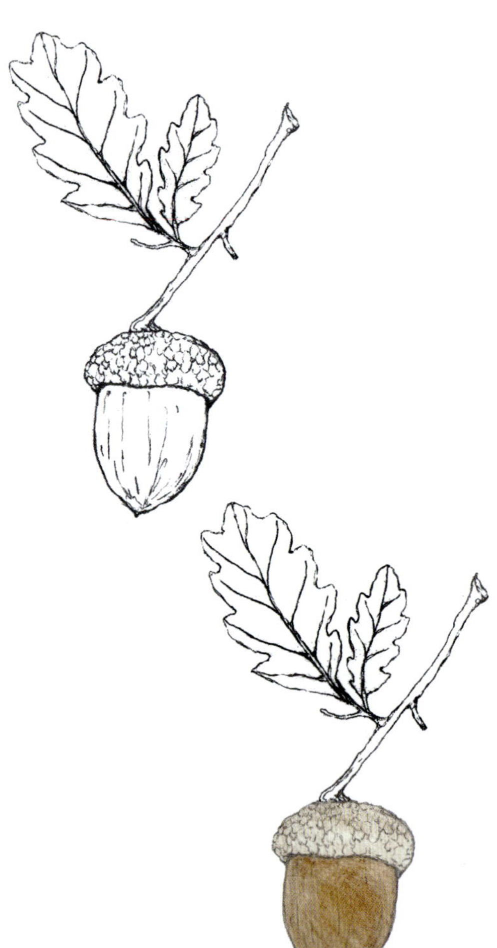

## Step 1: Draw the Outline

Starting on a sheet of cold-press watercolor paper, draw the acorn's outline, the stem, the branch and leaves with a sharp **HB** pencil using the corresponding template located in the back of the book (page 175).

## Step 2: Paint the Base Layer of the Acorn

For the top of the acorn, use a size 1 brush to mix a light wash of sepia and water. We want this to be a very pale gray–brown hue that is not saturated. Glaze this wash over the entire top of the acorn. Clean the brush and allow the paint to fully dry.

For the bottom of the acorn, use a size 4 brush to mix a midtone solution of Vandyke brown with a touch of burnt sienna. We want this to be a warm, burnt brown hue. Paint this wash over the entire body of the acorn and allow it to fully dry.

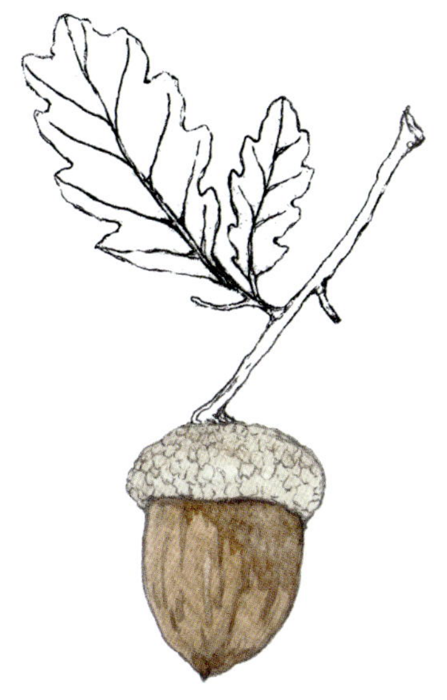

# Step 3: Paint the Shadows

To prepare the color that will be the shadows of our acorn, use a size 0 brush to mix the same warm burnt brown color of midtone Vandyke brown and burnt sienna. Layer downward strokes, beginning with short ones at the left-hand side of the acorn where it meets the cap. As you move toward the center and right, the brushstrokes will get longer, following the curves of the acorn shell. The brushstrokes toward the right of the acorn will reach about three-quarters of the way down the acorn. Paint the tip of the acorn with the same burnt brown and gradually work small short brushstrokes along the curve of the acorn's right-hand side. Allow the paint to fully dry before dipping back into the burnt brown mix and adding another layer to deepen the shadow tones. Finally, using the tip of the brush, add three to four small brushstrokes along the left-hand side of the acorn shell.

# Step 4: Add the Fine Details to the Acorn Cap

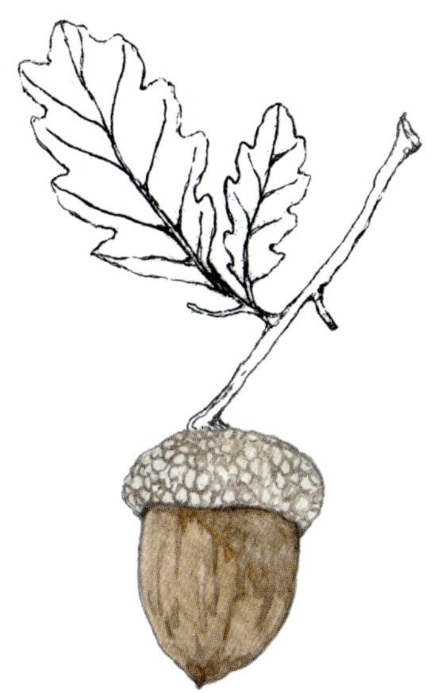

Using a size 3/0 brush, mix a simple midtone wash of sepia and water. Holding the brush at the ferrule to allow the most control over the brushstrokes, trace over the outlines of the pencil drawing using this wash, varying the weight of brushstrokes from using just the tip gently to using the natural flow of the bristles to create outlines. This will add texture and different weights to the strokes, giving natural shadows and texture.

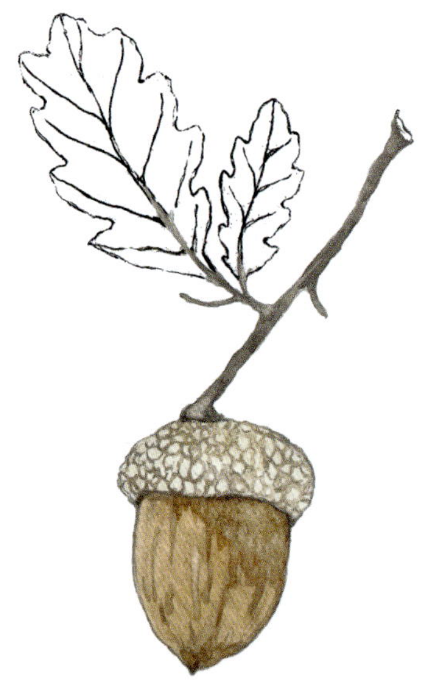

# Step 5: Paint the Branch

Using a size 0 brush, mix a heavy-tone wash of sepia and water. We want this color to be rich and dark, so ensure you mix in enough pigment. We do not want this color to be too transparent from mixing in too much water. Using the tip of the brush, carefully paint the entire branch, which also leads through the center stem of the leaves. Allow the paint to fully dry and clean your brush.

When the paint is fully dry and has an almost flat, matte appearance, dip the size 0 brush into water and wriggle the bristles into the center of the branch, directly where it meets the acorn. This will lift the paint up onto the bristles. Take your piece of paper towel and press it firmly onto this damp patch. The color will absorb and leave behind a subtle highlight.

# Step 6: Start the Leaves

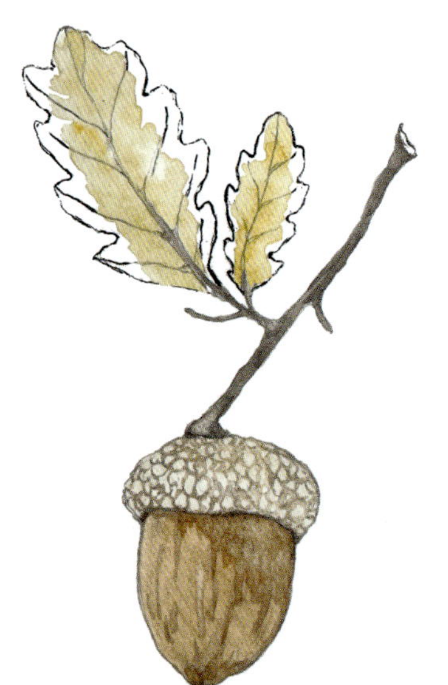

To prepare the color that will be the base layer for the leaves, use a size 1 brush to mix a midtone solution of yellow ochre with a swirl of raw sienna. Glaze this mixture over the center of the leaves, stretching the color almost to the edges of the leaf on the left- and right-hand sides. While the paint is drying, swirl the brush into raw sienna and drop the color at the tip of each leaf and along the center of the rib to the bottom leaf where it meets the stem, allowing the paint to naturally bleed into the damp base layer. When this fully dries, it will give the color a dappled effect.

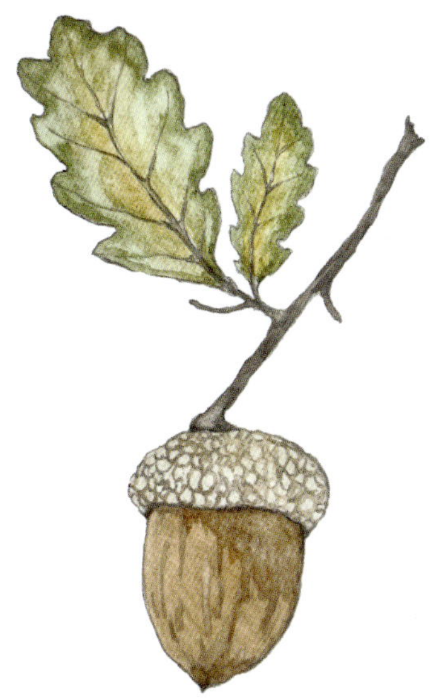

# Step 7: Complete the Leaves

Use a size 0 brush to mix a very pale wash of Hooker's green light and burnt sienna. We want the hue of color to be a muted, earthy green. Glaze this color over the edges of the leaf, gently blending the paint into the yellow base layer as it gradually reaches toward the center. Don't fully bring the green layer to the center, as we want some of the yellow to still peek through. While the paint is still wet, create a midtone solution on your palette of the same earthy green by swirling in some more Hooker's green light and a slight touch of sepia. Drop this color along the curved outlines of the leaf. The paint will bleed gently into the damp paper and create a seamless gradient from deep green to yellow in the center of the leaf when it dries.

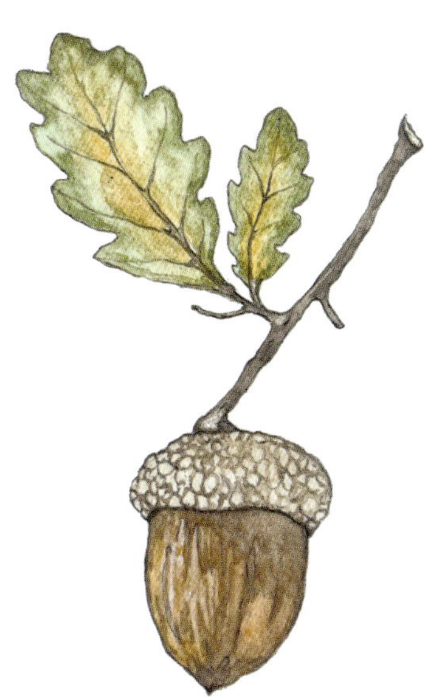

# Step 8: Add Luminosity and the Final Details

Squeeze a less than pea-size amount of acrylic white paint onto your palette. We will use this to create subtle highlights, which will really add a sense of realism and luminosity to the acorn. In our painting, light is naturally falling on the left-hand side, so this is where we will add our white paint. Using a size 3/0 brush, load a small amount of paint onto the bristles, and using light, controlled downward strokes, follow the curves of the acorn toward the left-hand side, moving toward the middle. Do not load the brush with paint, as we want the pigment layer to be quite thin to allow the base layer of watercolor to shine through. The acorn is now complete, well done!

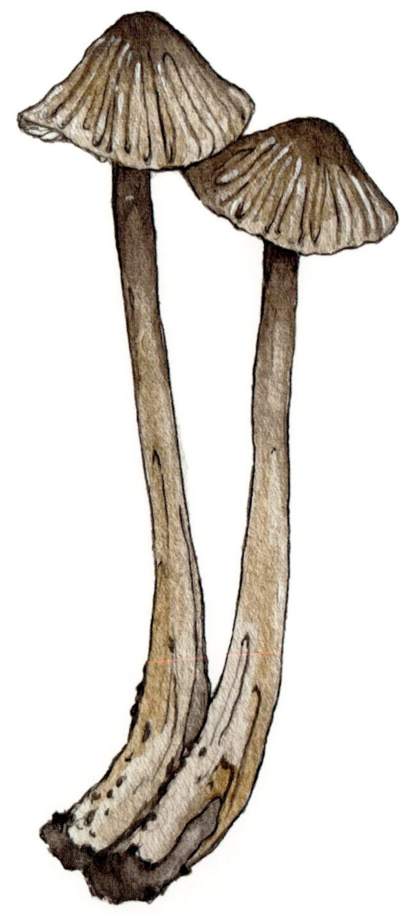

# Grooved Bonnet Toadstool

For artists and nature enthusiasts alike, grooved bonnet toadstools hold a truly captivating allure from their shape and details alone. Their delicate, ribbed caps and slender stalks make excellent subjects for a watercolor project and their palette of earthy shades can be a wonderful exercise in understanding the importance of subtleties when it comes to creating illustration and realism in painting.

# Materials Needed

A sheet of cold-press 140-pound (300-gsm) watercolor paper

HB pencil

Brushes

> Size 1

> Size 0

> Size 3/0

Watercolor paints

> Sepia

> Vandyke brown

> Yellow ochre

> Lamp black

Acrylic white

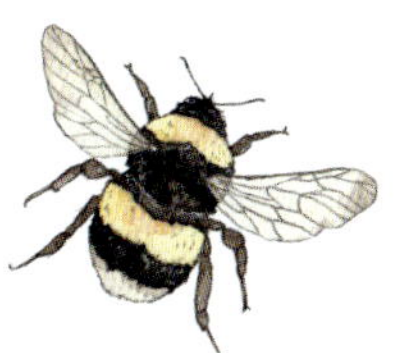

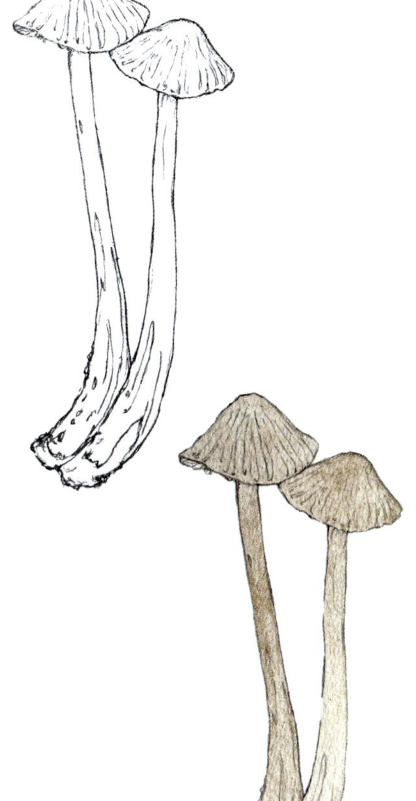

## Step 1: Draw the Outline

Starting on a sheet of cold-press watercolor paper, draw the grooved bonnet cap's outline, the details of the stem and the feathery flesh with a sharp **HB** pencil using the corresponding template located in the back of the book (page 175).

## Step 2: Paint the Base Layer

To prepare the color that will be the toadstool's base earthy brown, use a size 1 brush to mix a light glaze of sepia and water. We do not want this color to be too saturated; we want it to have a thin texture and a light gray–brown tone. Glaze this mixture over both caps and the stems. While the paint is still damp, dip the tip of the brush into pure sepia and load a small amount of the paint on the brush. Drop this into your light-tone mixture that you just mixed, which will deepen its color. Drop this now midtone mix of sepia onto the very tip of the toad-stool's caps, along the center of the stem of the left toadstool and along the bottom of stems where they meet the soil.

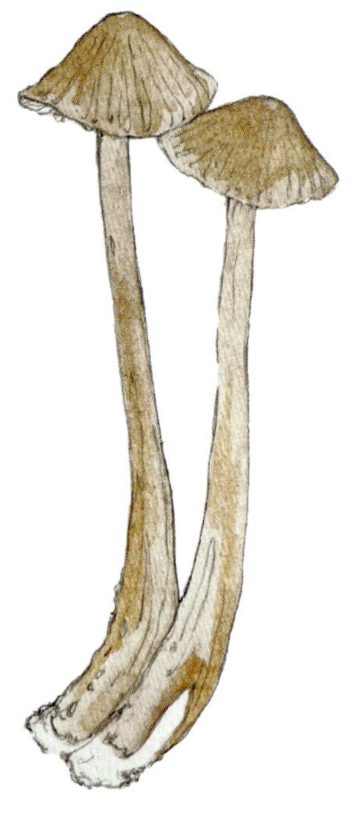

## Step 3: Add Color

Using a size 0 brush, mix together a midtone wash of Vandyke brown with a hint of yellow ochre. We want to warm up the Vandyke brown and create a warm, sunny orange–tone brown. Once the color is mixed, paint each toadstool cap, starting at the top and dragging the paint downward. Soften the edges so the paint is near transparent right at the edge of the cap where it meets the stem. Use the tip of the brush to paint the warm brown color from the center of the stems downward to the bottom where they meet the soil, focusing the color on the left-hand side of the stem on the left toadstool and the right-hand side of the stem on the right toadstool. While the paint is still damp, add another layer of this warm brown to the very tip of each cap and along the bottom of the right toadstool stem.

## Step 4: Paint the Shadows

For the shadow color, mix a mid- to dark-tone wash of sepia. We want the texture to be concentrated and thick and the color to be very dark, so ensure that enough paint is added so it is not overly diluted. Using a clean size 0 brush, gently drop this dark sepia on the top of each cap and on the underside of each cap where they meet the stem. Soften the edges downward with the bristles of the brush so the gradient of the color goes from dark to gradually lighter. Allow the paint to fully dry. Switch to a size 3/0 brush and load this dark sepia color onto the bristles. Trace along the ribs on the toadstool's cap using the tip of the brush, allowing the brush to naturally flow but holding it at the ferrule so you can keep the work tight and neat.

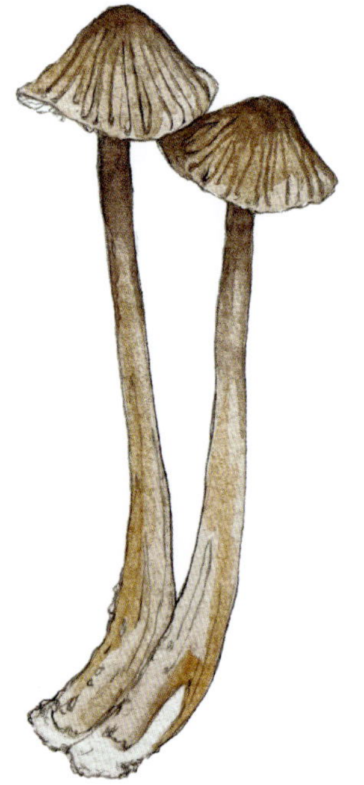

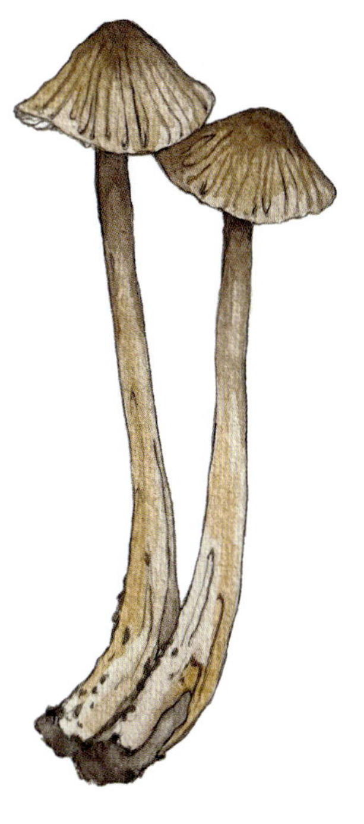

# Step 5: Add the Fine Details

Using a size 0 brush, mix a dark-tone solution of sepia with a hint of lamp black. This color will be used to paint both the soil and also to trace and define the feathery flesh of the grooved bonnet. Using the same size 0 brush, concentrate this dark brown right at the bottom of the toadstool, slowly bringing the paint upward to soften the edges, and fill the entire area of soil. While the paint is damp, swirl the brush back into this mixture and drop the color right at the bottom edge, which will deepen the tones of color and create a more defined gradient. Switch to a size 3/0 brush and load this color onto the bristles, tracing the outlines of your drawing where the flesh of the stem has subtle folds and pieces of soil traveling upward from the bottom.

# Step 6: Add the Final Details

Squeeze a less than pea-size amount of acrylic white onto your palette and dab in a clean size 3/0 brush to load a small amount of color onto the bristles. Carefully paint in between the ribs on the toadstool's cap to create subtle highlights and a gentle luminous effect, which will really define the cap's details. The toadstools are now complete, well done!

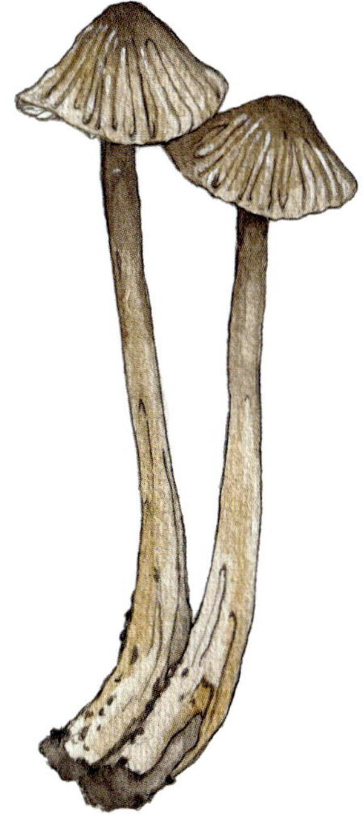

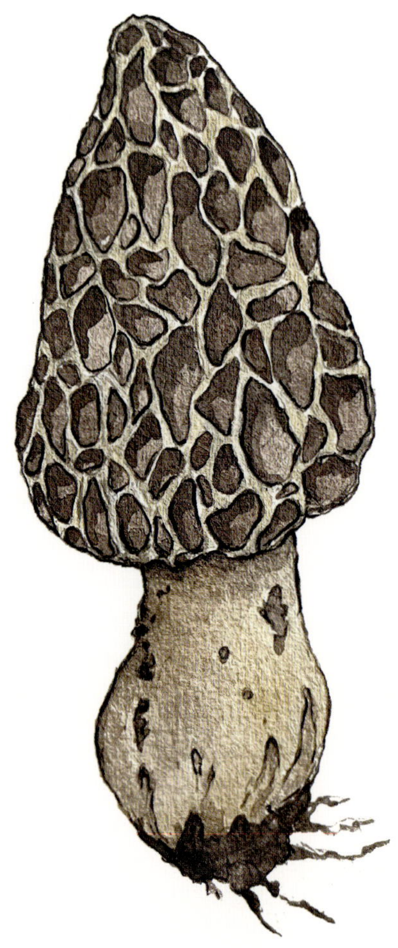

# Morel Toadstool

Often found nestled among forest undergrowth or peeking out from fallen leaves, morels are a captivating subject both to spot when out for a hike and also to paint with watercolor! Their delicate, honeycomb-like caps offer ample opportunity to explore not only form and texture but also to learn how to mix an earthy color palette, which I use very often in my own work.

# Materials Needed

A sheet of cold-press 140-pound (300-gsm) watercolor paper

HB pencil

Brushes

> Size 0

> Size 3/0

> Size 1

Watercolor paints

> Sepia

> Ivory black

> Raw sienna

> Chinese white

Acrylic white

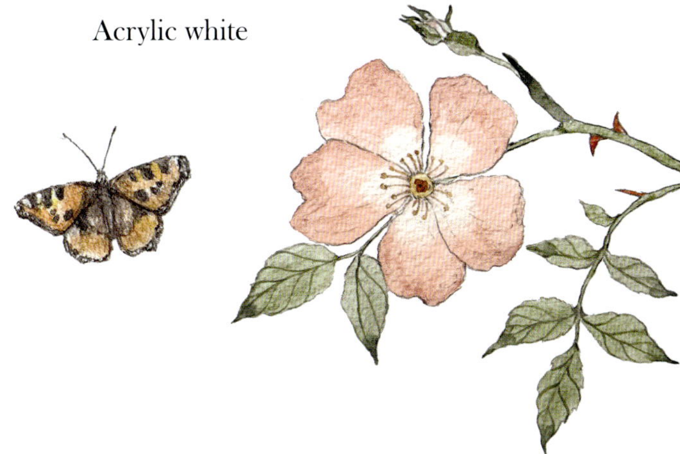

## Step 1: Draw the Outline

Starting on a sheet of cold-press watercolor paper, draw the morel cap's outline, the honeycomb-like patterns and the stem with a sharp **HB** pencil using the corresponding template located in the back of the book (page 175).

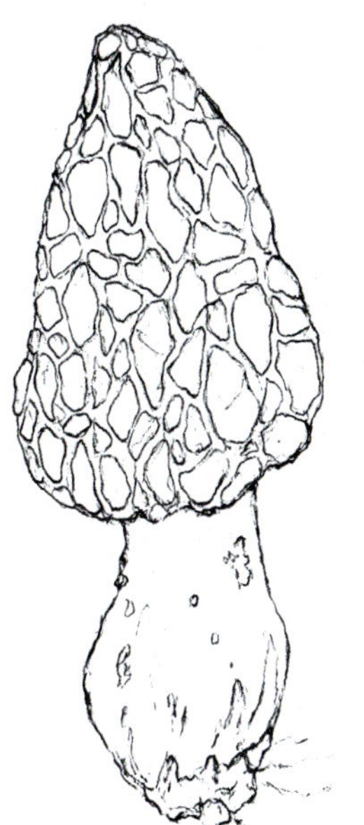

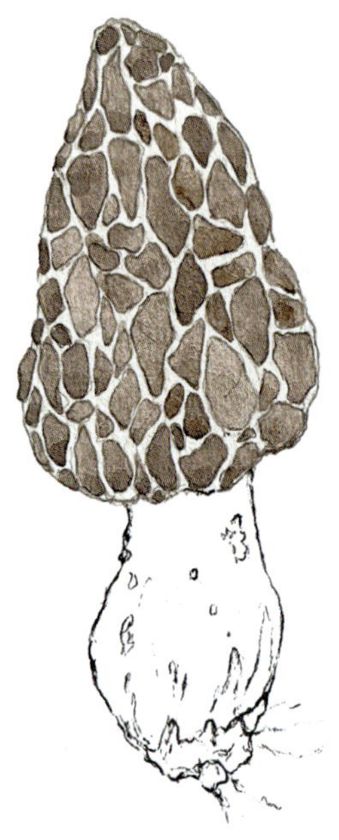

# Step 2: Paint the Cap Ridges

Prepare the color that will fill the honeycomb-like ridges that cover the morel's cap by using a size 0 brush to mix a midtone wash of sepia and water. We don't want this wash to be extremely dark or so diluted that it is pale and watery but a midpoint between the two. Carefully fill each concave ridge with this glaze. While the paint is still damp on the paper, swirl your brush back into sepia and drop this color right at the top of each damp ridge, which will cause the paint to gently disperse and, once fully dry, will give a very natural variation of tone of the same color.

# Step 3: Create a Three-Dimensional Effect with Shadows

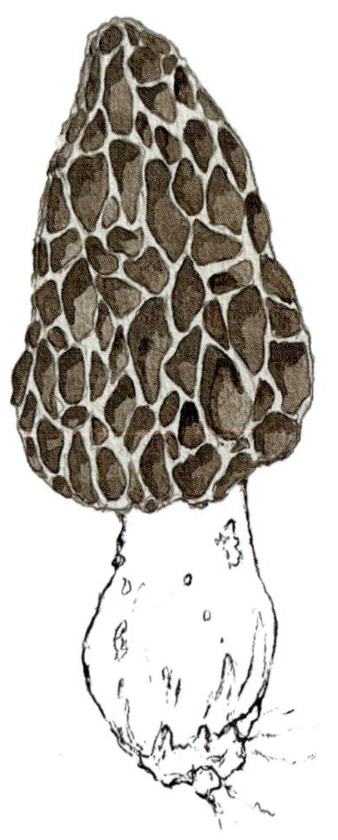

Using a size 3/0 brush, mix a dark-tone solution of sepia and a dab of ivory black with water. We do not want the mixed color to be black but a deeper saturation of sepia, so take care not to add too much ivory black, only the tip of a brush is needed. We want the texture of the mixed paint to be quite thick and less diluted than the midtone solution that we used for the base color in step 2. Paint along the top and slightly down the left-hand side of each ridge. We want the edges of the shadows to be sharp, so I recommend holding the brush at the ferrule to give you the most control of your line, allowing for tight and illustrative work.

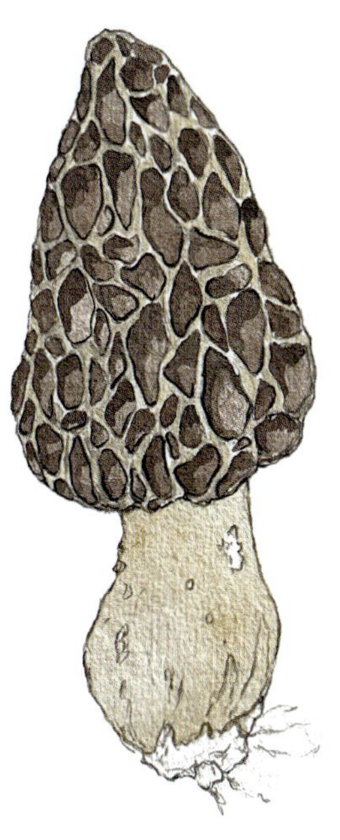

## Step 4: Paint the Rest of the Body

For the remaining part of the head surrounding the ridges, use a clean size 3/0 brush to mix a simple midtone solution of raw sienna and water. Next, squeeze a pea-size amount of acrylic white onto your palette and mix some into the raw sienna until you have a thick, earthy taupe color. Carefully paint around each of the ridges, dipping back into the acrylic sienna mixture when the paint runs dry. Allow the paint to fully dry.

For the morel's lower body, use a size 1 brush to mix a midtone wash of Chinese white and a dab of raw sienna until the color turns a rich, earthy cream. Glaze this entire solution over the morel's body. While the paint is still damp, dip a clean, damp 3/0 brush into raw sienna and lightly drop the color on the left-hand side at the top of the stem and to the right along the center of the stem. Allow the paint to fully dry.

## Step 5: Add the Shadows and Final Details

Using a size 0 brush, mix a rich solution of the same sepia and ivory black color we used in step 3. Fill in the bottom of the morel where the root system and soil are, using the very tip of the brush to fill in the tiny hairs on the roots. Next, dilute the sepia and ivory solution by watering it down until it is a very light brown–gray color. Glaze this along the left-hand side of the stem and underneath the cap where the most shadow would be. While the paint is still damp, swirl your brush gently into ivory black and very gently drop a tiny amount of the color along the top of the stem where the least amount of light would hit, darkening the color's tone. Clean and dry your brush, then gently stroke the bristles along these shadow layers to soften their edges and create a seamless appearance. The morel is complete! Good job!

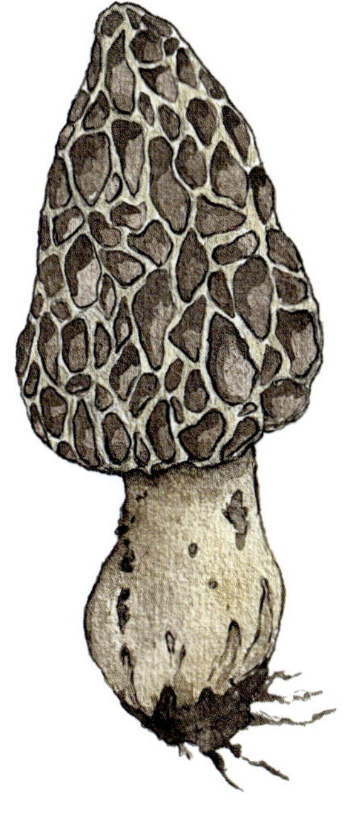

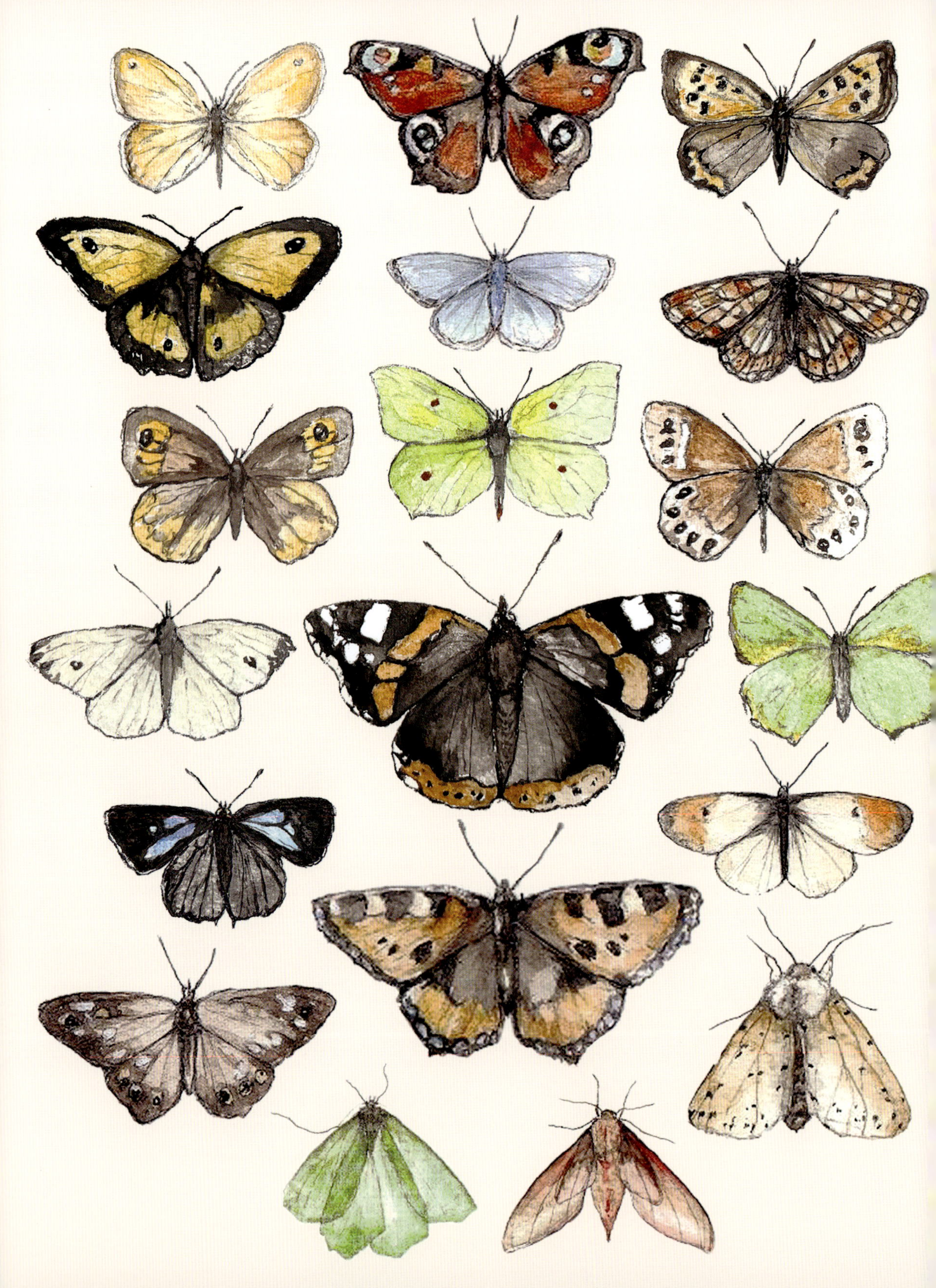

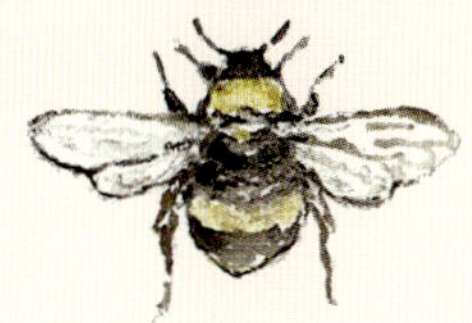

# Woodland Insects

Be prepared to grab your magnifying glass! In this chapter, we venture into the depths of the woodland to explore the beauty of its smallest inhabitants, from the garden snail (page 135) to those with wings that buzz through the air.

In this chapter, we will delve into the intricate details and vibrant colors of butterflies (pages 120 and 125). With their graceful flight and intricate wing patterns, butterflies are a symbol of beauty and transformation. We will focus on capturing the delicate details of their wings, the subtle gradations of color and the ethereal quality of their movements.

We will also learn about bumblebees (page 130). These industrious insects, with their fuzzy bodies and vibrant stripes, are essential pollinators in the garden. Learn to depict their fuzzy texture, the glossy sheen of their wings and the dynamic energy they bring as they go about their work.

Finally, we will learn how to paint a ladybug (page 140). With their cheerful red wings and black spots, ladybugs are beloved symbols of luck and good fortune. We will explore techniques for creating the smooth, rounded shape of their bodies, the glossy shine of their wings and the whimsical charm they exude, bringing their enchanting beauty to life.

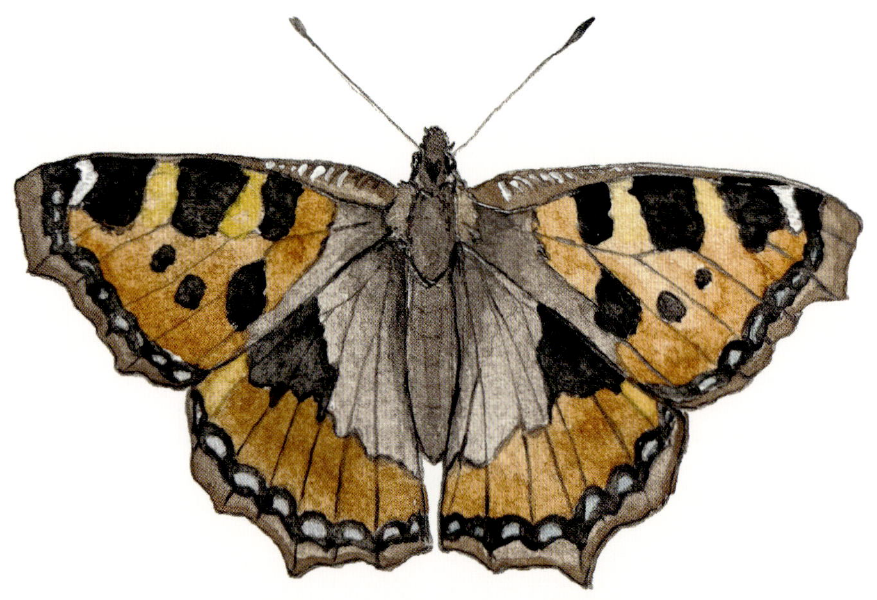

# Small Tortoiseshell Butterfly

The small tortoiseshell is among the most well-known butterflies in Ireland, and it always makes an appearance in my work if I ever feel the need for the addition of a winged companion. The striking and attractive patterning of its appearance at almost any time of the year has made it a familiar species. I would think it is one of the first images that comes to mind if anyone were to imagine the word "butterfly" due to its iconic wings. It is one of the first butterflies to be seen in spring and autumn, and I will often find them visiting the garden flowers in large numbers, which is always a pleasure to see!

# Materials Needed

A sheet of cold-press 140-pound (300-gsm) watercolor paper

HB pencil

Brushes

> Size 4

> Size 1

> Size 3/0

Watercolor paints

> Burnt sienna

> Yellow ochre

> Raw umber

> Sepia

> Vandyke brown

> Turquoise

> Lamp black

Acrylic white

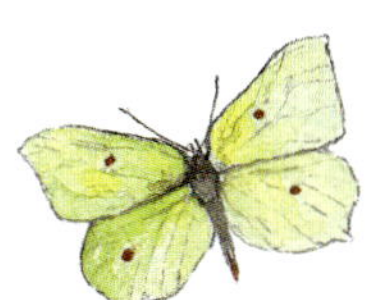

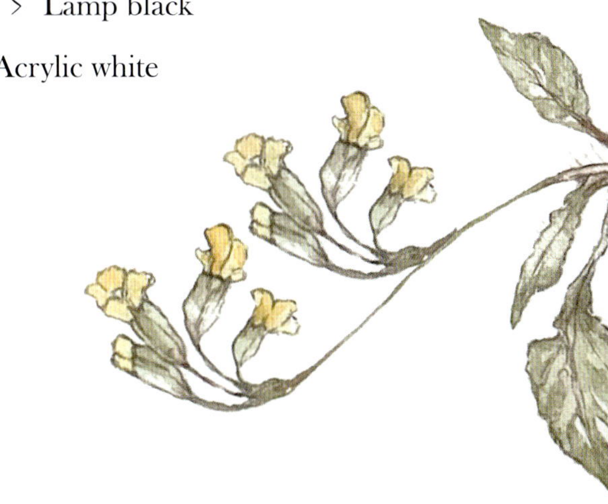

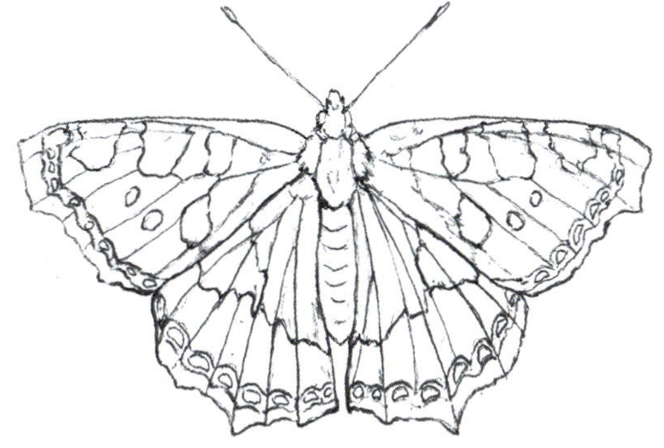

## Step 1: Draw the Outline

Starting on a sheet of cold-press watercolor paper, draw the butterfly's outline with a sharp **HB** pencil using the corresponding template located in the back of the book (page 177). There are a lot of details in this piece, so make sure to take your time, as butterflies do look their best and most realistic when the wings' patterns are as symmetrical as possible.

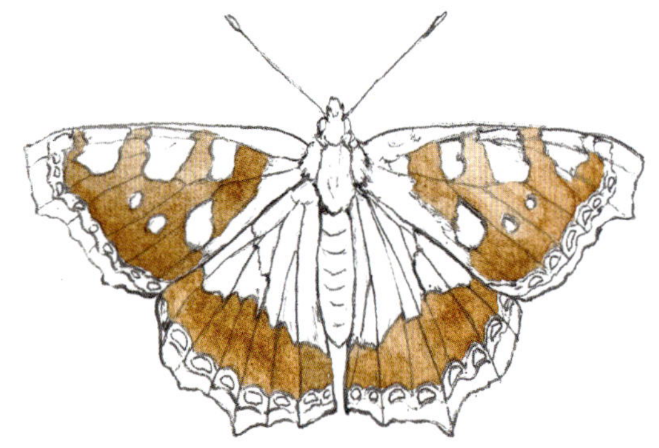

# Step 2: Paint the Main Body of the Wings

To prepare the color that will fill in the orange of the butterfly's wings, use a size 4 brush to mix a midtone saturation of burnt sienna with a dab of yellow ochre. We want this color to be a warm, copper rust hue. Glaze this color over the entire section of the wings we want to have an orange color, being careful to avoid the spots on the upper wings.

While the paint is still damp, swirl in a tiny amount of raw umber to the copper color, which will deepen the tone slightly. Load this paint onto the tip of the brush and glaze the bristles along the edges of the left- and right-hand sides of the upper wings, following the contour of the curve in toward the center. The paint will naturally bleed inward, leaving a deeper hue of color around the lower half of the upper wings. Complete the same step for the lower wings. Load the tip of the brush with the deep copper color and trace the bottom outline of the lower wings, causing a natural gradient as the paint bleeds into the lighter orange beneath it.

# Step 3: Paint the Abdomen and Inner Wings

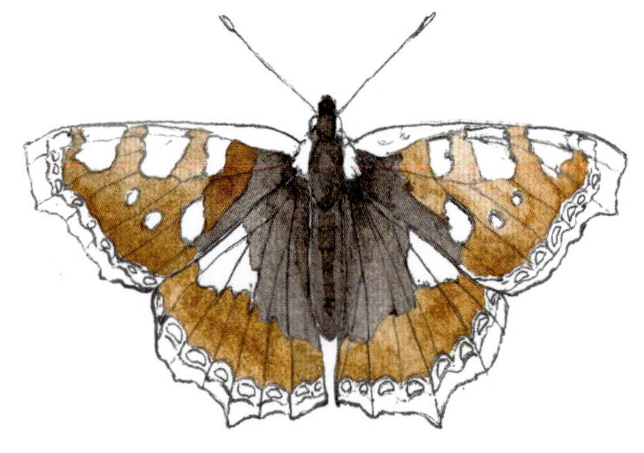

Using a size 1 brush, mix a midtone solution of sepia and water and load the color onto the brush. Glaze the abdomen and the inner wing sections that we want to be brown. While the paint is still damp, layer another glaze of deep brown onto the abdomen and inner sections of the wings nearest the center, softly spreading the paint outward. Allow the paint to fully dry.

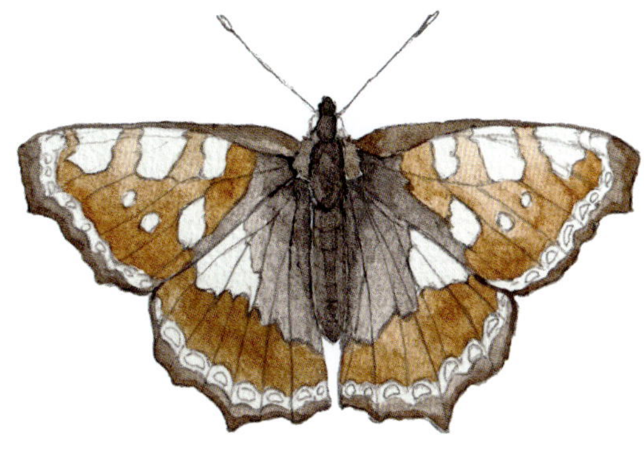

# Step 4: Paint the Outer Section of the Wings

To prepare the color that will fill the wings' outer sections, use a size 3/0 brush to mix a simple midtone saturation of Vandyke brown. Load the bristles with color and fill the outer contours of the upper and lower wings. While the paint is still wet, add another layer of color around the outermost edge, which will create a deeper outline along the edge of the top and bottom wings. Finally, fill in the tiny sections of fur that intersect the abdomen and upper wings with a layer of this brown mixture.

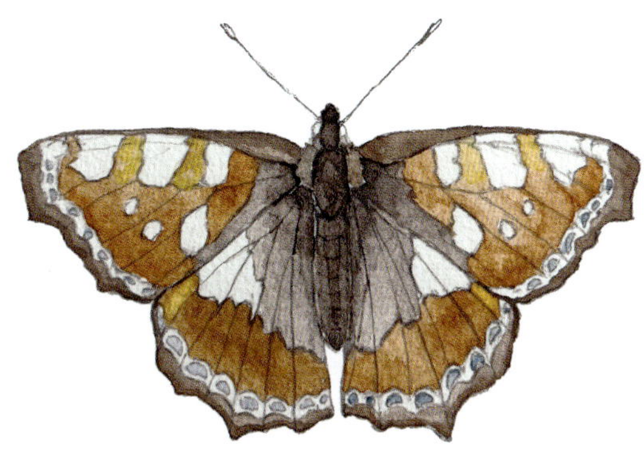

# Step 5: Add Pops of Color

Using a clean size 1 brush, mix a midtone solution of yellow ochre and water. We want this color's consistency to be not too watery but also not too thick that it appears matte and heavily saturated. It should be sunny but not too pale and diluted. Load the color onto the brush and dab the sections of the upper half of the top wings in between the dots that are not yet filled with color. Soften the edges of the paint downward so they blend into the orange base layer below it.

For the bottom wings, add a single dab of yellow on the uppermost section of orange on the left and right sides of the lower wings.

Next, use a size 3/0 brush to mix a light-tone solution of turquoise and water. Load the paint onto the tip of the brush and carefully fill in each of the singular dots that are arranged in a curved formation along the left- and right-hand sides of the upper and lower wings.

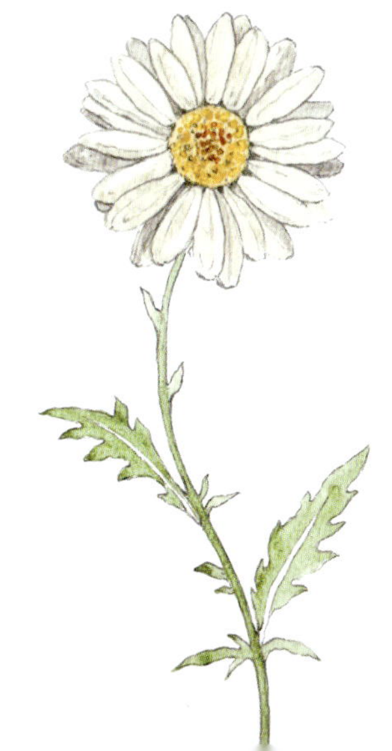

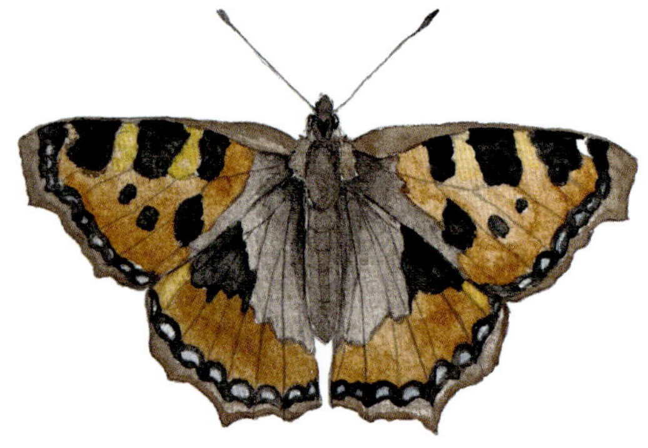

# Step 6: Create Definition on the Wings

Using a size 1 brush, mix a heavily saturated solution of lamp black and water. We want this color to be thick and matte and not overly diluted with water. Load the brush with this inky black hue and carefully fill in the remaining sections of the wings that have not yet been filled in with color: the spots on the upper and lower wings and the curved lines that hold the blue dot patterns along the curvature of the outside of the wings.

Switch to a size 3/0 brush and load the tip of the brush with this same inky black pigment. Carefully trace in the antennae and fill in the eyes at the top of the butterfly's abdomen.

# Step 7: Add the Final Details

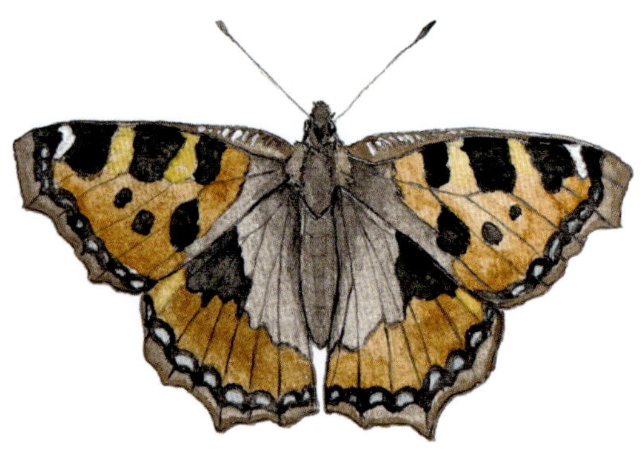

Using the same inky solution and the tip of the size 3/0 brush, carefully define the veins that are on the upper and lower wings. Trace around the outlines of the abdomen to define each section.

Finally, squeeze a less than pea-size amount of acrylic white onto your palette and load a small amount of color onto the tip of a clean size 3/0 brush. Hold the brush at the ferrule in order to have the most control of the brushstrokes and dab two dots of white into the eyes. Paint short dabs of white along the upper outline of the upper wings. Finally, fill in the two dots on the far side of both the upper left and right wings. Allow the paint to fully dry. The butterfly is complete! Good job!

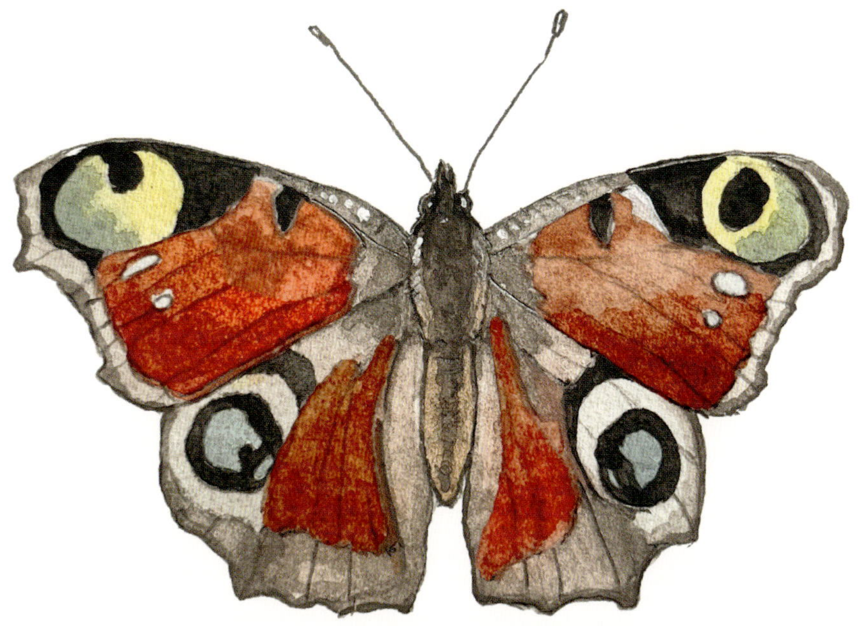

# Peacock Butterfly

The peacock butterfly is probably the most beautiful of all the Irish species of insects. The large, unmistakable eye spots on each of the hind wings, which resemble those on a peacock's tail, are what give this striking butterfly its name. The colorful, striking patterns not only serve as a defense mechanism of camouflage for this beautiful butterfly, but they also make a wonderful project for painting a large rainbow palette of color!

# Materials Needed

A sheet of cold-press 140-pound (300-gsm) watercolor paper

HB pencil

Brushes

> Size 4

> Size 1

> Size 3/0

Watercolor paints

> Light red

> Chinese white

> Yellow ochre

> Indian red

> Sepia

> Ivory black

> Lemon yellow

> Cobalt blue

> Burnt sienna

Acrylic white

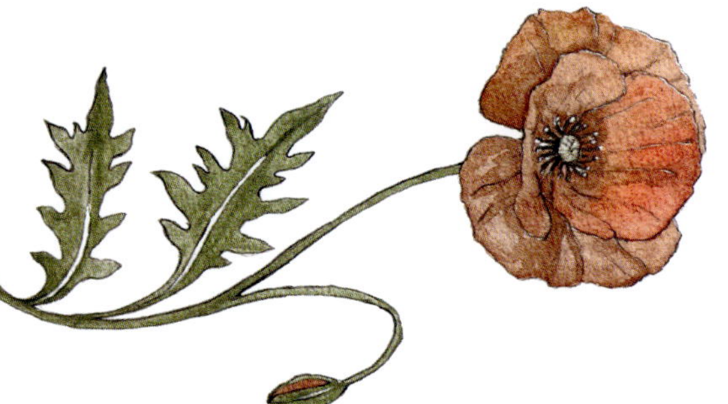

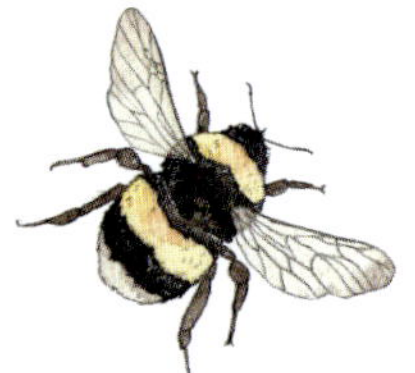

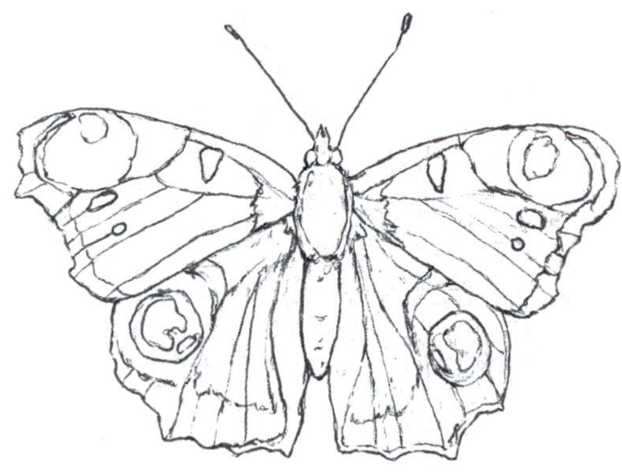

## Step 1: Draw the Outline

Starting on a sheet of cold-press watercolor paper, draw the butterfly's outline with a sharp HB pencil using the corresponding template located in the back of the book (page 177). There are a lot of details in this piece, so make sure to take your time, as butterflies do look their best and most realistic when the patterns of the wings are as symmetrical as possible.

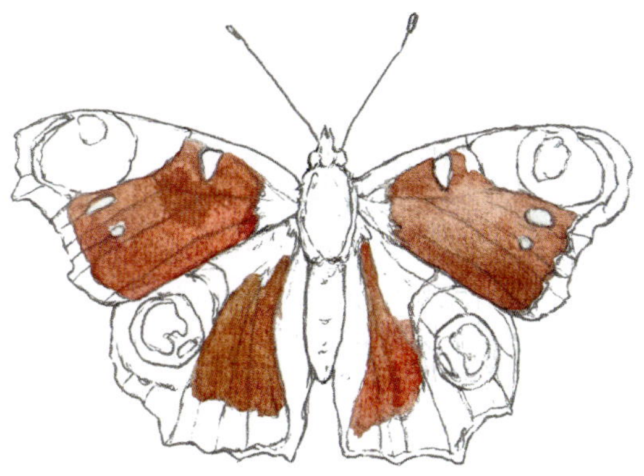

## Step 2: Paint the Main Body of the Wings

Using a size 4 brush, prepare your color that will fill the main body of the butterfly's wings by mixing a rich concentration of light red. To do this, dip your brush into your water and load the brush with pigment. We do not want it to be a mixture that is pale and thin. Flood the inner body of the butterfly's upper and lower wings with your deep red mixture. Allow the paint to fully dry.

## Step 3: Paint the Outer Wings

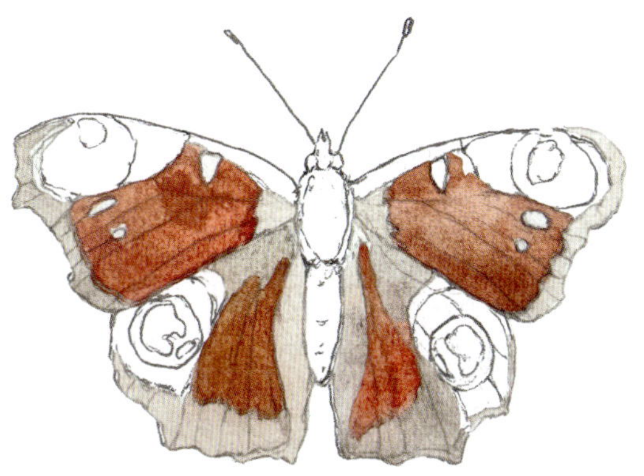

To prepare the color that will be the outer section of the butterfly's wings, mix a midtone solution of Chinese white with a dab of yellow ochre. We want this color to have a warm, cream hue and not a pale yellow, so ensure you do not add too much ochre. Load the paint onto a size 1 brush and glaze the outer section of the wings that surround the red center of both the upper and lower wings.

## Step 4: Create Deeper Hues of Red

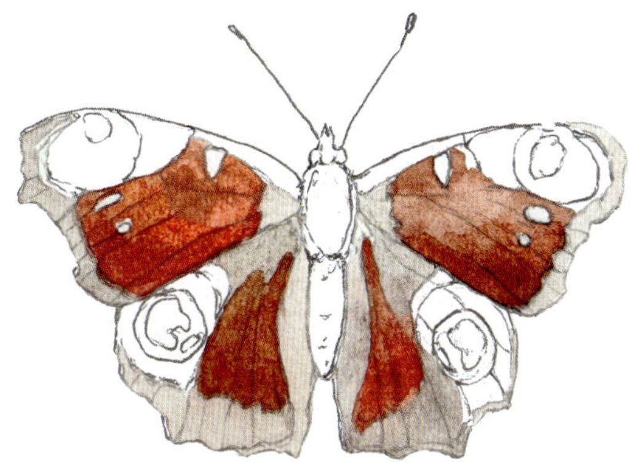

Next, we want to go back to our red center section of the upper and lower wings and deepen the red hues to create shadow layers. Using a clean size 1 brush, create a midtone mixture of light red with a swirl of Indian red and a tiny dab of sepia. This will create a deeper shade of warm red. Dab this mixture along the bottom curves of the upper wings, softening the edges of the paint layer upward so they blend seamlessly into the bottom layer of light red paint.

Load the brush with another layer of this deep wine color and glaze the central red sections of the bottom wings fully from top to bottom. Allow the paint to fully dry.

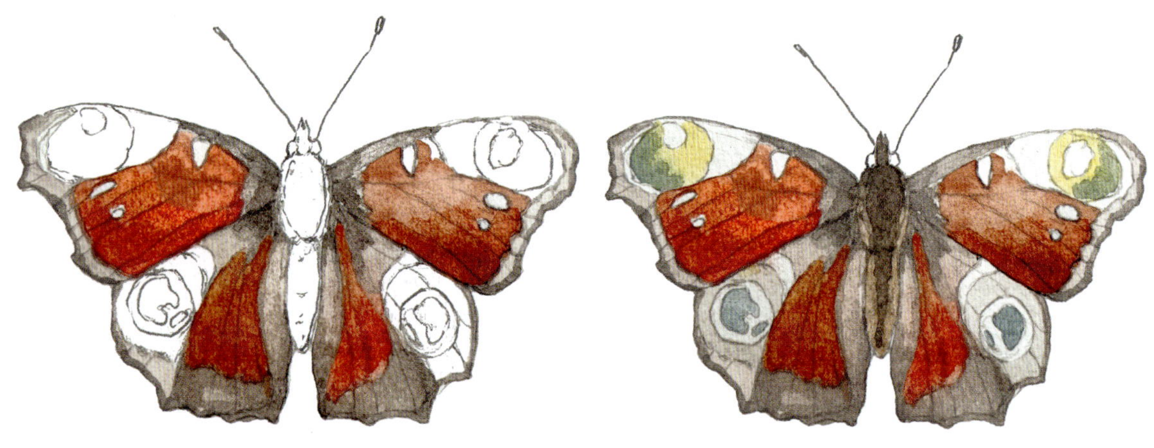

## Step 5: Paint the Edges of the Wings

To prepare the color that will be the outline for the upper and lower wings, use a size 3/0 brush to mix a simple light saturation of ivory black and water. We want this color to be a pale, charcoal gray. Load the paint onto the brush, and using the tip, trace inside the contours of both the upper and lower wings. Build up a concentration of the gray color at the center, where the wings grow from the body. On the bottom set of wings, paint the contour only to the halfway point and on the side of each wing that is closest to the body. Glaze the entire outer section of the wings surrounding the red centers with gray, creating a soft gradient of high concentration of color at the bottom, gradually softening as it bleeds toward the center of the wings.

## Step 6: Add Pops of Color

For the colors that will fill the eyes of the butterfly's wings, we need to create two washes of color. Using a clean size 3/0 brush, mix a simple midtone saturation of lemon yellow hue and water, and paint the top spots on the upper wings. While the paint is still damp, clean the brush and use it to mix a simple midtone saturation of cobalt blue. Load the paint onto the brush and drop the color onto the outer left- and right-hand sides of the yellow spots on the upper wings. As the yellow base layer is still damp, the blue paint will naturally bleed and flow around the contours of the upper spots.

For the lower spots, load more of this cobalt blue solution onto the brush and fill in the two spots that sit in the inner eye of the lower wings.

To prepare the colors that will fill in the butterfly's body, use a size 1 brush to mix a simple midtone solution of burnt sienna and glaze this as a base layer over the entire central body of the butterfly, leaving the eyes blank. While the paint is drying, clean your brush and use it to mix a simple midtone solution of sepia and water. Load this dark brown onto the tip of the brush and fill in the entire upper section of the body with brown. As the color travels downward along the abdomen, paint only a central line, leaving a pop of burnt sienna on either side.

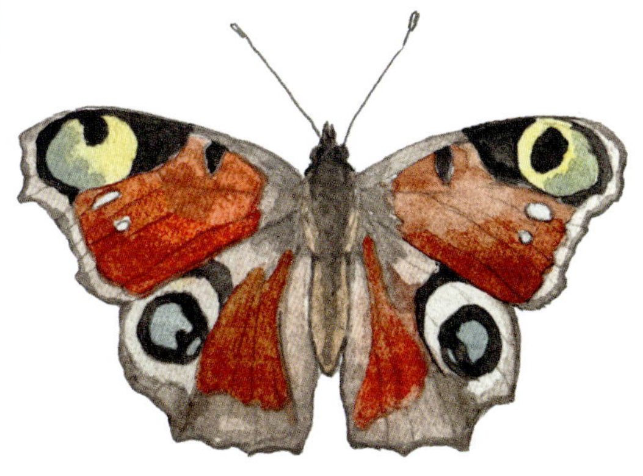

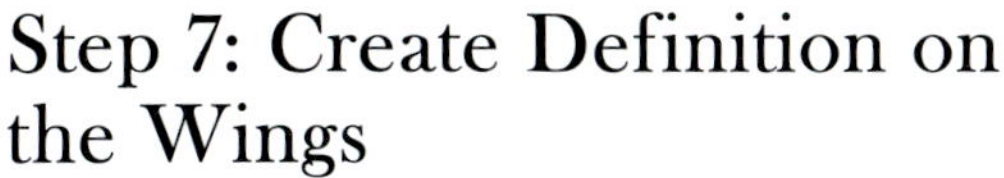

# Step 7: Create Definition on the Wings

Using a clean size 1 brush, mix a heavily saturated solution of ivory black and water. We want this color to be thick and matte and not overly diluted with water. Load the brush with this inky black hue and carefully fill in the remaining sections of the eyes surrounding the yellow and blue spots and the small dotted and semicircular details sitting above and beside the eyes on the wings. Switch to a size 3/0 brush and load the tip of the brush with this same inky black pigment. Carefully trace in the antennae and fill in the eyes at the top of the butterfly's abdomen.

# Step 8: Add the Final Details

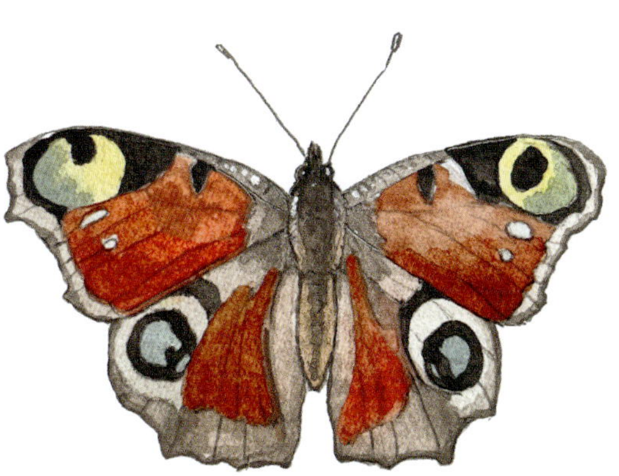

Using the same inky solution and the tip of the 3/0 brush from step 7, carefully define the veins that are on the upper and lower wings. Trace around the outlines of the abdomen to define each section. Using a clean, damp size 1 brush, mix a light-tone solution of yellow ochre and Chinese white to create a light, creamy tan mixture. Use the tip of the brush to drop in color on the lower wings, just above the eye where the blue and black was painted. When this is dry, it will give a very subtle highlight.

Finally, squeeze a less than pea-size amount of acrylic white onto your palette and load a small amount of color onto the tip of a clean size 3/0 brush. Hold the brush at the ferrule in order to have the most control of the brushstrokes, dab two dots of white into the eyes and paint short dabs of color along the upper outline of the upper wings to the point where they meet the black of the eyes on the wings. Fill in the two dots on either side of the left and right wings with white paint. In the center section of the abdomen, paint short, feathery brushstrokes traveling downward along the left- and right-hand sides. The butterfly is complete, well done!

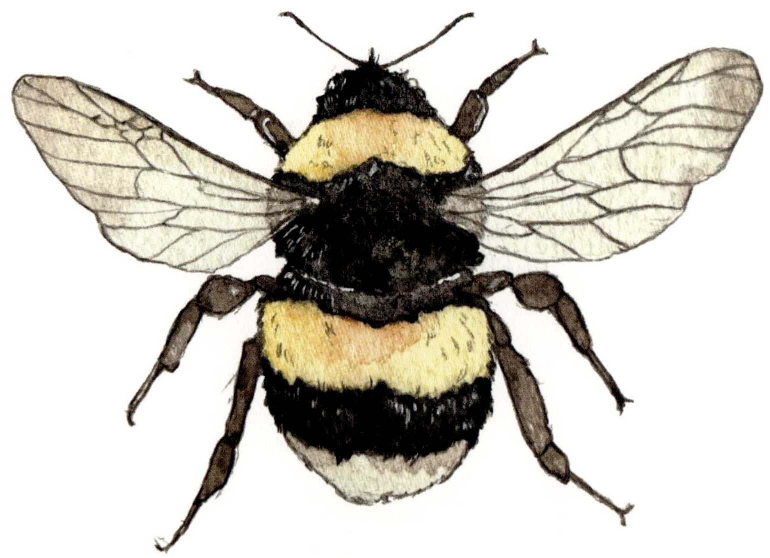

# Bumblebee

The delicate wings, intricate patterns and vibrant colors of a bumblebee make them excellent little subjects to study for watercolor painting. Capturing the unique texture of their fuzzy bodies can provide valuable practice building texture, while their iconic striped and simplistic colors lend to a really visually stunning result without feeling too overwhelmed by having to mix a wide and varied palette of tones.

# Materials Needed

A sheet of cold-press 140-pound (300-gsm) watercolor paper

HB pencil

Brushes

> Size 1

> Size 0

> Size 3/0

Watercolor paints

> Cadmium yellow

> Burnt sienna

> Lamp black

> Vandyke brown

> Chinese white

Acrylic white

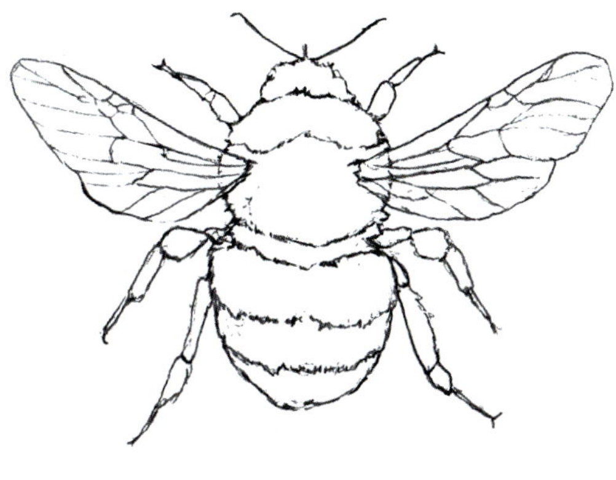

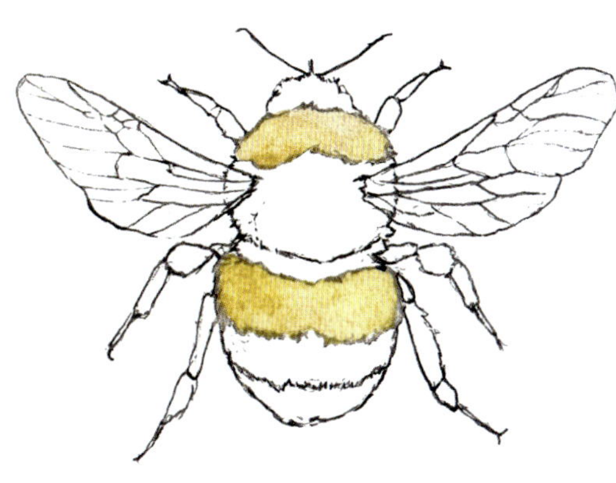

## Step 1: Draw the Outline

Starting on a sheet of cold-press watercolor paper, draw the bumblebee's outline with a sharp HB pencil using the corresponding template located in the back of the book (page 177). Note that the texture on the body of the bee is quite loose and fuzzy, and the bumblebee's legs have little individual hairs on them. Adding these little details will really bring a sense of realism to your finished painting.

## Step 2: Paint the Yellow Fur

To prepare the color that will be the yellow fur on the bumblebee's body, use a size 1 brush to mix a midtone wash of cadmium yellow hue with water. We do not want this mixture to be too wet or too thick and saturated. Once mixed, glaze this solution into the two sections where we want the yellow to be on the body. Keep your brushstrokes short and quick, as we want the body to have a fuzzy appearance. Once the paint layer is fully dry, dip the brush back into the yellow mix and dab the tip of the brush on the left-hand side of each section to build up a sense of texture through layering of color, softening the edges so the paint will blend seamlessly into the paper.

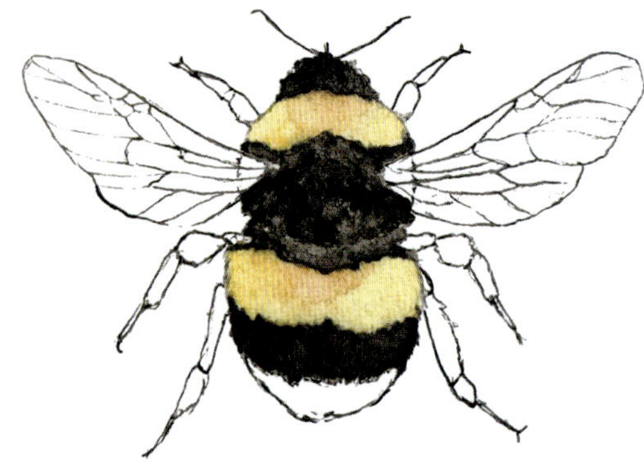

# Step 3: Paint the Black and Add the Shadows

For the shadows on the yellow sections of the bumblebee's body, mix a light solution of cadmium yellow hue with a tiny hint of burnt sienna to give the color a more earthy tone. Using a size 0 brush, outline the top of each yellow section. Soften the edges downward to blend into the base layer.

To paint the bumblebee's fuzzy black sections, use a size 1 brush to mix a midtone solution of lamp black and water. We want to be able to see the texture of the brushstrokes on the page, so make sure that the hue is not too dark, as this will create a saturated matte effect that will hide detail. To prevent smudging, I recommend painting and allowing each section to fully dry one at a time. Load your brush with the solution, and with a light touch, carefully outline the black areas of the bumblebee's body and head following the natural contours and shapes. Then, gradually fill in the outlined sections with the diluted lamp black, using short, downward brushstrokes to mimic the texture of the bumblebee's fuzzy coat. Pay close attention to the direction of the brushstrokes, allowing them to follow the downward flow of the bee's fur for a realistic effect.

Switch to a size 3/0 brush and dip it back into your midtone black. Holding the ferrule of the brush and using just the tip of the bristles, carefully paint the antennae.

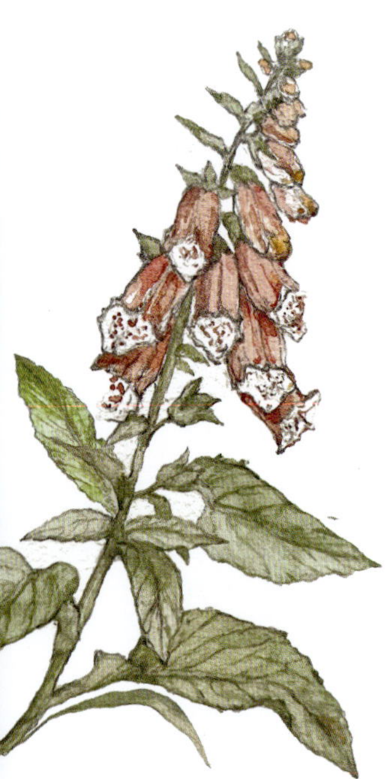

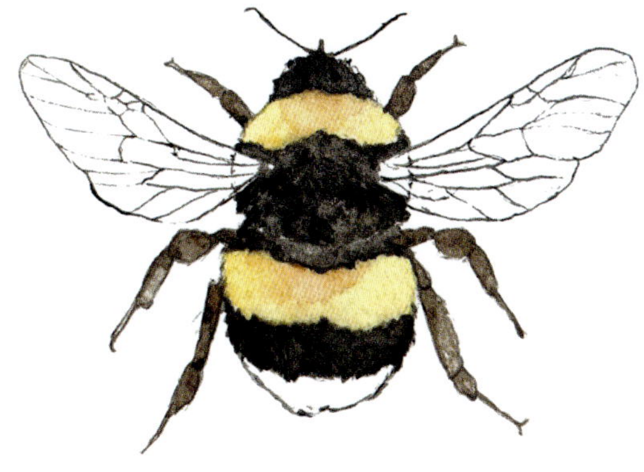

# Step 4: Paint the Legs

For the bee's legs, use a clean size 3/0 brush to mix a midtone solution of Vandyke brown and water. Using fluid brushstrokes, delicately glaze this color to fill each leg with the brown hue. Allow the paint to fully dry before you add the next layer to create depth and shadow. Load the midtone brown back onto the brush, and using the tip of the brush, paint in the segments where the legs meet the body with two additional washes of the color. Add one additional layer to the middle section of each leg. For the bottom sections of the legs, we want to create the illusion of light, so use the tip of the brush to paint one layer of the wash along the left-hand side of each leg. Use the tip of the brush to carefully define the miniscule hairs on the legs and the joints where the sections of leg meet.

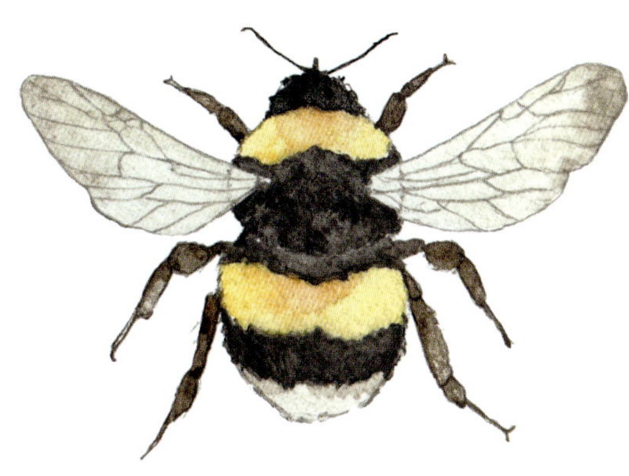

# Step 5: Add the White

For the wings and bottom of the bumblebee's body, we want to mix a warm cream solution. Using a size 1 brush, mix a midtone solution of Chinese white with a tiny hint of burnt sienna. Make sure not to add too much burnt sienna, as we want to warm up the white hue and not create a pale orange, so less is more when it comes to creating this hue. Paint this color over the left and right wings and on the very bottom of the bumblebee's body. While the paint is still damp, use a size 0 brush to mix a light solution of Vandyke brown and water. Drop this color along the outer side of each wing, allowing the paint to bleed inward and blend into the cream base. Using the same brush and color, carefully outline the top of the white section of the body where it meets the black above it and leave it to fully dry.

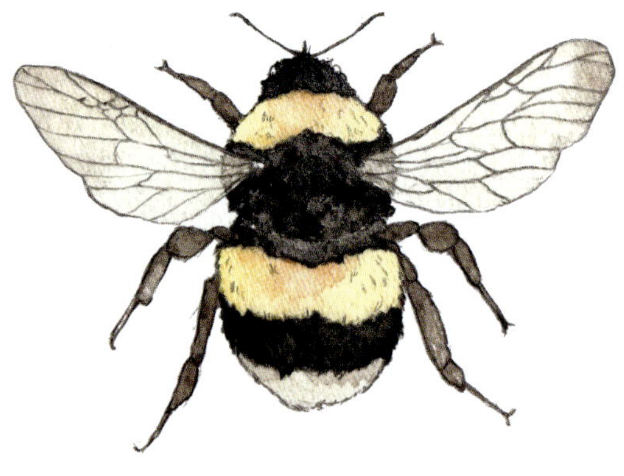

# Step 6: Define the Wing Details

To create more definition and shadow on the wings, use a clean size 0 brush to mix a light-tone wash of lamp black. Glaze this simple solution on the tiny triangular-shaped sections where the wings intersect with the body, creating the illusion that the wings are transparent and we can see the black fur due to how delicate they are. Allow this to fully dry before we begin defining the wings' fine details.

Use a size 3/0 brush to mix a midtone solution of Vandyke brown with a hint of lamp black. Carefully and slowly trace along the inner details of the wing. As this work is fine and detailed, I would recommend holding the brush at the ferrule so you have the most control over the flow of the line, which will keep your work neat.

Use this same deep brown solution and brush to define the tiny fuzzy downward hairs on the left and right sides of the yellow sections of the body. Keep your brushwork short and use only the tip of the brush to get the best results.

# Step 7: Add the Final Details

Finally, squeeze a less than pea-size amount of acrylic white out onto your palette. Using a clean size 3/0 brush, load a small amount of paint onto the tip of the brush and define the tiny hairs along the black sections of the body. Use tiny downward strokes to build the texture of fur, focusing mainly on the upper right-hand side of each section. To define the legs, outline along the joints by following the natural curved shapes from your drawing. Finally, paint each eye with a small dot of white. The bumblebee is now complete, great job!

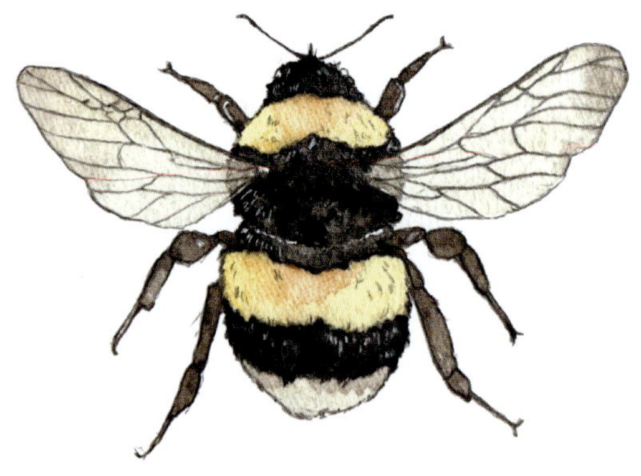

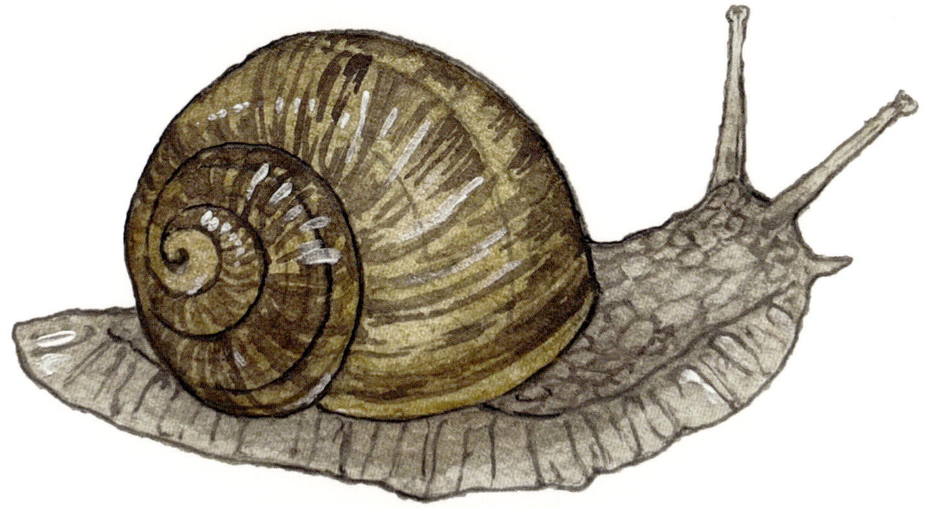

# Garden Snail

I have always thought of the snails, paired with their spiral shells, as a testament to the wonders of nature's design. They truly reward observation. When we really stop and take a closer look, so many fascinating intricacies are held on an often-overlooked creature due to their miniature size and slow, gentle demeanor. As an artist, you can learn to echo the patient, deliberate movements of a snail. It is in that simple trick of learning to move at one's own pace that there is true precision!

# Materials Needed

A sheet of cold-press 140-pound (300-gsm) watercolor paper

HB pencil

Brushes

> Size 4

> Size 3/0

> Size 0

Watercolor paints

> Raw sienna

> Yellow ochre

> Sepia

> Raw umber

Acrylic white

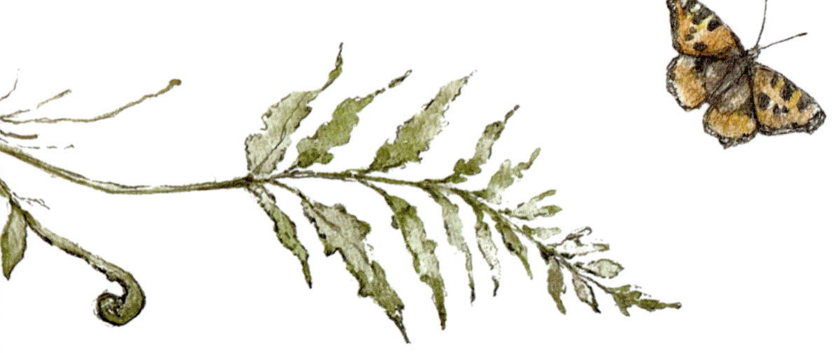

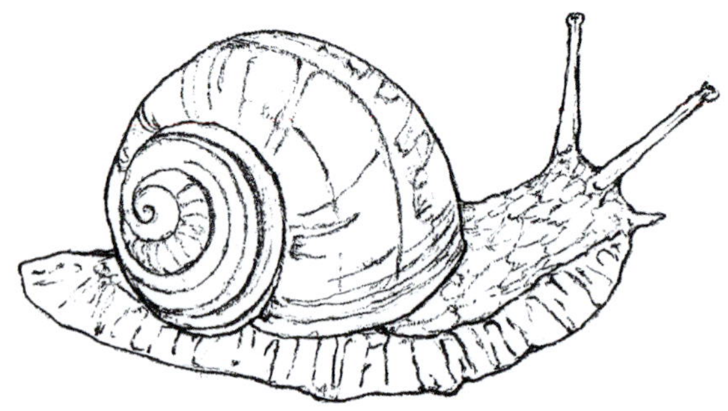

# Step 1: Draw the Outline

Starting on a sheet of cold-press watercolor paper, draw the snail's outline, the fine details of the shell and the body with a sharp **HB** pencil using the corresponding template located in the back of the book (page 177).

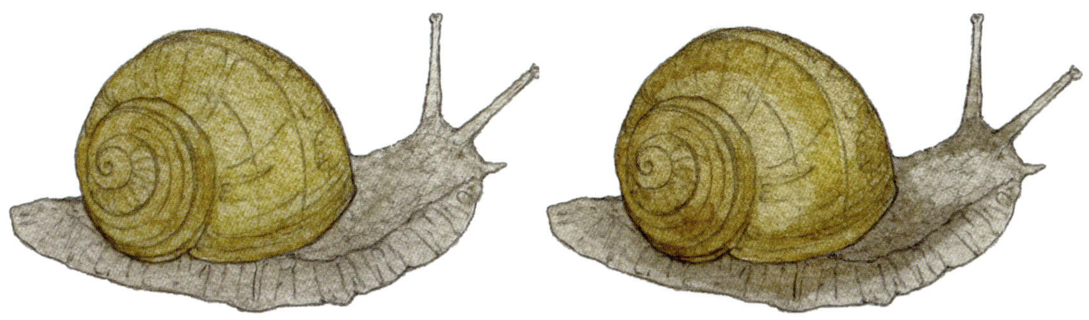

## Step 2: Paint the Base Layer

Using a size 4 brush, mix together a midtone wash of raw sienna with a tiny dab of yellow ochre to warm the tone. Glaze this mixture over the entire spiral shell. While the paint is still damp, dab the tip of the brush with pure raw sienna and gently drop the color into the center-right part of the outer spiral and along the inner outline of the bottom of the shell.

Next, we will prepare the mixture that will be used as the base layer for the body. Use a clean size 4 brush to mix together a simple light-tone solution of sepia and water. We want this color to be a very pale wash that is a very light gray–brown. Glaze this color over the entire body. For the antennae, switch to your size 3/0 brush, but use the same color, as the work is much finer and more intricate.

## Step 3: Create the Shadows

For the shadows of the snail's shell, use a size 0 brush to mix together a light-tone solution of raw umber with a tiny dab of raw sienna. We want this color to be a warm brown and the consistency to be watery, as we do not want the shadows to be too dark. Begin at the bottom of the shell, dragging the brush along the inner outline, and soften the edges by pulling the paint gently upward toward the right-hand side of the spiral and the right-hand side of the shell that is closer to the head. Next, dip the brush back into the warm brown and follow the inner outline of the spiral, starting right at the center. As the spiral winds outward, trace the left-hand side with the shadow glaze, making sure your brush follows the curvature of the lines on the drawing. As the shadow reaches the part of the shell that is closer to the head, bring the paint outward, so it is tracing not only the inner left-hand side outline but running into the center of the shell.

(Continued)

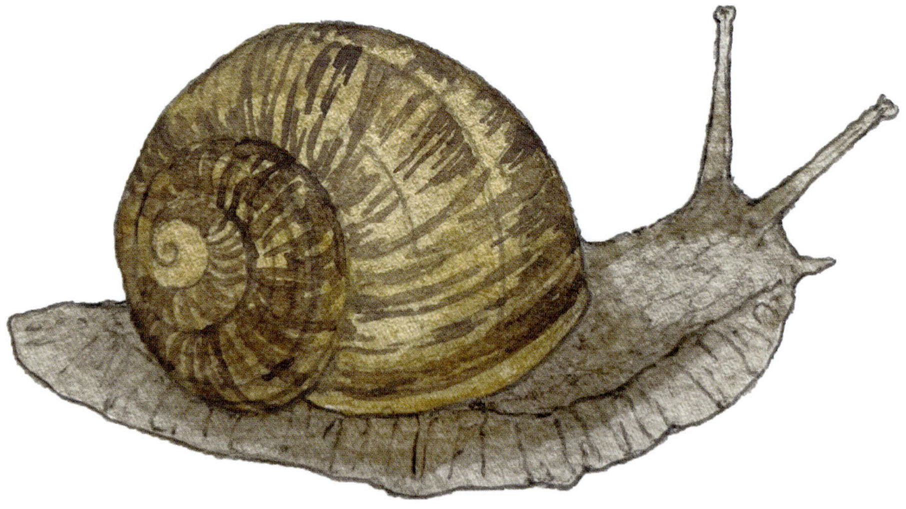

For the shadows on the snail's body, use a clean size 0 brush to mix a light-tone solution of sepia and water. We want this color to be a pale glaze and not too dark and thick. Glaze over the part of the body where it meets the shell and gently drag the paint downward to soften the edges. Paint along the inner outline of the upper body, following to and up to the tip of the antennae.

# Step 4: Paint the Lines of the Shell

To paint the intricate lines on the snail's shell, begin by using a size 3/0 brush to mix a midtone solution of raw umber and water. Hold the brush at the ferrule where your hand will have the most control and load the bristles with the sepia solution, ensuring it's not too watery or too thick. Using the fine tip of the brush, carefully apply thin, curved lines along the spiral of the shell, following its natural contours. Vary the pressure on the brush to create lines of different thicknesses, mimicking the organic patterns found in nature. To prevent smudging, take your time and allow each line to dry slightly before adding adjacent lines. The lines will be quite close and tight together as the spiral curves closer inward toward the center and more spaced out and longer as the body of the shell widens.

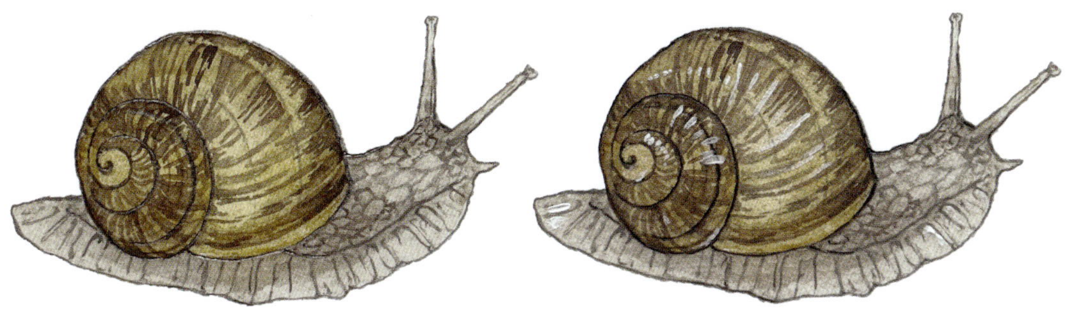

# Step 5: Create the Creases and Details of the Body

Using a clean size 3/0 brush, mix a midtone solution of sepia and water—not too runny or too thick. Using the tip of the brush, slowly and carefully paint along the intricate pattern lines from your template on the body of the snail. Pay attention to the direction and shape of the lines; everything is soft and organic and rounded with no sharp edges, so allow your bristles to have movement while still holding close to the ferrule to keep the essence of the drawing quite illustrative.

# Step 6: Add the Highlights

Squeeze a less than pea-size amount of acrylic white paint onto your palette. Ensure that the base layer of the painting is fully dry and load a small amount of the white onto the tip of a clean size 3/0 brush. It is important to identify areas of the shell where light would naturally hit, such as the uppermost curves and edges. In this painting, the most light will fall and focus on the center-right of the shell. Begin by painting left to right on the curves of the shell, starting with dots at the left that broaden to longer lines that follow the natural curves of the shell. As the spiral tightens toward the center, paint the highlights as tiny strokes. Finally, add a small curved stroke at the bottom of the shell. The snail is now complete, well done!

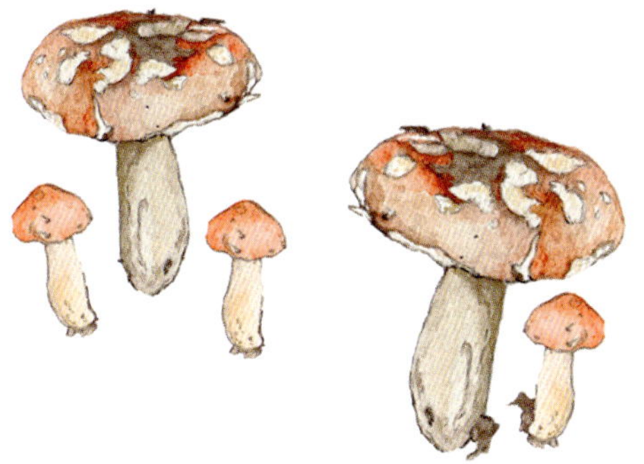

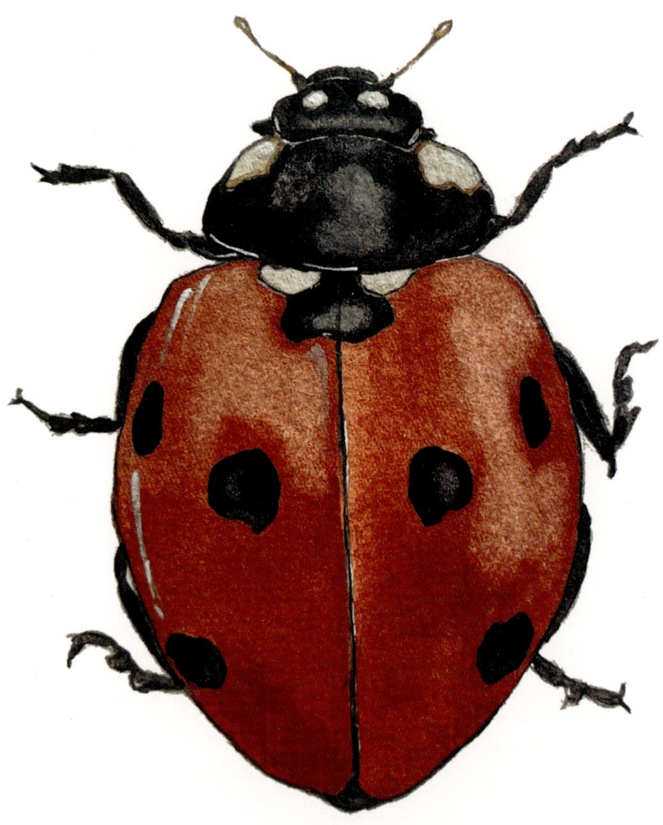

# Ladybug

Ladybugs not only captivate me with their delicate beauty and intricate patterns, but I find they hold such wonderful inspiration when it comes to a subject matter for watercolor painting! Once we take the time to observe such tiny, yet quietly elegant creatures, we can see that they hold a magical balance of vibrant hues, yet also a symmetry within each tiny dot on their wings. This is an excellent project for beginners, as only some simple shading and highlight techniques can bring flat layers of color alive.

# Materials Needed

A sheet of cold-press 140-pound (300-gsm) watercolor paper

HB pencil

A piece of paper towel

Brushes

> Size 4

> Size 0

> Size 3/0

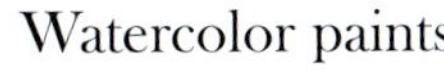

Watercolor paints

> Cadmium red

> Chinese white

> Lamp black

> Yellow ochre

Acrylic white

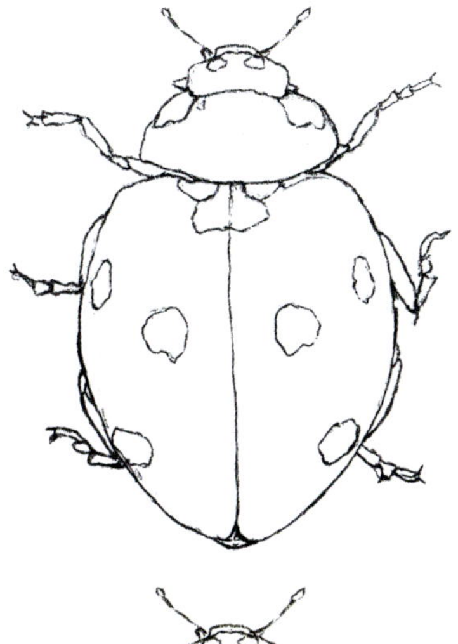

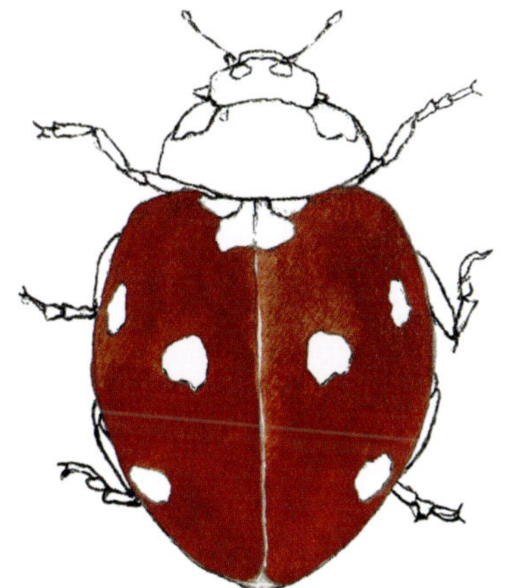

## Step 1: Draw the Outline

Starting on a sheet of cold-press watercolor paper, draw the ladybug's outline with a sharp **HB** pencil using the corresponding template located in the back of the book (page 179). Note that the spots on the ladybug's back are not perfectly round and follow an organic rounded shape that will add a true sense of realism to our finished piece.

## Step 2: Paint the Wings

Using a size 4 brush, prepare your color that will fill the body of the ladybug by mixing a rich concentration of cadmium red hue. We want the hues to be rich and vibrant, so we are aiming for a thicker mixture of paint and water. To do this, dip your brush into your water and load the brush with pigment. Flood the body of the ladybug's wings with your deep red mixture. Don't worry if some of the paint seeps into the spots, as these will be filled in later with a heavy mixture of black. We want the entire body that is covered in red to have a consistent finish that appears almost matte, so if your brush is running out of paint, repeat the process to reload your brush with paint until all of the body is filled in. Allow the paint to fully dry.

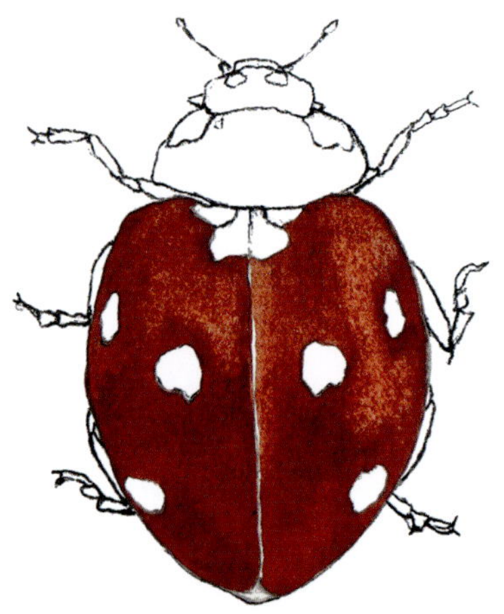

## Step 3: Create the Highlights

Creating highlights will give the appearance of "shine" on the ladybug's wings and provide a three-dimensional effect. We want the top of wings near the head to have a lighter appearance. Wet a clean size 0 brush with water and wriggle it onto the top central section of the wings. Then, press down a piece of dry paper towel firmly onto these damp sections until the paint has been absorbed and lifted.

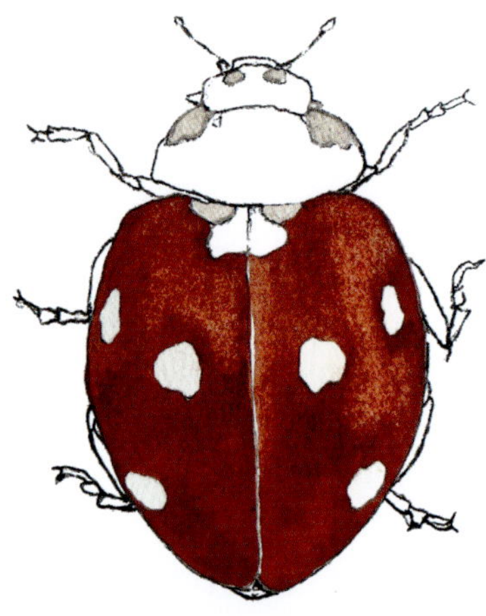

## Step 4: Start the Head

Now, we want to start adding life to the head of the ladybug. Wet a size 0 brush and swirl it into Chinese white. We do not want this mixture to be as thick as our red wing base, so add more water to create a more diluted solution. Using this white mixture, fill in the small sections of the head.

## Step 5: Paint the Spotted Details

Using black is what will really give our ladybug life. We want our black paint to be heavily pigmented to give an appearance of a matte finish, so just as we did in step 2 with our cadmium red hue, we want this paint-to-water ratio to have an identical thick consistency. Dip a clean size 0 brush into water and swirl it into lamp black until the brush is loaded with paint. As we don't want the appearance of shadows or highlights, only solid blocks of black color, we want to ensure that the color stays consistent. Reload your brush as necessary as you are filling in the black sections. Start the process by filling in the head first, taking care not to bleed into the pieces of white that we painted in step 4. Then, fill in the spots along the ladybug's back.

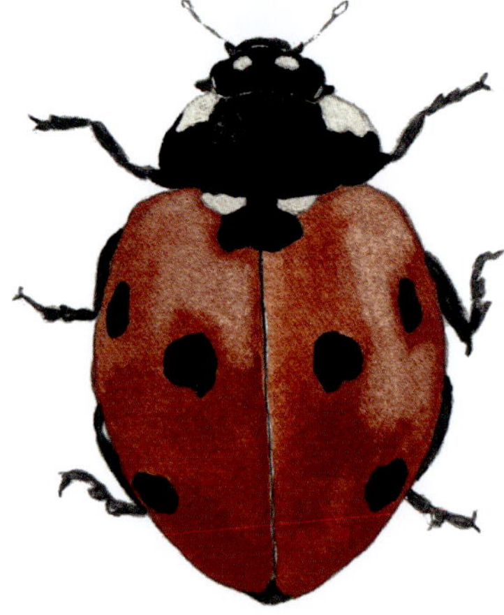

For the finer outlines of the wings, legs and antennae, use a size 3/0 brush with this black mixture. Let the paint fully dry.

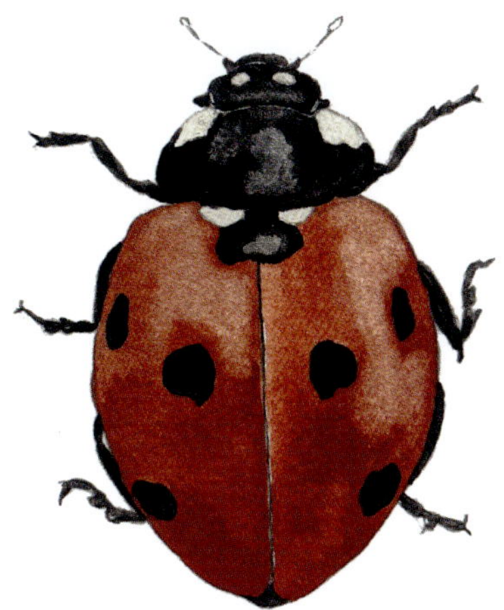

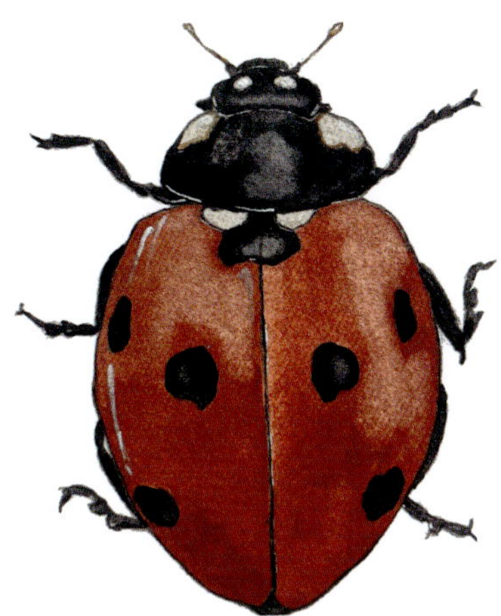

## Step 6: Create More Highlights

We want to carry through this "shine" effect to the ladybug's head by creating highlights. Dip a clean size 0 brush into water and wriggle it just in the center of the upper and lower section of the head. Press a dry paper towel into these damp sections and lift to find the paint has been absorbed, leaving a paler patch underneath to create a shine-like highlight.

## Step 7: Add the Final Details

These finishing steps will add so much character to our ladybug. Dip a clean, dry size 3/0 brush into a small blob of acrylic white paint and, focusing on the left wing, draw three downward lines that curve around the shape of the wing. The top two lines are short and the bottom line is slightly longer. Dip your brush again into acrylic white and outline the bottom of the head where it meets the wings and the bottom of the very top section of the head.

Completely clean the same brush with water. We now want to outline the larger white sections on the head that we created in step 4. Dip your brush into water and swirl it into yellow ochre until you have a thick, glossy mixture on the brush that isn't pale and diluted. Outline the white sections on the bottom of the head with this mixture. The ladybug is now complete, great job!

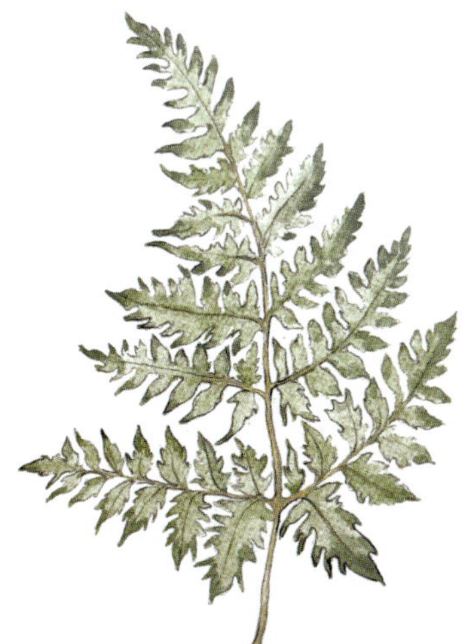

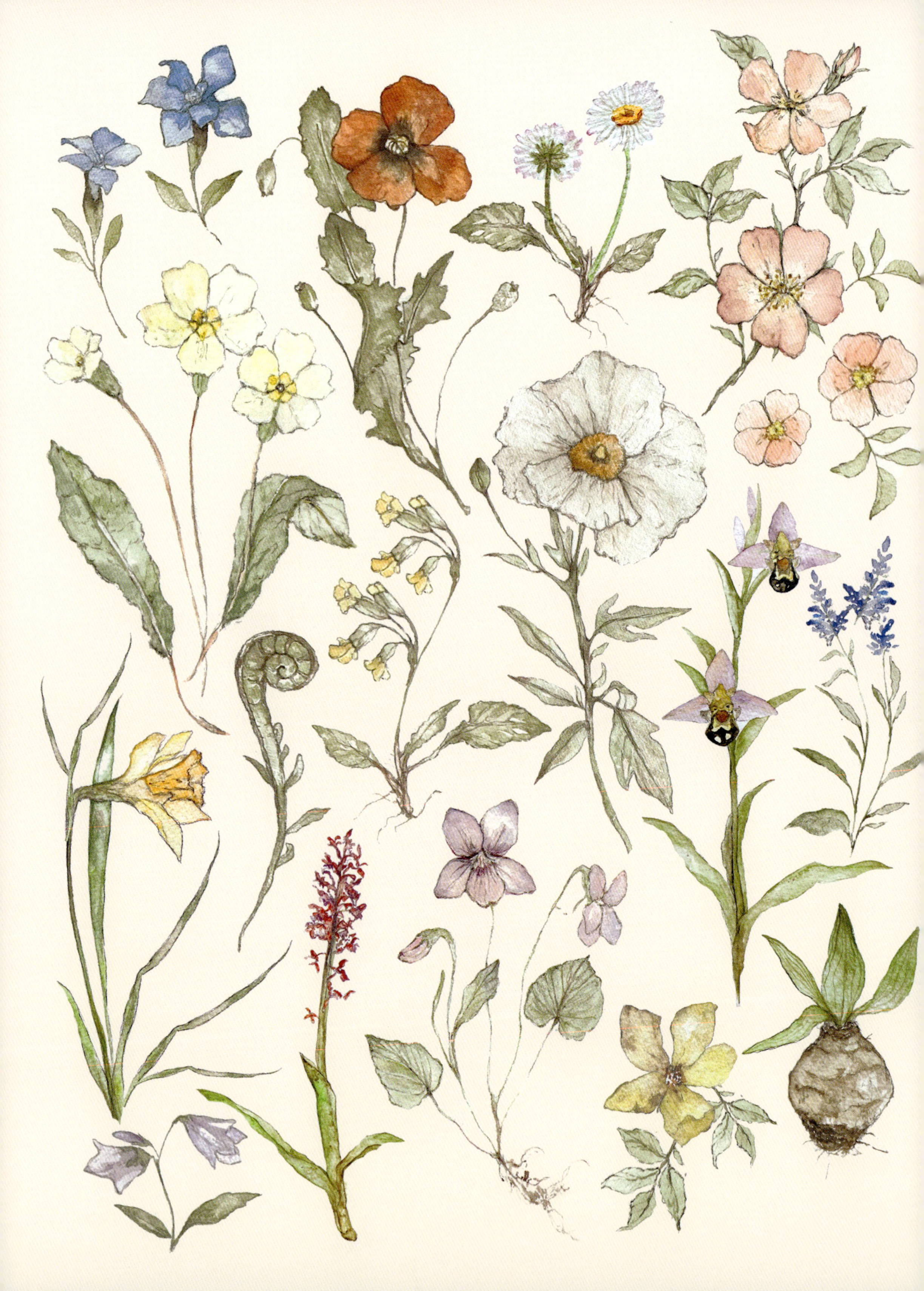

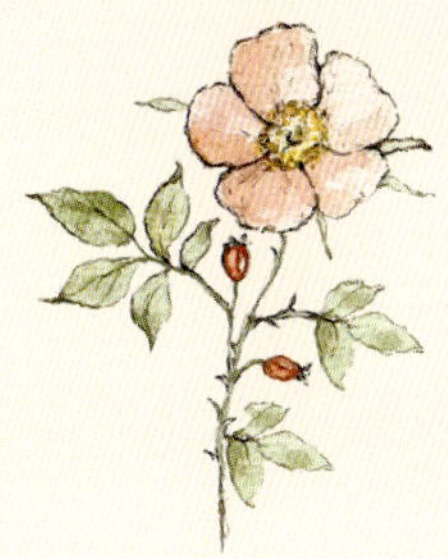

# Forest Flora

Welcome to Forest Flora, a chapter devoted to capturing the
exquisite beauty and diversity of flowering plants found in the
depths of the woodland.

In this chapter, you will find yourself immersed in the timeless beauty of
one of nature's most beloved treasures. From the delicate leaves of the
dog rose (page 146) to the crisp symmetry of the daisy's petals (page 154),
from the graceful unfurling of fern fronds (page 159) to the fiery
splendor of the poppy's bloom (page 162), every botanical specimen
holds a unique charm. You will soon find that botanicals offer an
endless source of inspiration and opportunity to explore—
and master—newfound techniques.

You will gain confidence in your ability to blend colors, create depth and
convey the intricate beauty of fine details on leaves and petals. Along-
side specific techniques for each flower and plant, we will also explore
broader watercolor methods, such as layering washes, using wet-on-wet
techniques and incorporating fine details with precision.

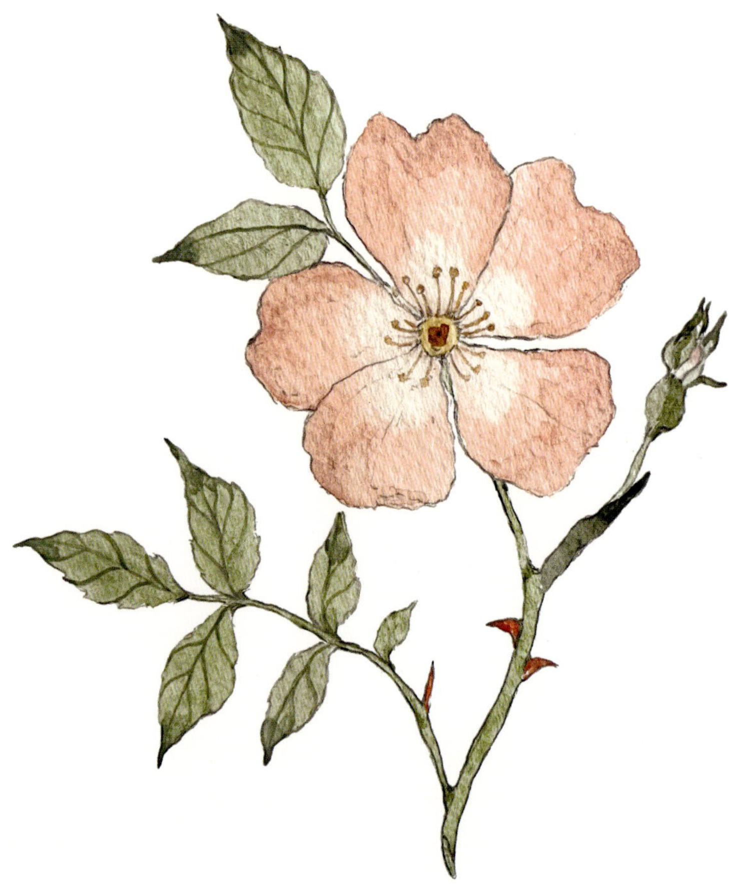

# Dog Rose

I adore wild roses for their timeless beauty and, of course, their captivating
fragrance. These little plants are known to grow in only a teaspoon of soil in
the summer months, so I am always reminded of what it means to be
resilient when I see them shoot up among the cracks of rocks in May!
Their soft pink petals also make for a wonderful subject to paint, as
we will learn to emphasize delicacy through painting shadows
and sheer layers of color.

# Materials Needed

A sheet of cold-press 140-pound (300-gsm) watercolor paper

HB pencil

A piece of paper towel

Brushes

> Size 3/0

> Size 4

> Size 0

Watercolor paints

> Yellow ochre

> Permanent rose

> Burnt sienna

> Hooker's green light

> Vandyke brown

> Indian red

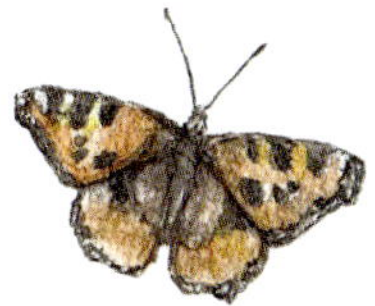

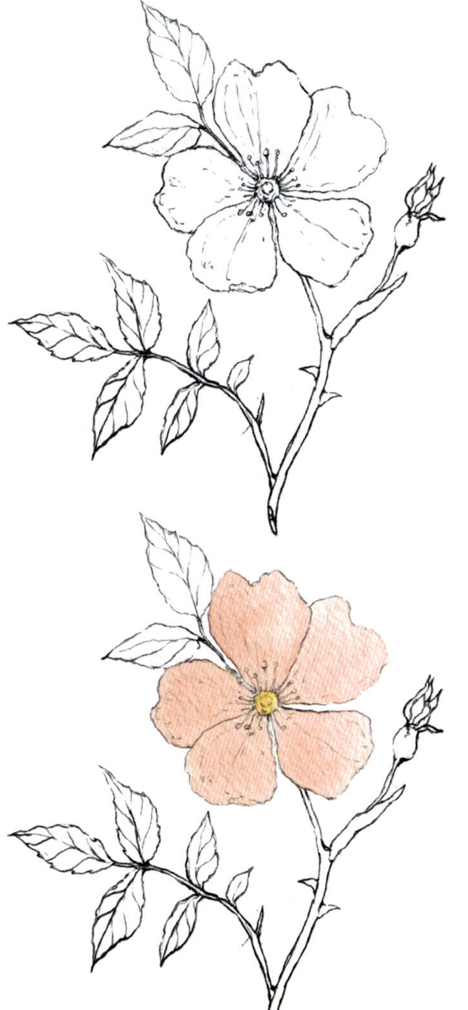

## Step 1: Draw the Outline

Starting on a sheet of cold-press watercolor paper, draw the rose petals' outline, the flower center, the stem and the leaves and their veins with a sharp HB pencil using the corresponding template located in the back of the book (page 179).

## Step 2: Paint the Head of the Flower

Using a size 3/0 brush, mix a midtone solution of yellow ochre and water. Paint this right in the center of the rose from where the petals grow.

To prepare the color that will be the base layer painted over the petals, use a size 4 brush to mix together a simple midtone wash of permanent rose and water. Glaze it over each petal until there is a consistent layer of color covering the entire head of the flower. Allow the paint to fully dry.

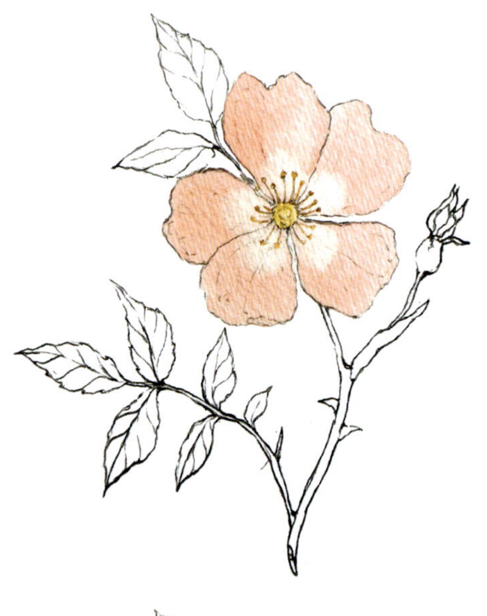

# Step 3: Create the Highlights

Dip a clean size 0 brush into water and wriggle it on the very bottom of each individual petal, causing the paint to lift up and sit on top of the paper. Taking a clean, dry paper towel, press the paper firmly, which will absorb the paint and leave behind a delicate highlight.

Using a size 3/0 brush, create a midtone solution of burnt sienna. Using just the tip of the brush, paint in the stamens that fan around the center of the flower. Holding the brush close to the ferrule will give you more control over the lines and can allow you to have a more illustrative and tidy finish.

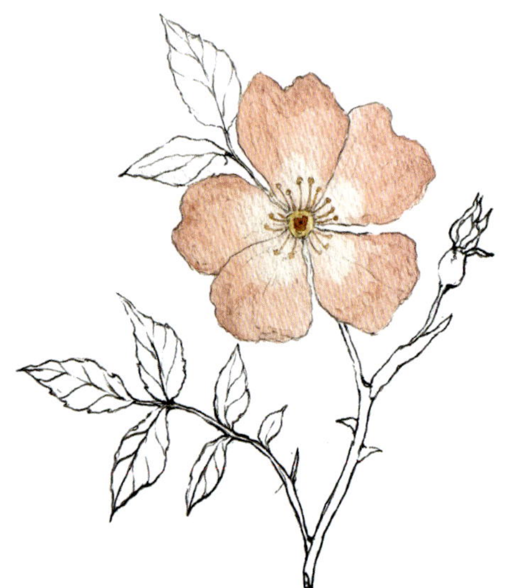

# Step 4: Create the Shadows

Using a size 0 brush, mix a midtone solution of permanent rose and glaze this mixture over the edge of each individual petal. This will deepen the petals' edges and folds by using a deeper tone of the same color that we used for the base of the rose, giving a more natural and realistic effect. Clean and dry the brush, and gently stroke the bristles over the edges of the shadow tones that are closer to the center to soften them and have them blend seamlessly into the base layer.

Deepen the center of the rose by using a size 3/0 brush and the same midtone solution of burnt sienna we used in step 3. Paint a tiny irregular circle shape using just the tip of the brush.

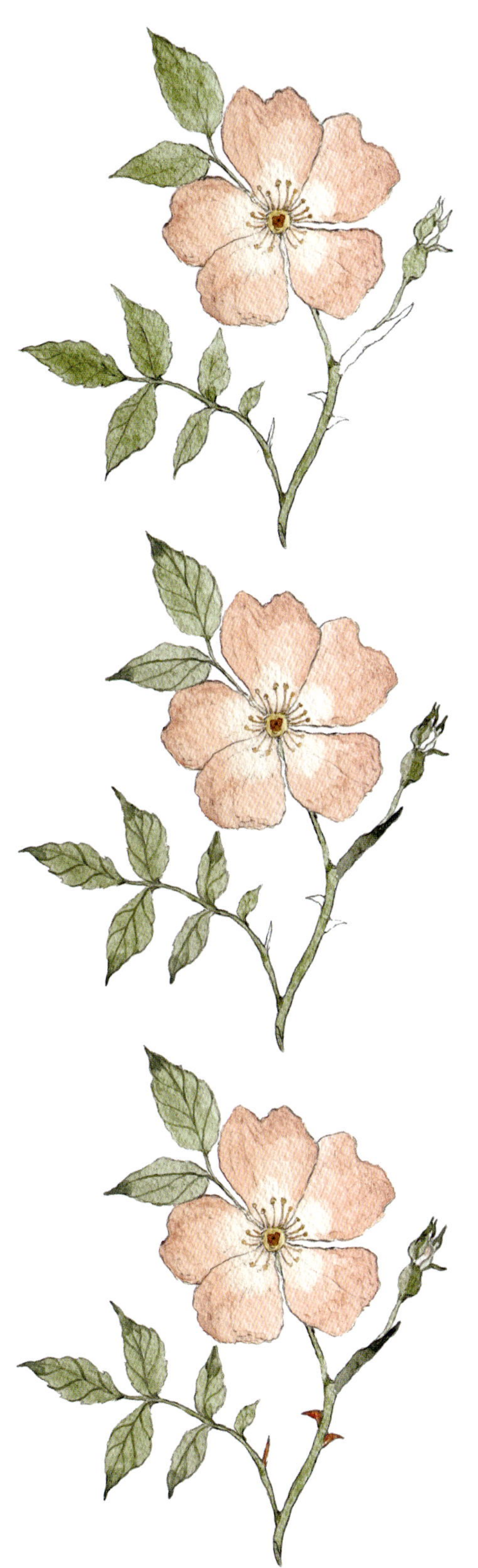

## Step 5: Paint the Leaves, Bud and Stem

Using a size 0 brush, create a midtone glaze of Hooker's green light and paint the entire stem, leaves and outside of the flower bud. While the paint is still damp, swirl your brush back into the green and gently dab along the very tips of the leaves, allowing the darker pigment to softly disperse inward to create a natural layered shadow. Dip back into the green and trace along the very bottom of the stem upward to the center. Make sure not to paint the thorns or the singular leaf on the right-hand side of the stem.

## Step 6: Define the Leaf Details

Using a size 3/0 brush, create a light mix of Hooker's green light with a tiny dab of Vandyke brown to make it a deeper tone of green. Using just the tip of the brush, paint the tips of the leaves and the curves of the serrations along the edge of the leaf, as well as the inner rib stems. Glaze the entire singular leaf on the right-hand side, the right-hand side of the bud and the very bottom of the stem. While the paint is still wet, swirl your brush into Vandyke brown and drop it right at the very top of each individual leaf.

## Step 7: Add the Final Details

To prepare the color for the thorns and singular rosebud that is yet to blossom, use a clean size 3/0 brush to mix a simple midtone solution of Indian red and water. We want this to have a high pigment but not too strong as to overpower the delicacy of the soft pink petals. Using the tip of the brush, fill in the thorns that run up the stem. Dip your brush back into the water and swirl it into your Indian red solution, which will lighten it. Use this to lightly glaze the inside of the bud. The dog rose is now complete! Good job!

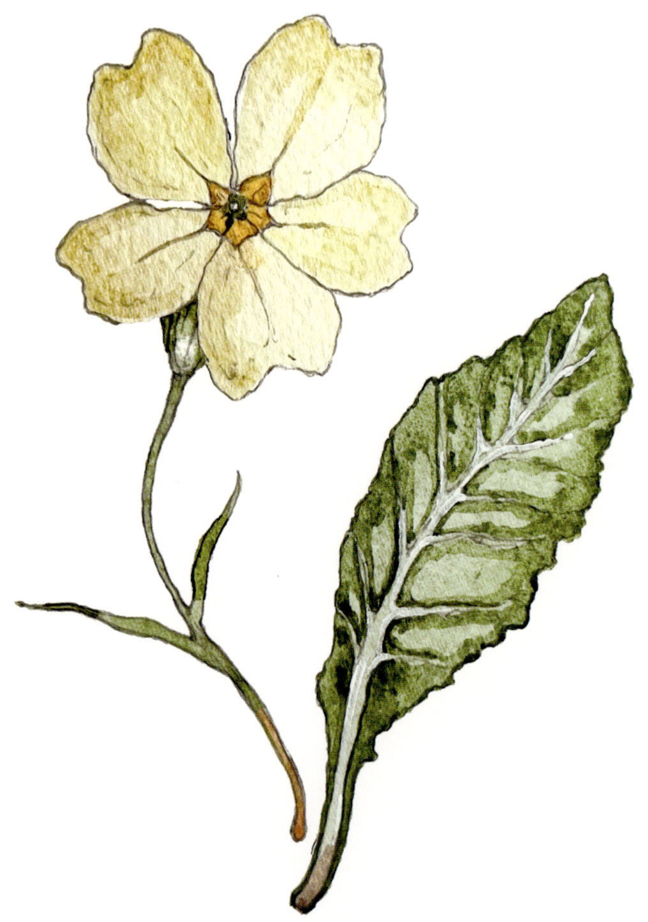

# Primrose

For me, primroses are a sign of hope and resilience. As they often bloom in
early spring, they always signal a sure arrival of warmer weather after months of
dark evenings and winter dormancy in the garden. Their soft pastel hues can
really add a quiet yet captivating beauty to any painting. I often include
them in my work as their sunny velvety petals are simplistic in shape,
yet very visually effective!

# Materials Needed

A sheet of cold-press 140-pound
(300-gsm) watercolor paper

HB pencil

Brushes

> Size 4

> Size 1

> Size 0

> Size 3/0

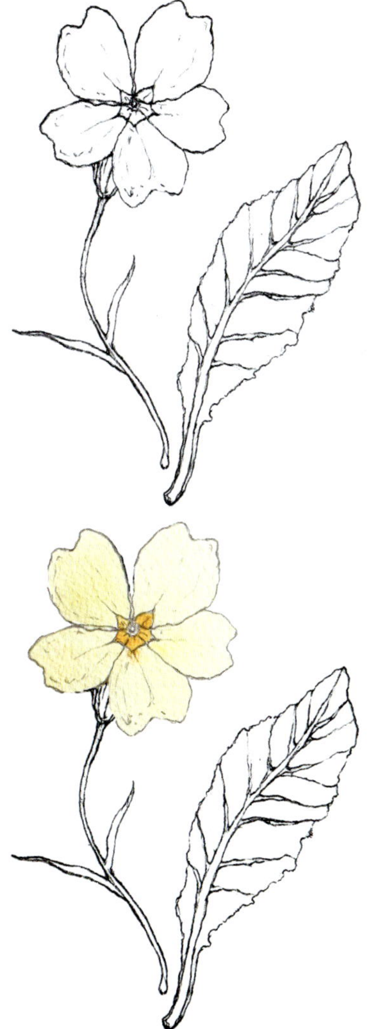

Watercolor paints

> Yellow ochre

> Chinese white

> Raw sienna

> Raw umber

> Hooker's green light

> Burnt sienna

Acrylic white

## Step 1: Draw the Outline

Starting on a sheet of cold-press watercolor paper,
draw the primrose petals' outline, the flower center,
the stem and the leaves with a sharp HB pencil
using the corresponding template located in the
back of the book (page 181).

## Step 2: Paint the Head of
the Primrose

To prepare the color for the base layer of the petals,
use a size 4 brush to mix a simple light-tone solution
of yellow ochre with a tiny dab of Chinese white.
We want this to be a pale, pastel yellow hue. Glaze
this wash over each individual petal, taking care
not to paint the very center of the flower. While
the paint is still damp, dip your brush back into
your pastel yellow mixture and glaze another layer
of the paint on the left-hand petals. Dab the tip of
the brush at the bottom-center of each petal where
it meets the middle of the flower. This will drop in
a tiny amount of color that will create subtle depth
and tone. Allow the paint to fully dry.

(Continued)

For the center of the flower, use a size 1 brush to prepare a midtone wash of raw sienna and water. Carefully fill in each section in the flower's center. Allow the paint layer to fully dry.

## Step 3: Add the Shadows

Prepare the shadow color by using a clean size 1 brush to mix a midtone solution of yellow ochre with a dab of raw umber to create a muted, earthy yellow. In our painting, the light will naturally fall to the right-hand side of the petals, so we will focus the majority of the shadows on the left-hand side of the flower. On the left-hand side's petals, work from top to bottom. Using light brushstrokes to trace along the curves at the top of each petal, blend the paint completely downward toward the center so the paint will transition from darker to lighter over the entire petal. Make sure to soften the edges to create a seamless transition between light and shadow, ensuring a natural and realistic appearance. On the right-hand side's petals, define only the outline of the top of the petals and trace the center fold toward the center.

To define the very center of the flower, using a size 3/0 brush, blend a dark-tone mixture of Hooker's green light and raw umber and fill in the tiny section from where all of the petals grow. Use the tip of the brush to define the petals' center folds.

## Step 4: Paint the Leaves

Using a size 0 brush, create a midtone glaze of Hooker's green light and paint the entire stem and leaves. While the paint is still dry, swirl your brush back into the green and gently dab along the stem's tip where it joins the primrose flower, allowing the darker pigment to softly disperse inward to create a natural layered shadow.

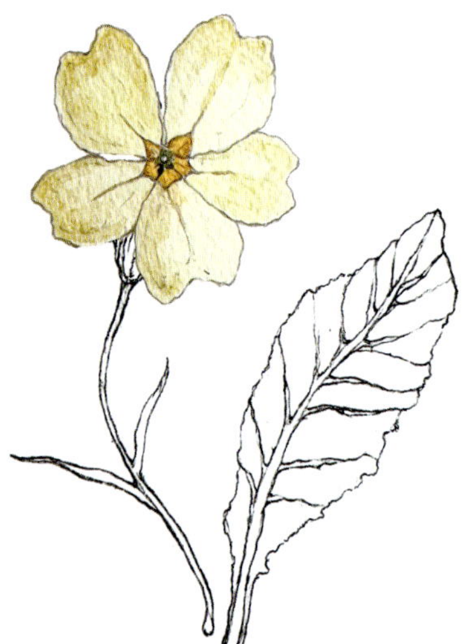

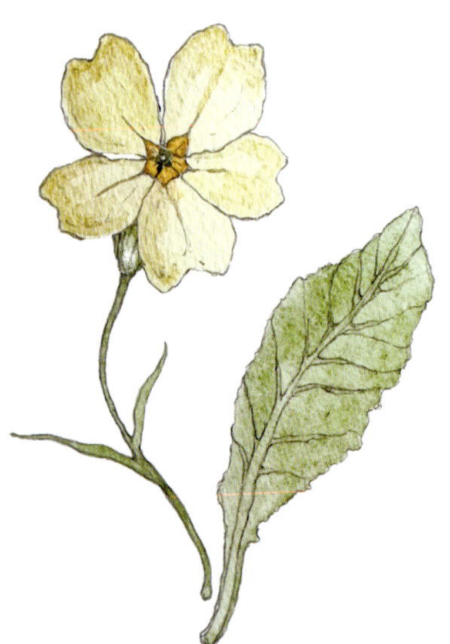

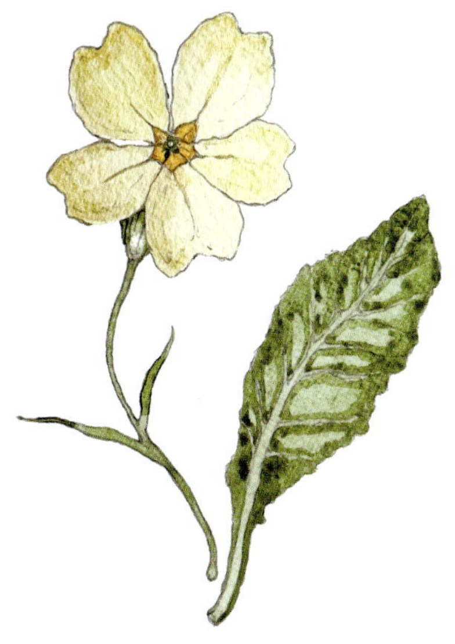

## Step 5: Create the Defining Details on the Leaf

We now want to define the detailed areas that surround the veins on the leaf and divide them into different sections of darker green. First, glaze an extremely thin layer of clean water over the entire right-hand side's singular leaf. We do not want the water to be sitting and pooled on top of the paper; we want the paper to be slightly damp but not wet. Using a size 1 brush, mix a midtone solution of Hooker's green light with a swirl of raw umber to create a deep, warm green hue. While the paper is still damp, use the tip of the brush to drop color along the edges of the leaf and following the curves of the veins inward toward the center rib.

Using this same color and brush, use the tip to paint the very top of the stem where it meets the flower and the tips of the leaves on the flower's stem.

## Step 6: Add the Final Details

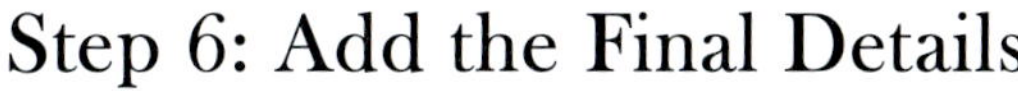

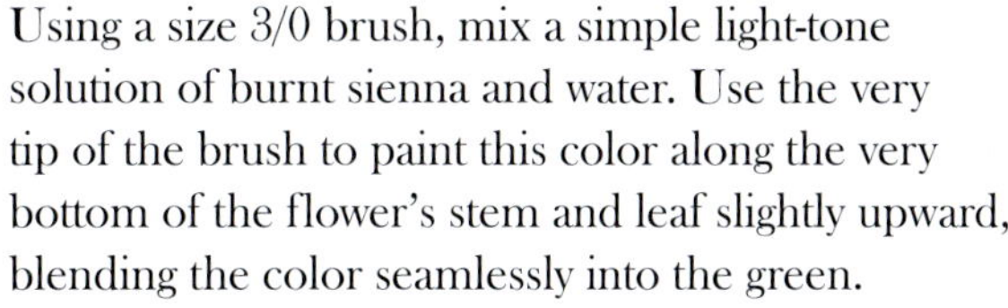

Using a size 3/0 brush, mix a simple light-tone solution of burnt sienna and water. Use the very tip of the brush to paint this color along the very bottom of the flower's stem and leaf slightly upward, blending the color seamlessly into the green.

Finally, squeeze a small amount of acrylic white onto your palette. Using a size 0 brush, load a small amount of paint onto the tip of the brush. With a steady hand, carefully trace the center rib veins, following their natural direction and shape curving up through the center of the leaf. Gently trace the tiny veins that grow outward from it. The primrose is now complete, well done!

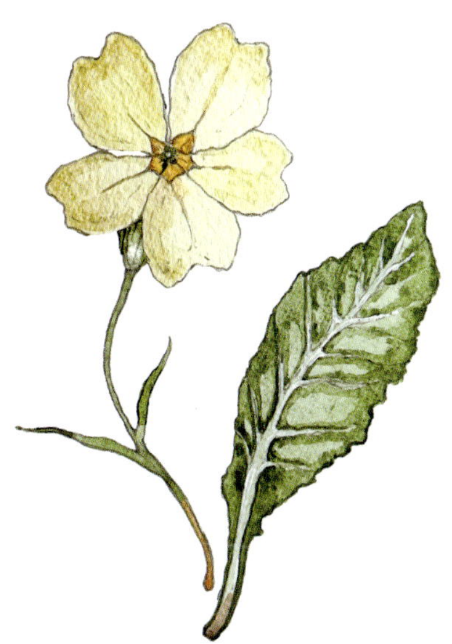

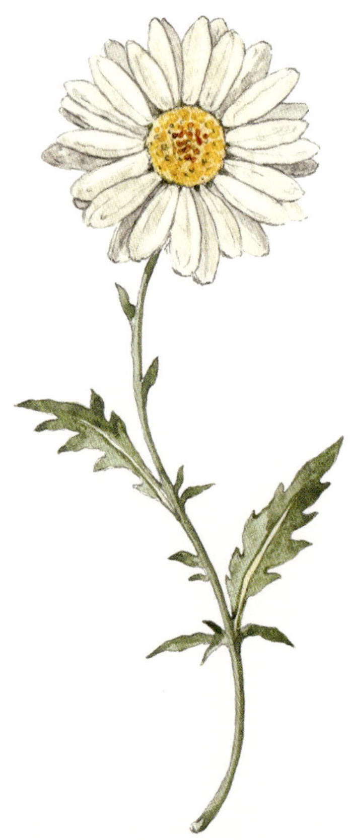

# Daisy

I love painting white flowers. For me, their petals portray calmness, tranquility
and purity. The aim is to capture the white of the paper within a pattern of
subtle shadows. They make an excellent project for beginning watercolor painting: When executed with the proper care, we learn that, in this case, less is
more. The degree of subtlety required to paint white upon a white background
will make you feel very accomplished when you see your finished piece.

I can assure you that if you are like me, you will immediately
want to start painting another picture!

# Materials Needed

A sheet of cold-press 140-pound (300-gsm) watercolor paper

HB pencil

A piece of paper towel

Brushes

> Size 0
> Size 3/0

Watercolor paints

> Chinese white
> Yellow ochre
> Raw sienna
> Burnt sienna
> Lamp black
> Hooker's green light
> Vandyke brown

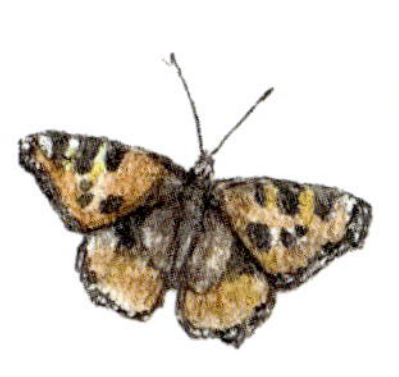
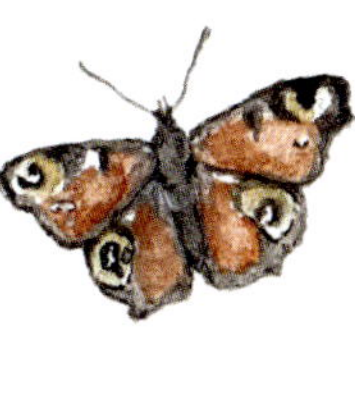

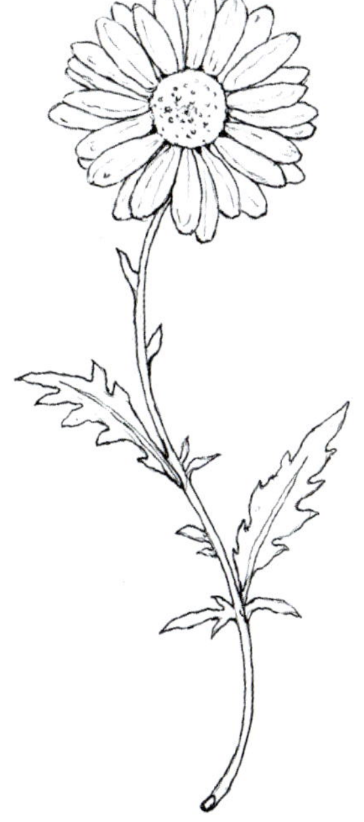

# Step 1: Draw the Outline

Starting on a sheet of cold-press watercolor paper, draw the daisy's outline with a sharp **HB** pencil using the corresponding template located in the back of the book (page 179). The form of a daisy, especially its petals, is quite uniform and smooth rather than soft, fluffy and organic, so make sure that your line is strong and confident to outline each rounded shape on the head where all of the petals grow.

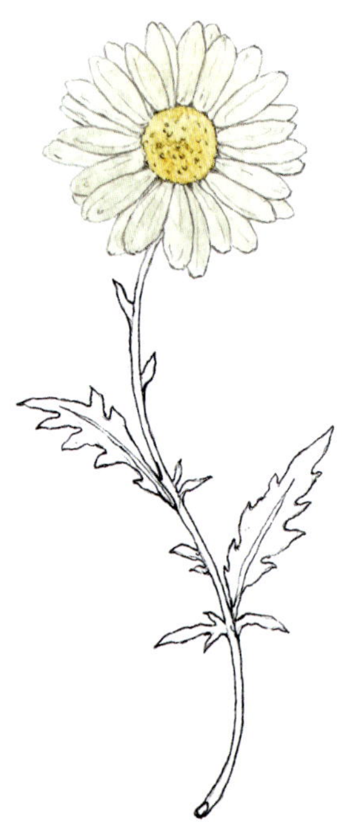

## Step 2: Paint the Head of the Daisy

Prepare the base color for the petals by using a size 0 brush to mix a light wash of Chinese white with the tiniest dab of yellow ochre. We want this to appear as a very light and warm cream and not a light yellow, so if you find the color is too overpowered by yellow, keep adding in white and slight dilutions of water until the desired color is achieved. Paint this light wash over the entire head of petals and allow the paint to fully dry.

Next, for the center of the daisy, prepare a simple light wash of yellow ochre and water. We want this wash to be light, as we will be progressively layering it to give a dappled effect, so add slightly more water. Build up the color in the center by glazing the area two to three times, allowing each layer to fully dry in between. Finally, add another layer on top, but this time simply dab the center in random spots to give a very subtle "dotted effect" where the pollen of the daisy sits.

## Step 3: Add the Shadows and Highlights

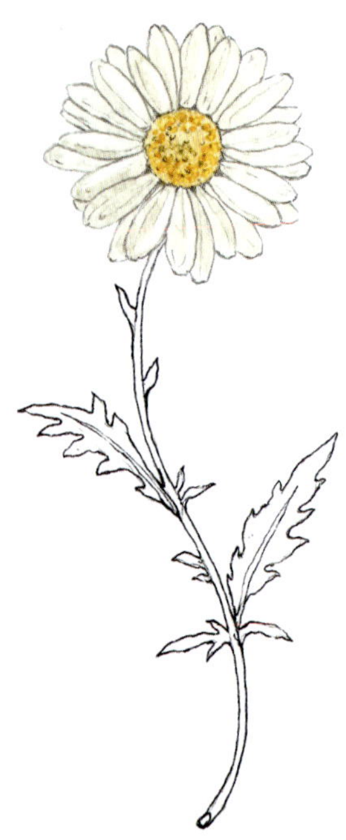

Dip a size 3/0 brush into clean water and wriggle the brush along the right-hand side of each petal, which will lift the color from the paper. Using a clean paper towel, press heavily down on these damp sections. The paint will absorb onto the towel, leaving behind a subtle highlight that will give the illusion of the daisy catching sunlight.

Next, we will prepare the color for the depth of the daisy's center. Using a size 3/0 brush, mix together a midtone wash of raw sienna with a tiny dot of burnt sienna to deepen it slightly. Using the very tip of the brush, gently and softly create little broad dots all around the inner edge of the daisy's center.

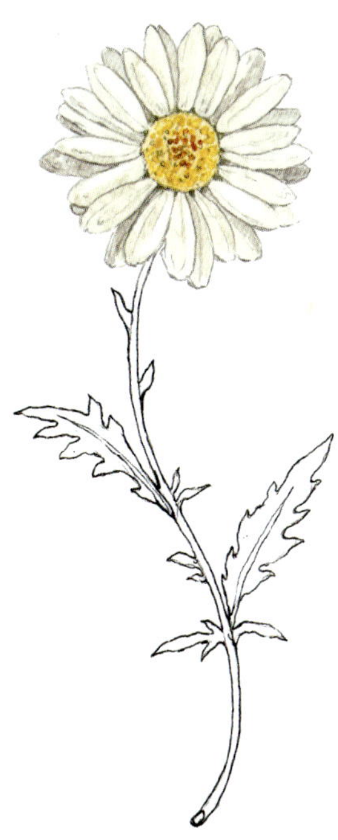

# Step 4: Add Depth and Layers

To create a three-dimensional effect on the petals, use a clean size 3/0 brush to mix together a very diluted solution of lamp black, adding enough water to make it a very light gray. Gently paint this wash on the very bottom petals on the stack that surround the daisy's center. Paint just around the center of the daisy to create central depth. While this first layer of black is drying, clean your brush and swirl it into burnt sienna to create a midtone solution. Create little painted dots right at the daisy's center. Clean your brush and dip it back into our lamp black mixture to create a second layer. Paint over the outline of the daisy's center in between the petals and on a bottom petal roughly every quarter of the way around the daisy. This will create more shadows and really give the impression that the daisy is bursting with petals.

# Step 5: Paint the Stem and Leaves

Using a size 0 brush, create a midtone glaze of Hooker's green light and paint the entire stem and leaves. While the paint is still damp, swirl your brush back into the green and gently dab along the very tips of the leaves, allowing the darker pigment to softly disperse inward to create a natural layered shadow. Dip back into the green and trace along the very bottom of the stem upward to the center. Make sure not to paint the inner stem vein of the leaves.

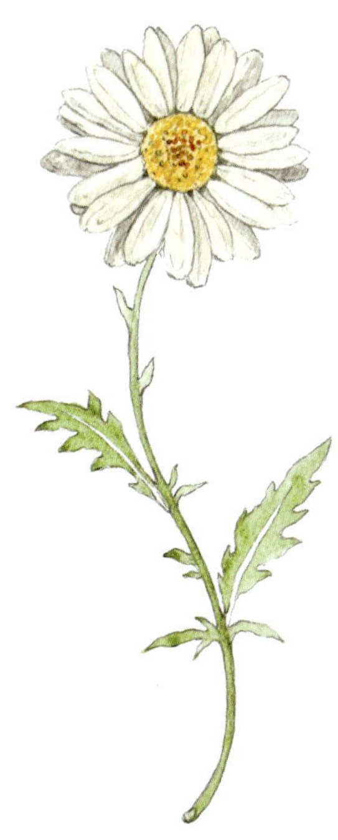

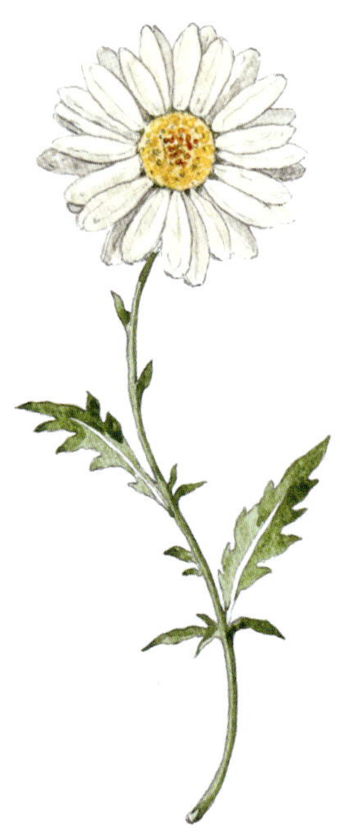

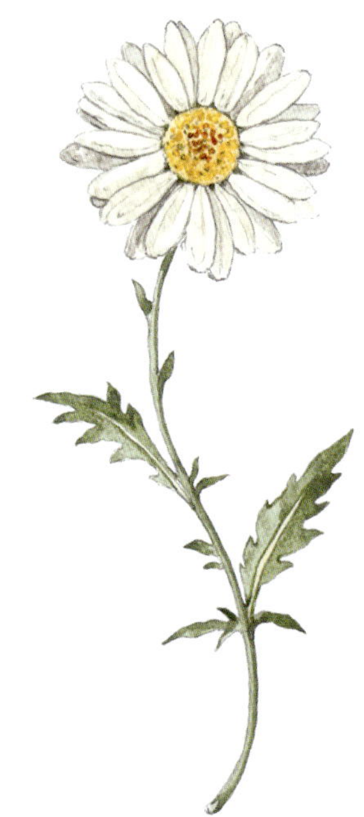

# Step 6: Add the Stem and Leaf Shadows

Using a clean size 0 brush, create a light mix of Hooker's green light with a tiny dab of Vandyke brown to make it a deeper green tone. Paint the tips of the leaves and right at the top of the stem where it meets the head, gradually bringing the paint down to soften it. As this is a light mix, allow the paint layers to fully dry, then dip back into your green mixture and repeat the steps once more, softening each time.

# Step 7: Add the Final Details

Using a size 3/0 brush, mix a light mixture of yellow ochre and water. Paint inside the central rib of each leaf. The daisy is complete! Well done!

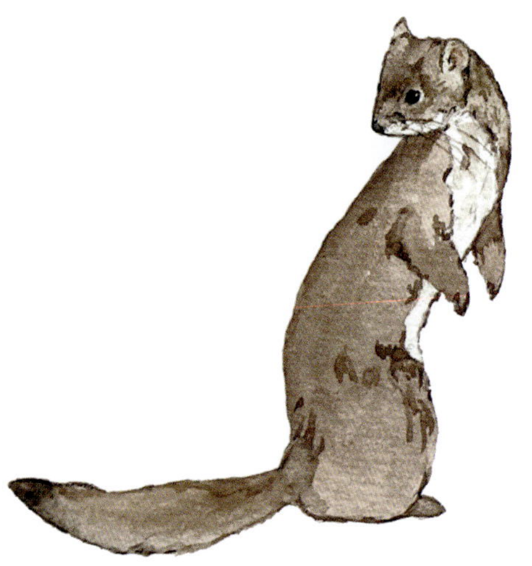

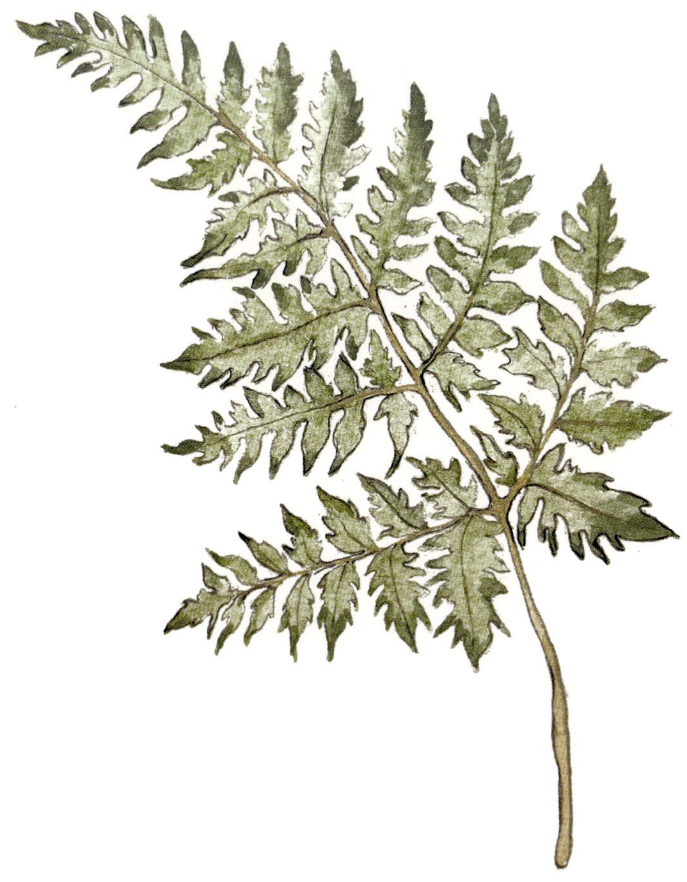

# Fern

Ferns hold a unique allure for me due to their graceful and intricate foliage and also due to their iconic status in the region of the west of Ireland, where I live. When they are fully in bloom, their unfurling fronds in various shades of green could be mistaken for belonging in any Japanese garden! They are also a joy to paint as a botanical subject. The repetition of their form lends well to mastering fluid painting techniques of subtle shading and rhythm.

# Materials Needed

A sheet of cold-press 140-pound (300-gsm) watercolor paper

HB pencil

A piece of paper towel

Brushes

> Size 0

> Size 3/0

Watercolor paints

> Sap green

> Hooker's green light

> Sepia

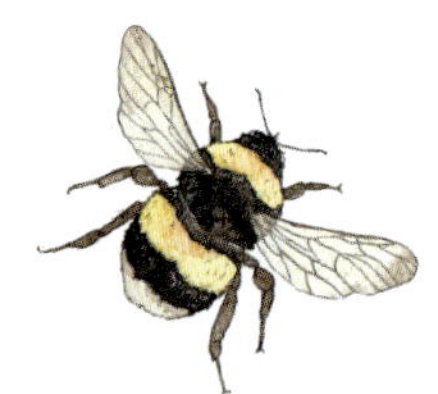

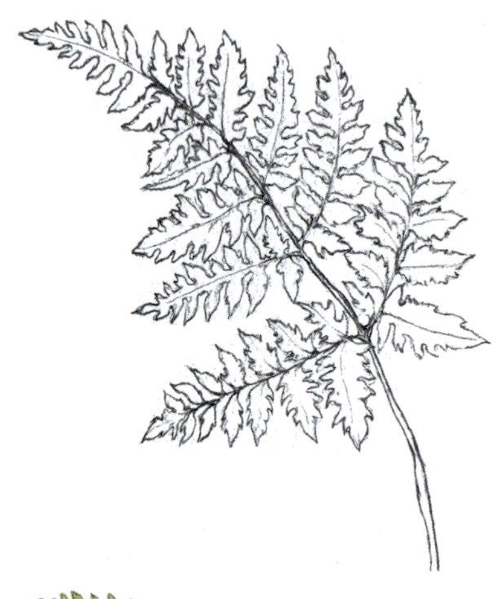

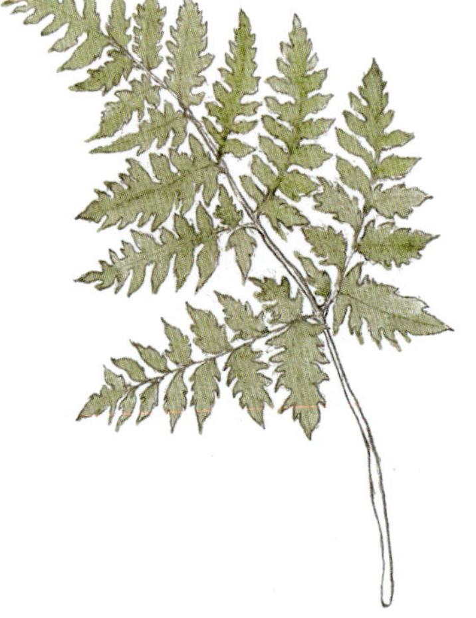

## Step 1: Draw the Outline

Starting on a sheet of cold-press watercolor paper, draw the fern's outline with a sharp HB pencil using the corresponding template located in the back of the book (page 181). Sketch in finer details, lightly using your pencil to emphasize the soft, fluffy, organic outlines on the outer leaves.

## Step 2: Paint the Leaves

For the leaves that make up the plant's main body, create a midtone shade of sap green mixed with water. We want this to act as a glaze, so it cannot be too thick but equally not too pale. This will be the base, so it should still be vibrant. Using a size 0 brush, apply this sap green glaze into the entirety of the fern, stem and leaves, ensuring that you do not paint outside the lines of the drawing as we want the plant's leaves to remain organically symmetrical and uniform.

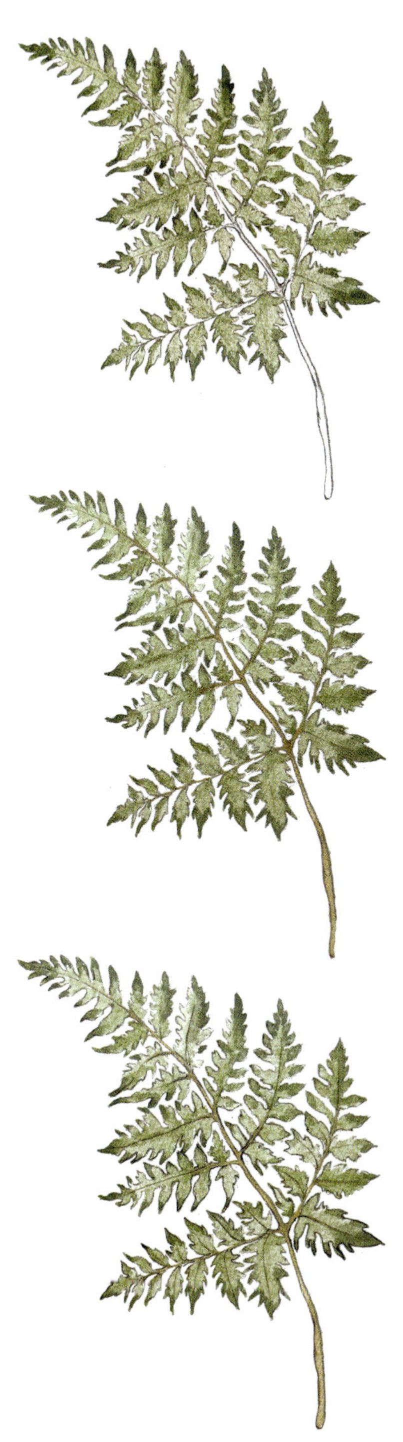

## Step 3: Create the Shadows

To prepare the color that will act as our shadows on the leaves, dip a clean size 3/0 brush into water and swirl it into Hooker's green light until the bristles are fully coated in color. Add this to your palette and clean the brush. Then, dab the brush into a small amount of sepia and mix this into the Hooker's green light that is on your palette. Once they are combined, begin to paint the tips of each individual leaf, working downward and softening the edges of your dark green mixture each time.

## Step 4: Paint the Stem

For the stem, use a clean size 3/0 brush to mix a very simple midtone solution of sepia. We want to ensure that there is a balance of the paint not being too thick but also not too watery that the color will not show without layering multiple times. Using your midtone mix, paint in the stem from top to bottom and take note that the stem extends halfway through each leaf.

## Step 5: Add the Final Details

Dip a clean 3/0 brush into water and wriggle it along the dappled parts of the base green we laid out on the leaves in step 2. This does not need to be done on every leaf, only every third or fourth. We want to create the illusion of moving light. Do not wriggle the brush into the areas of dark green, as we want to keep the shadows vibrant. On these damp patches where we had worked our brush, press a clean, dry paper towel, which will lift the paint and leave subtle highlighting. The fern is now complete, well done!

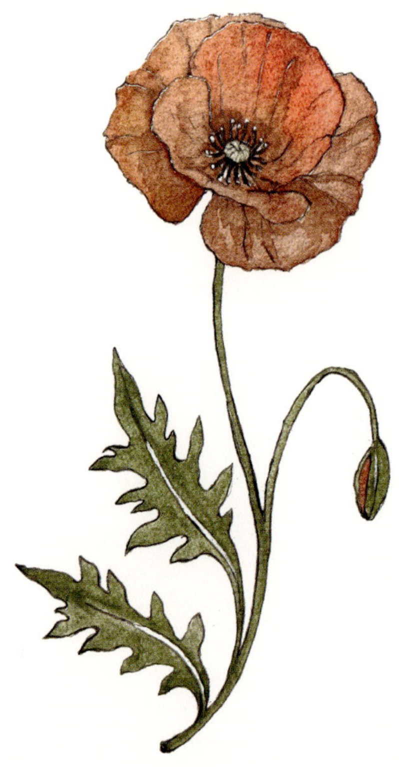

# Poppy

Every year, I look forward to seeing the explosion of vibrant red from the poppy hidden among the tall grass in the garden. Their seeds are often included in "bee bombs," which you can scatter among the garden and which include a range of wildflowers that will bring droves of hardworking bees to the grasses of the garden or woods once they are left to thrive wildly without trimming. I love the simple, old-fashioned appeal of the poppy. The blooms open quite fast and fade away quickly, so I try to paint them before the wind blows their delicate petals away until the following year. This project will allow us to explore how effective shading and highlights can be—and how they can really bring a botanical piece to life—with a few simple touches of a brush.

# Materials Needed

A sheet of cold-press 140-pound (300-gsm) watercolor paper

A piece of paper towel

HB pencil

Brushes

> Size 4

> Size 3/0

> Size 0

Watercolor paints

> Light red

> Yellow ochre

> Burnt sienna

> Lamp black

> Hooker's green light

Acrylic white

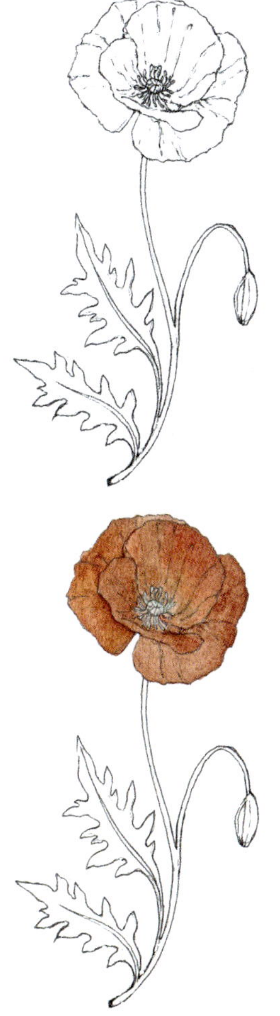

## Step 1: Draw the Outline

Starting on a sheet of cold-press watercolor paper, draw the poppy's outline, its petals, the stem and the leaves with a sharp HB pencil using the corresponding template located in the back of the book (page 181).

## Step 2: Paint the Petals

Begin by mixing a midtone wash of light red and yellow ochre until they form a warm and sunny red color. Poppies naturally hold a red in their petals that could almost appear as a deep burnt orange, so take into consideration that we want our wash to be a warm red with an obvious hint of yellow to create the base. Using a size 4 brush, glaze over the entire head of the poppy, gently moving the paint around and taking care to avoid the flower's center and the little tendrils growing from it. Switch to a size 3/0 brush to paint in the smaller and finer spaces around the center of the flower so you keep your lines neat and tidy.

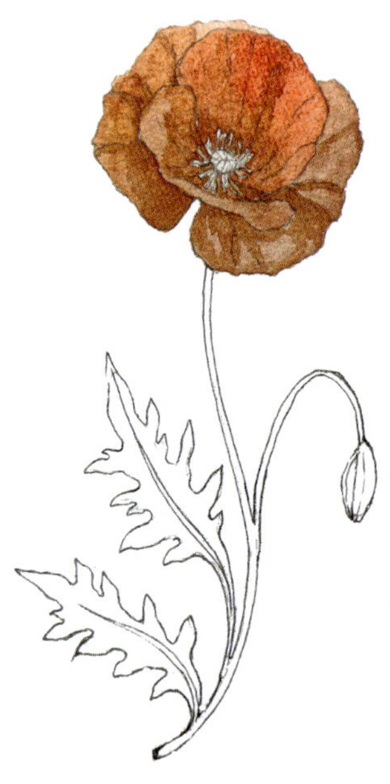

## Step 3: Create the Petal Shadows

Prepare the color for the deeper tones of the poppy by mixing a midtone wash of light red with a touch of burnt sienna. We want this color to appear deeper, a brown-tone red that will act both as the delicate surface veins of the petals and as the shadows. Using a size 0 brush, paint the bottom petals and center of the flower lightly with your wash, focusing from the center where the shadows are darker, then softening as you work outward toward the edges of the petals.

Next, using a size 3/0 brush, paint on the petals' veins that grow outward from the center. Use very gentle sweeps for this and just the tip of the brush to allow for tight work and accurate tracing of the lines from our template. We want these veins to have hard, defined edges, so allow the paint to fully dry, and build them up in one to two layers so they will be visible and not appear soft.

## Step 4: Paint the Center of the Poppy

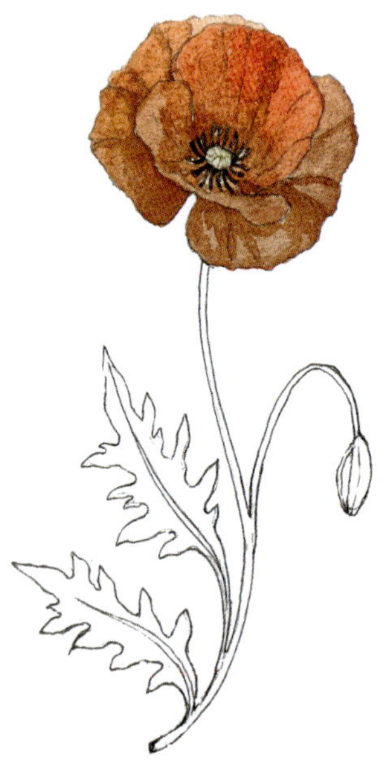

Use a clean size 3/0 brush to mix two separate basic washes: one of a light solution of water and yellow ochre, the other of a thick, deep-tone solution of lamp black. As we want the black tendrils to really stand out, ensure that your black mixture is not too diluted with water. We want it almost to appear like black ink on your palette.

Begin by going from light to dark. Load your light yellow ochre mixture onto the brush and glaze over the center bud. Allow this to fully dry.

Clean your brush and load it with the deep black mixture. Hold the brush at the ferrule to gain the most control and delicately paint each tendril surrounding the bud. Allow the paint to fully dry.

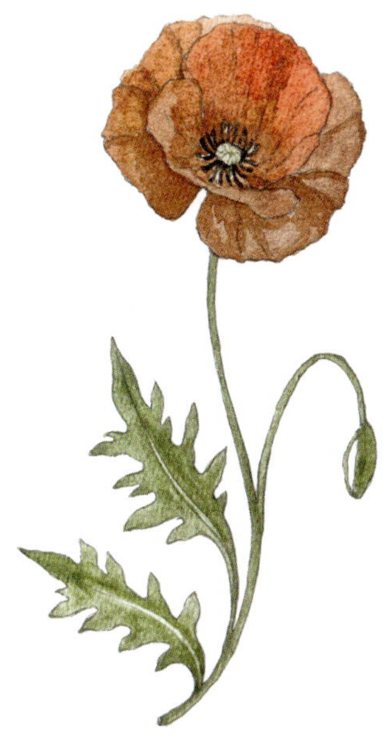

## Step 5: Fill in the Stem and Leaves

For the stem base, we will need a basic mix of Hooker's green light and water. We want this mixture to be midtone, so make sure that there is not so much water that it is almost transparent but also not too thick that it appears highly pigmented and difficult to spread. Using a size 0 brush, begin by painting the leaves. Focus on the centers of the leaves first (this is where the highest concentration of color will be) painting around the stem and softening the color by gently pushing the paint to the edge of each leaf where the color's concentration will get lighter. While the leaves are drying, dilute the midtone green mixture with water to create a more lightly saturated solution, and use this light-tone green to paint along the inner stem of the leaves from top to bottom and the right hand bud that has not yet blossomed. While the paint is still damp, coat the closed bud on the right hand side with another layer of light-tone green to create greater depth. When the leaves are dry, coat the centers around the stem with another layer of the light-tone green mixture, gently softening the edges.

## Step 6: Add the Final Details

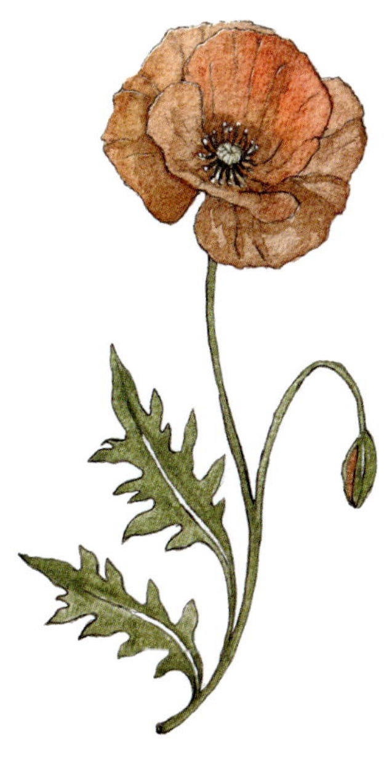

To finish off our poppy, using a size 3/0 brush, fill in the right-hand bud with our sunny red mixture that we used in step 2. Clean your brush and squeeze a less than pea-size amount of acrylic white paint onto your palette. Dip the brush into the white and dot the top of each individual tendril with a tiny amount of this paint. Next, using the absolute tip of your brush, dip back into the white and follow the line on the center of each leaf to create the middle rib. Finish off by once again dipping into the acrylic white and lightly tracing the petal vein outlines on the top inner center petal. The poppy is now complete! Well done!

# Templates

For beginners, templates offer a pathway to understanding form and structure. It's not about copying but about learning—observing how lines connect, how shapes form, and how details bring a subject to life. Tracing can help train the eye to see these elements and replicate them more easily in freehand drawing with more practice.

In this chapter, each template matches with a corresponding project. How I recommend using the templates is layering a blank piece of watercolor paper over the picture you're tracing, holding them both up on a bright window, and trace using a sharp HB pencil. If you feel confident enough, you can even try copying the template freehand onto your piece of watercolor paper. This is a great way to practice and hone your drawing skills, as well as experiment with proportion and whether you would like your picture to be bigger or smaller.

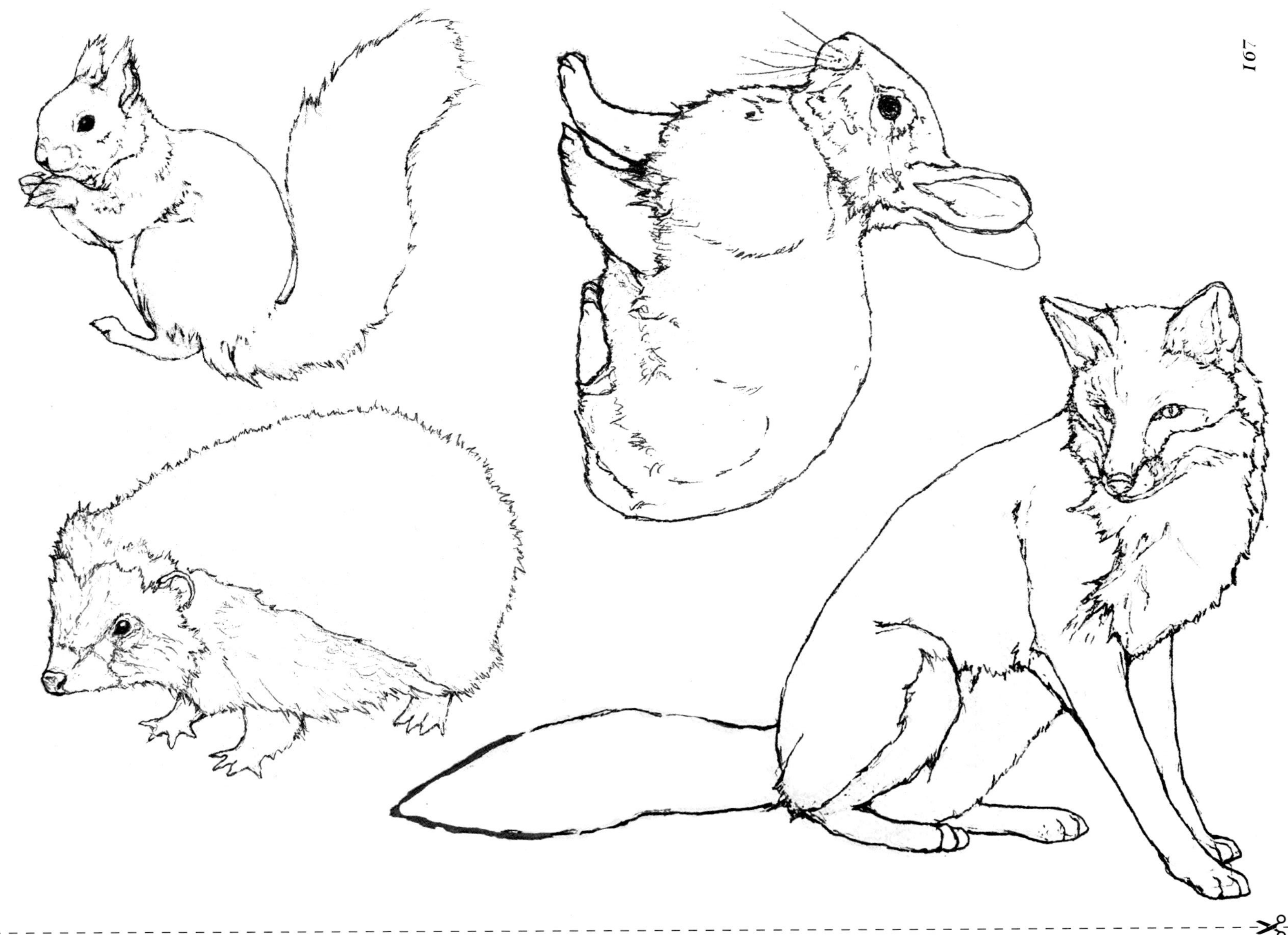

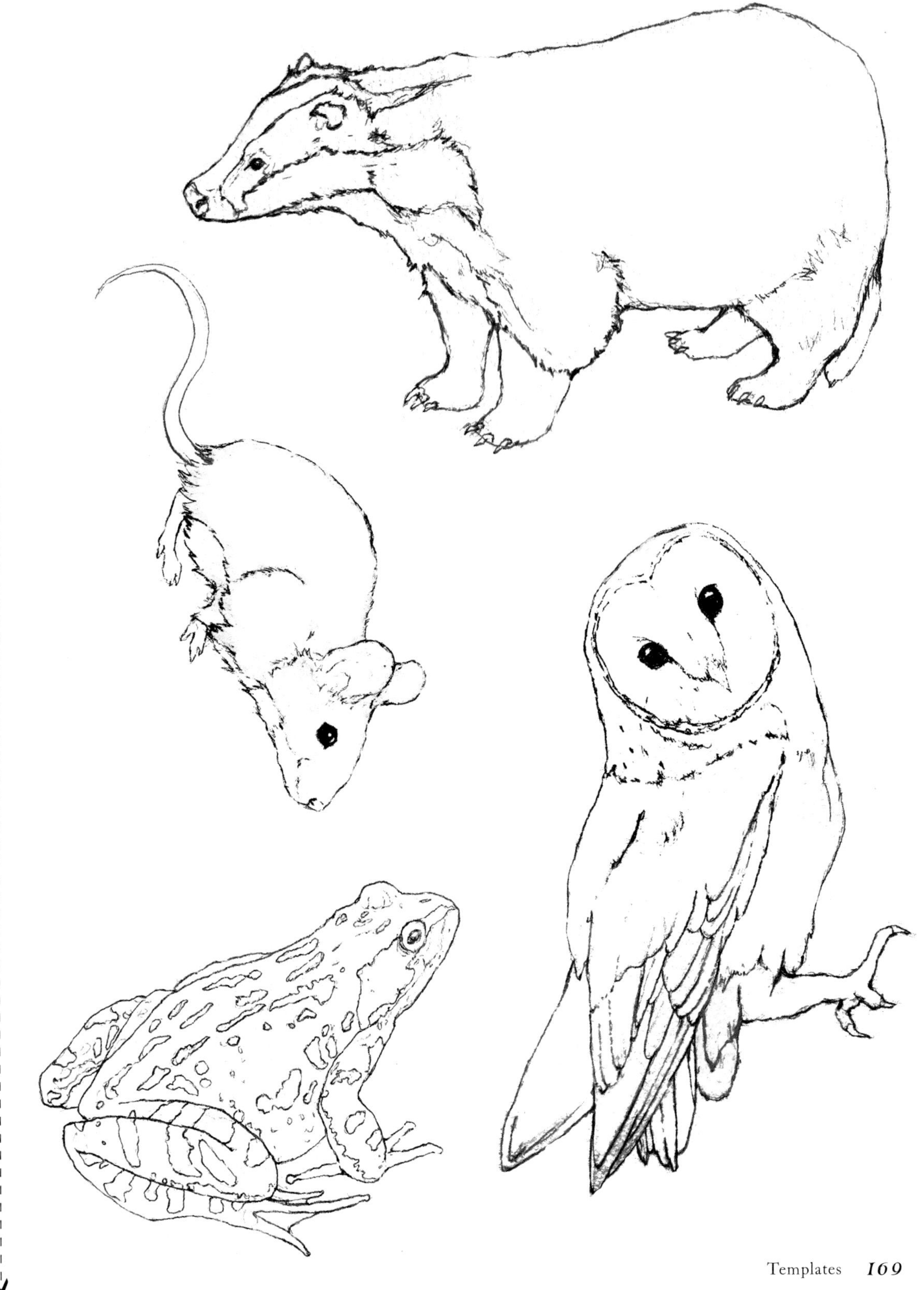

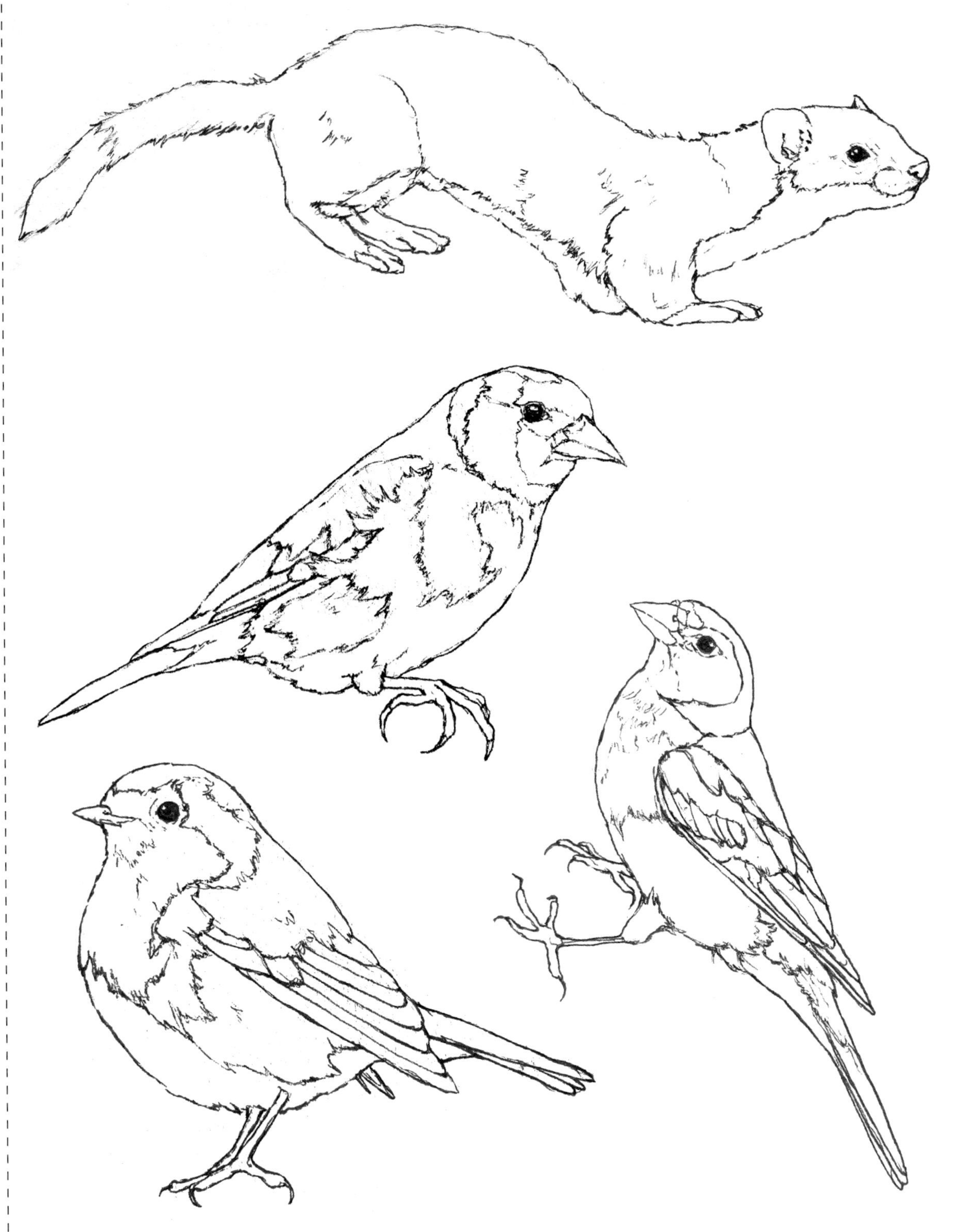

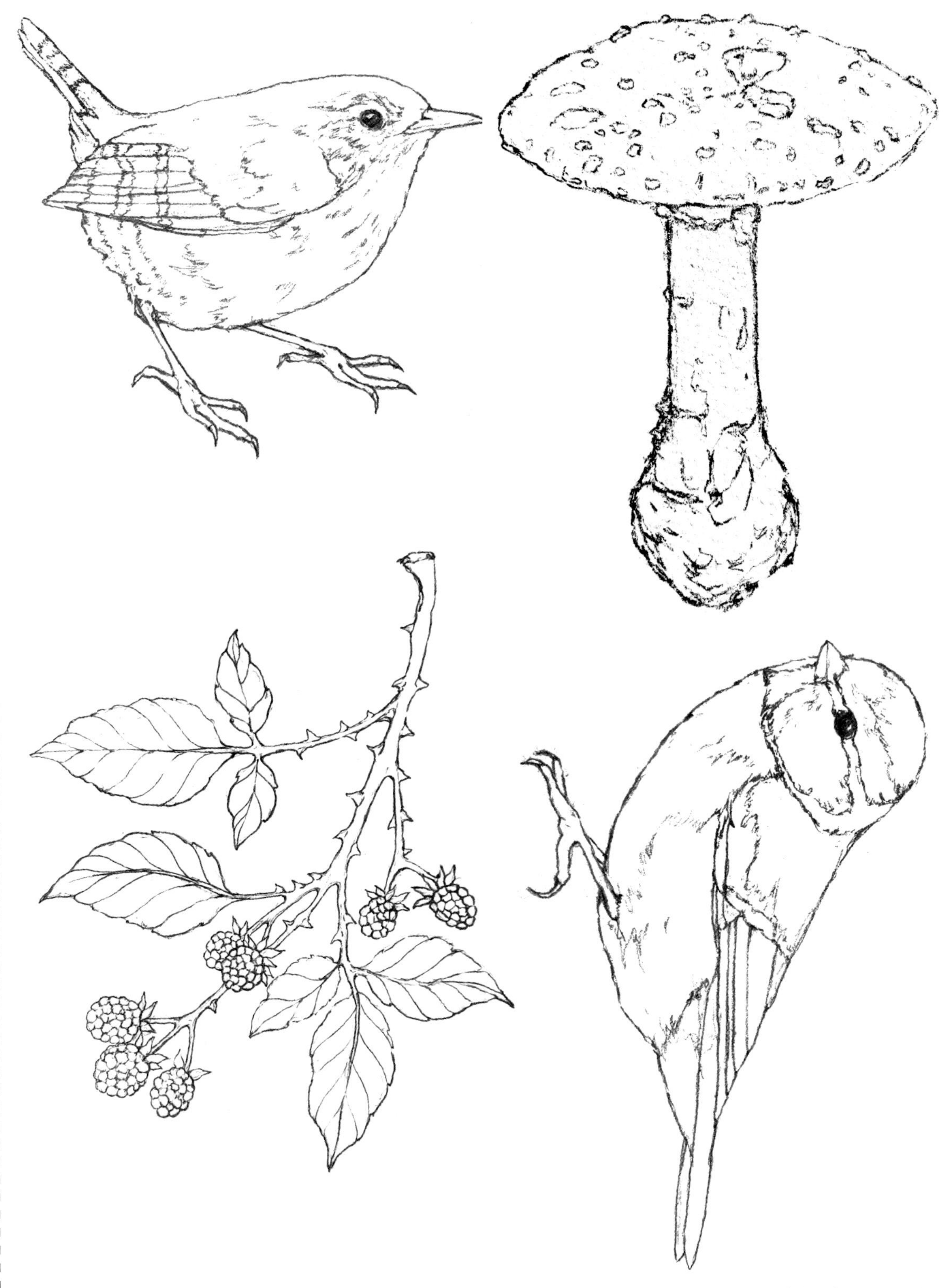

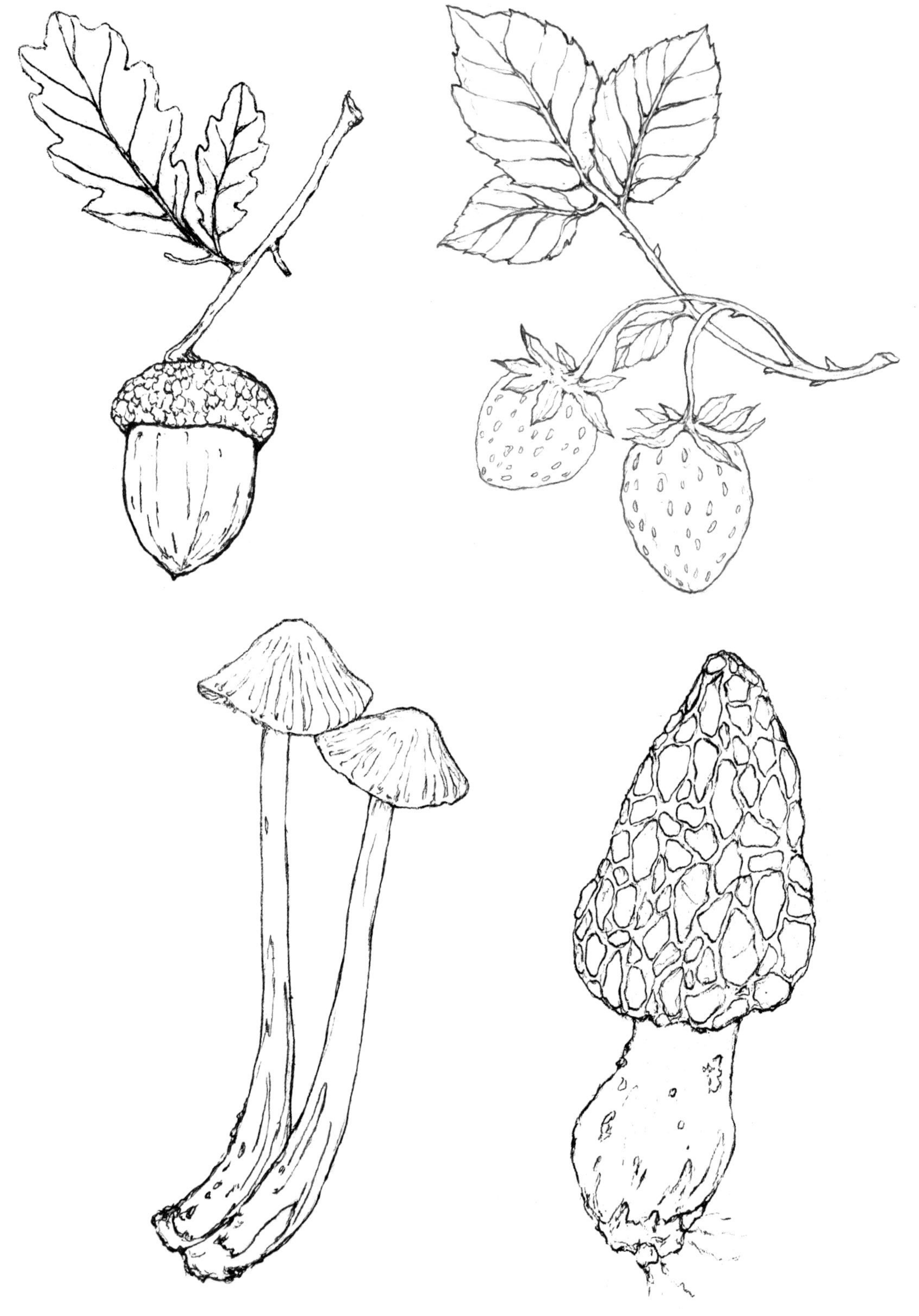

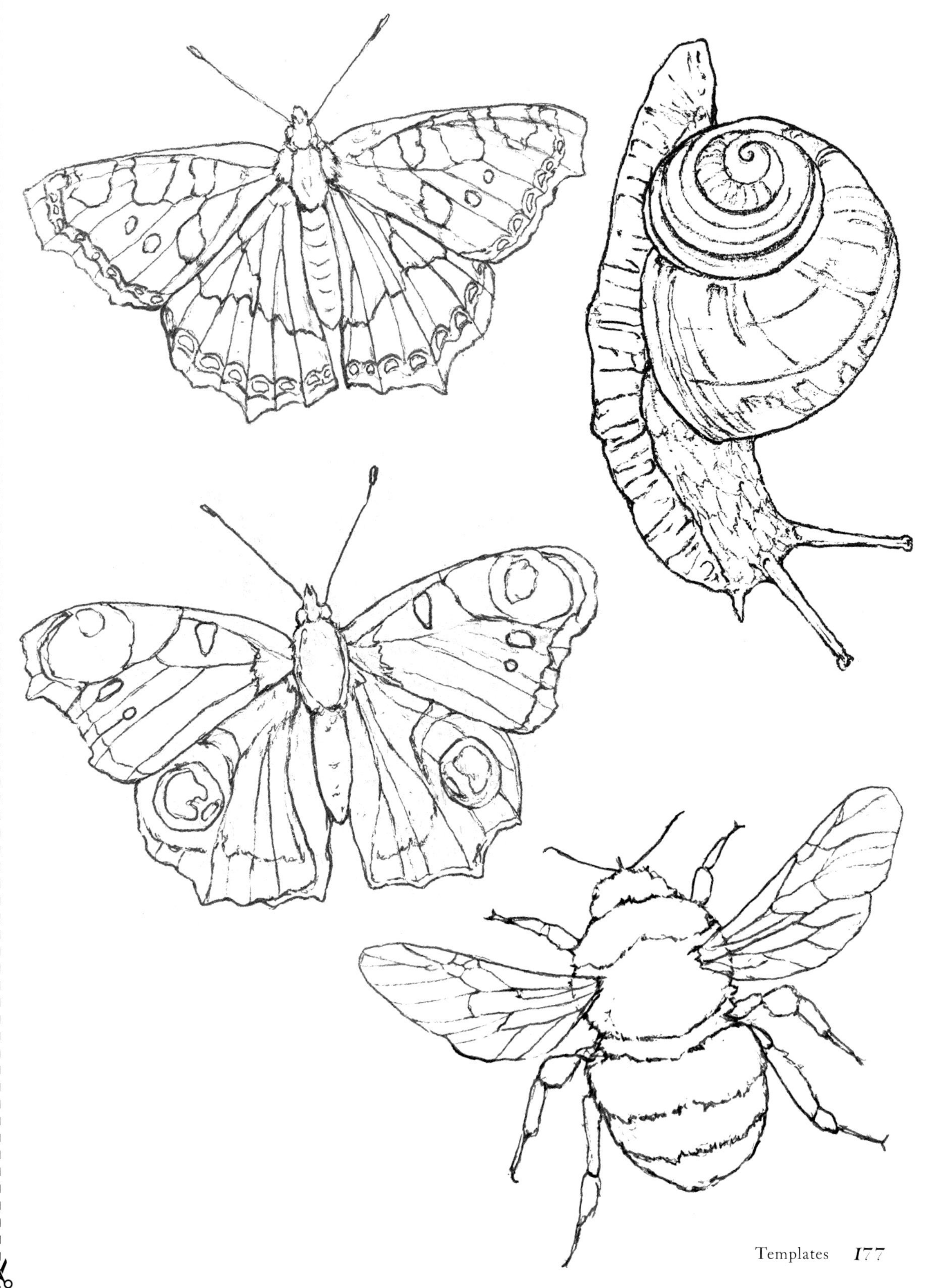

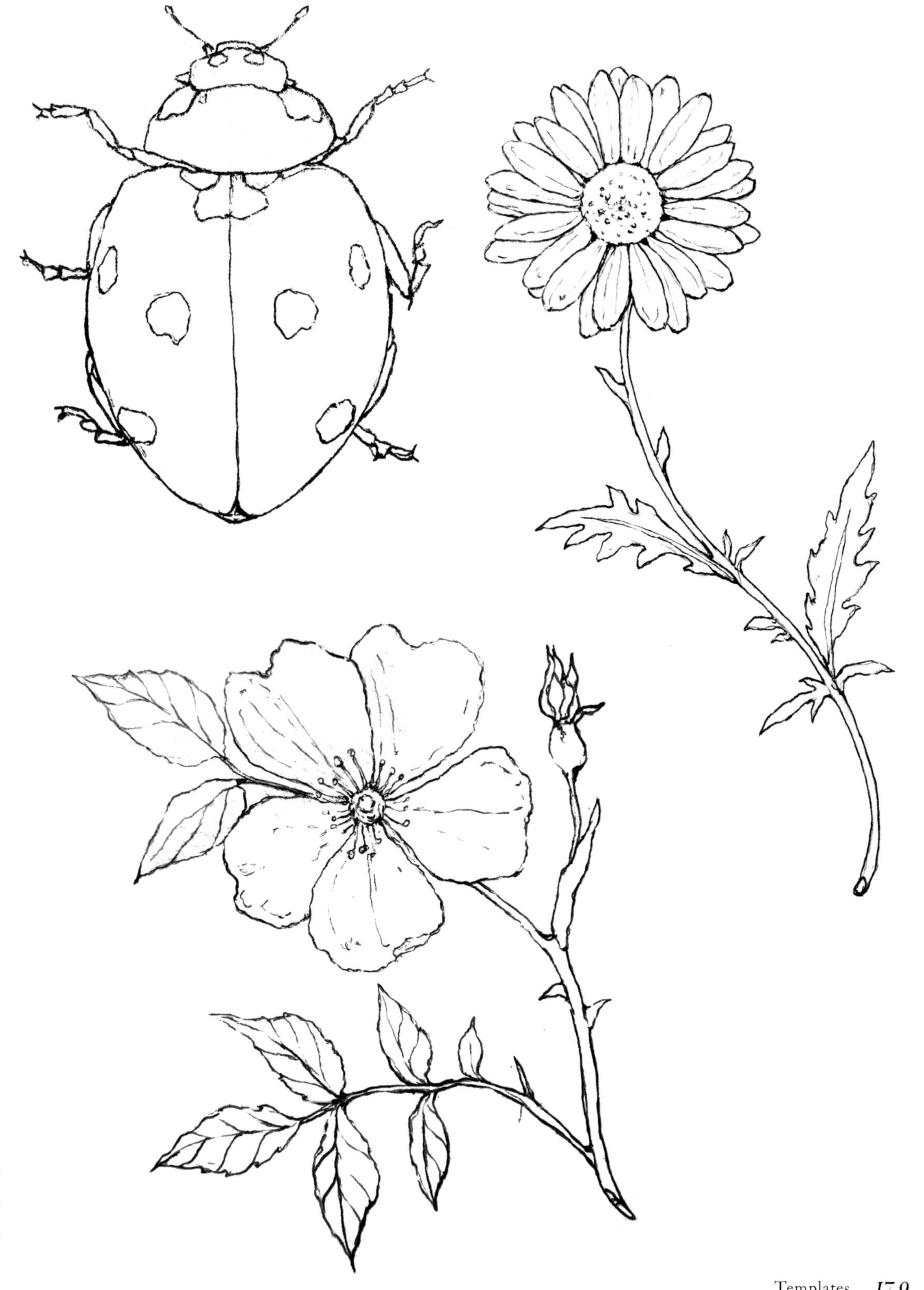

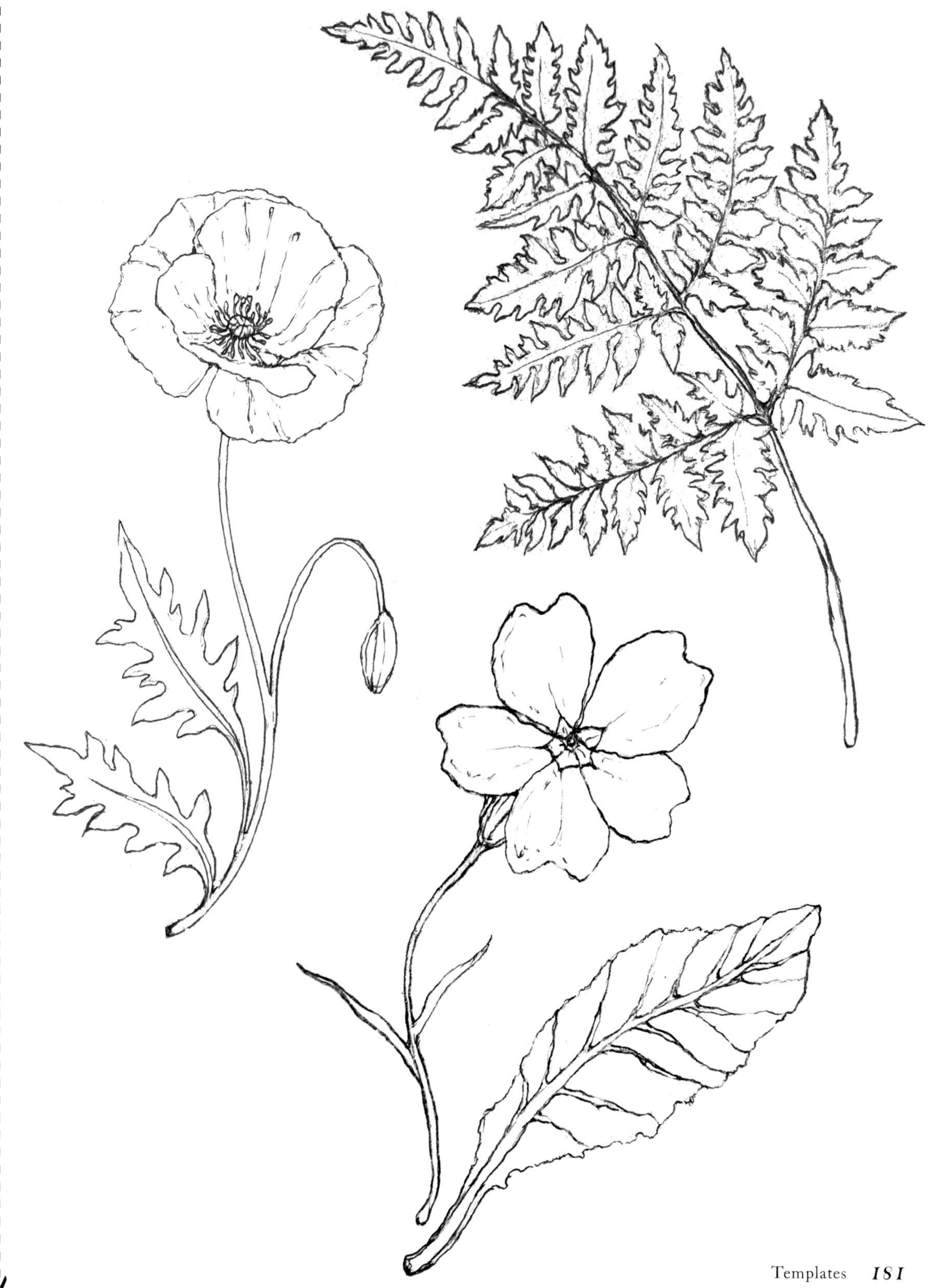

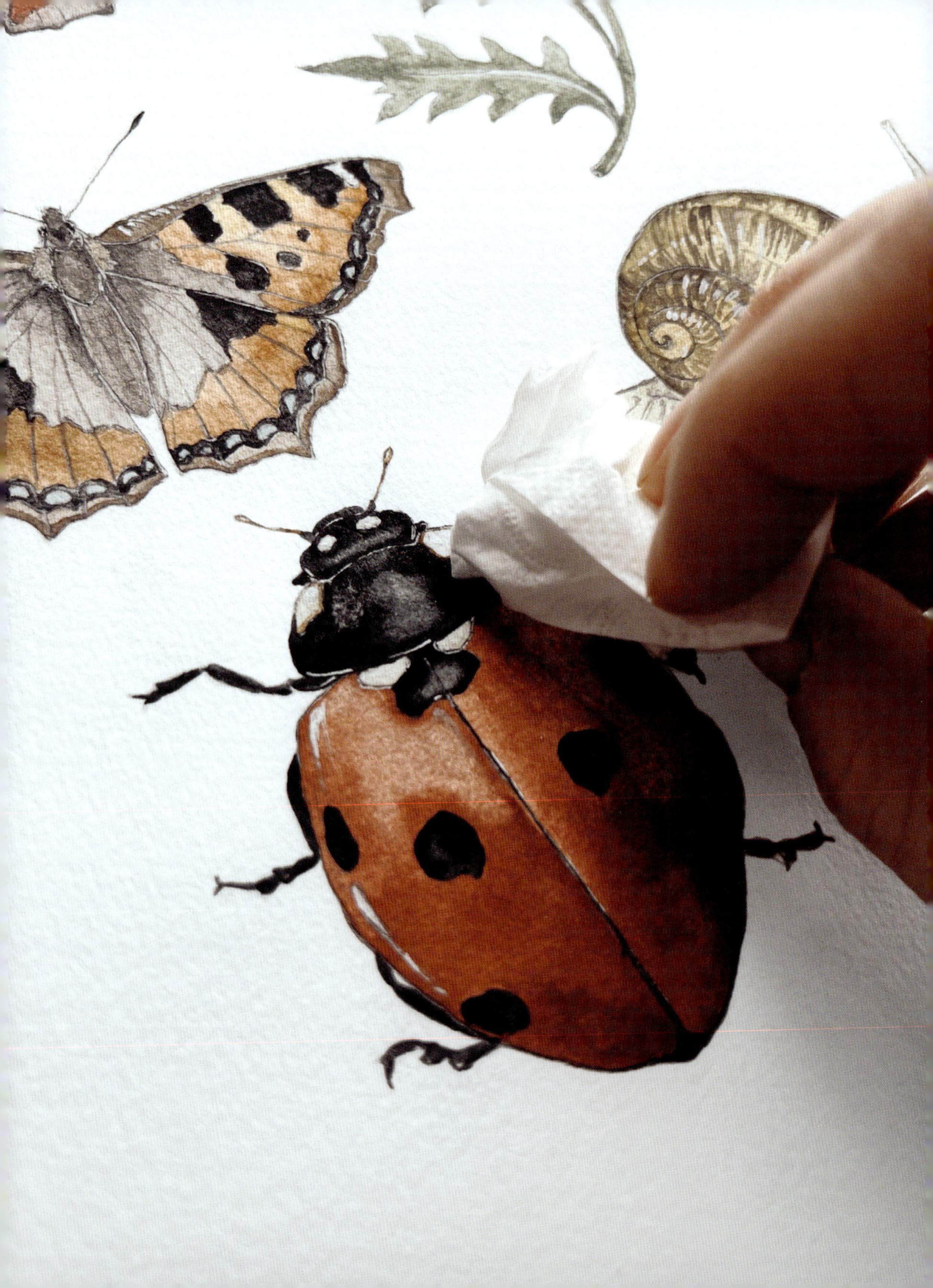

# Acknowledgments

I would like to heartfeltly thank my friends and family, for their unwavering encouragement and support for all that I create.

A very grateful thank-you goes to the most amazing team at Page Street who gave me this opportunity and have worked tirelessly and cheerfully to bring this book to life. It has been a pleasure!

Thank you to Krystle and Sarah, who have calmly nurtured this project, handling the often-complex material with such good humor and efficiency, which has helped me capture my vision with accessibility, vibrancy and freshness.

Last but not least, to my customers, students and readers, who are always supportive and encouraging of my work. These pages are, as always, for you.

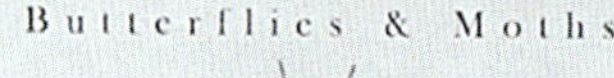

## Butterflies & Moths

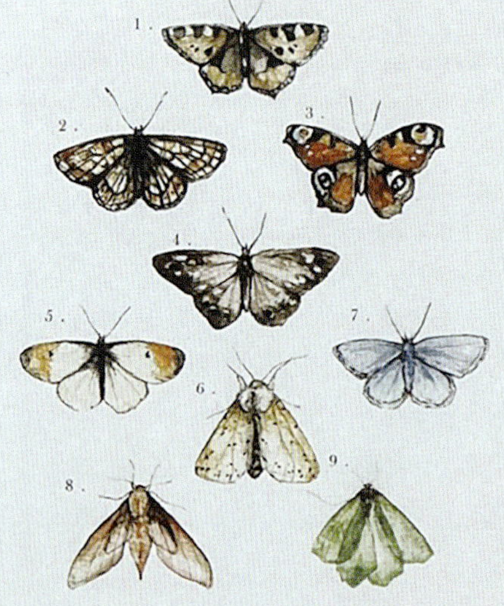

1.Small Tortoiseshell 2.Marsh Fritillary 3.Peacock
4.Speckled Wood 5.Orange Tip 6.White Ermine
7.Common Blue 8.Elephant Hawkmoth 9.Large Emerald

## Woodland Fauna

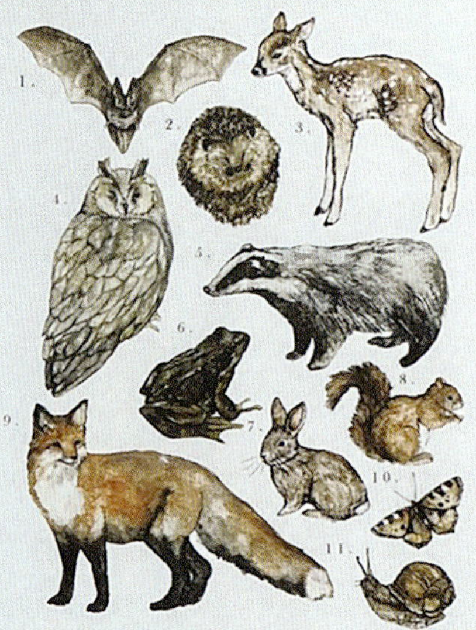

1.Horseshoe Bat 2.Hedgehog 3.Deer 4. Long Eared Owl
5.Badger 6. Frog 7. Rabbit 8. Red Squirrel
9. Red Fox 10. Small Tortoiseshell Butterfly 11. Garden Snail

## Garden Birds

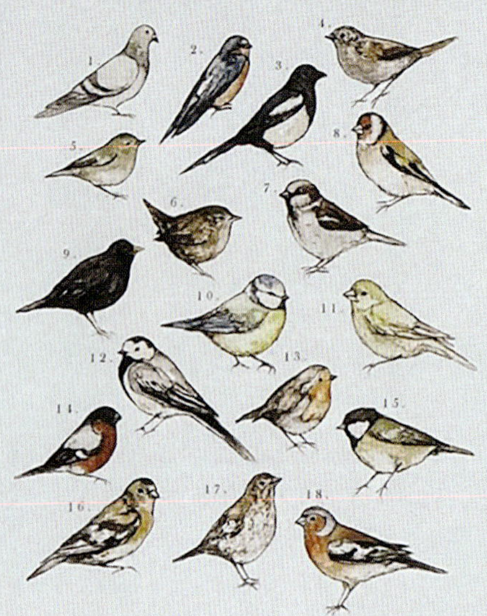

1.Pigeon 2.Swallow 3.Magpie 4.Dunnock
5.Chiffchaff 6.Wren 7.Sparrow 8.Goldfinch 9.Blackbird
10.Bluetit 11.Greenfinch 12.Pied Wagtail 13.Robin
14.Bullfinch 15.Great Tit 16.Brambling 17.Thrush 18.Chaffinch

## Toadstools

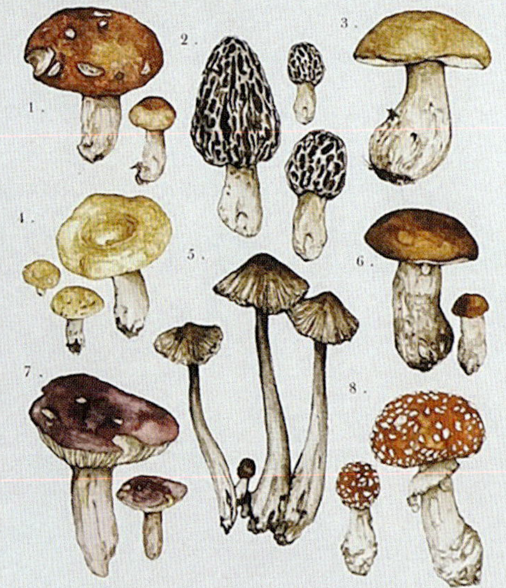

1.Fragile Brittlegill 2.Half-Free Morel
3.Saffron Bolete 4.Ochre Brittlegill
5.Grooved Bonnet 6.Red Aspen-Oak Bolete
7.Primrose Brittlegill 8.Fly Agaric

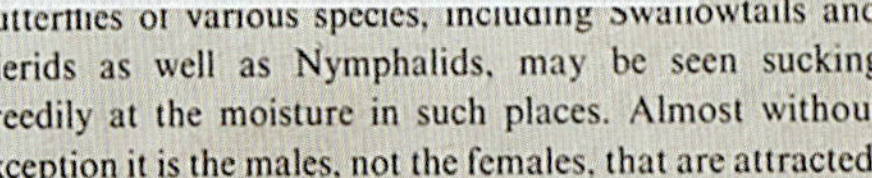

ylvain; Ge. Gr[...]

d more magn[...]

l (*Limenitis* [...] and is one of those species in Britain but unfortunately [...] aspen. [...] hose of the Purple Emperor, [...] butterflies of various species, including Swallowtails and Pierids as well as Nymphalids, may be seen sucking greedily at the moisture in such places. Almost without exception it is the males, not the females, that are attracted.

# About the Author

Jane Carkill is an illustrator and textile designer on the west coast of Ireland. She studied fine art textiles at the Atlantic Technological University's School of Design & Creative Arts. She is fascinated by natural ephemeral beauty and intricate detail and combines a love of folklore, narration, myth and story with a precise style of illustration to capture an essence in nature that is both magical and nostalgic. Flora and fauna are the ultimate inspirations for her work, which portrays the distinctive elements and characteristics of her everyday experiences in the countryside.

She began sharing her work under the name Lamblittle in 2012, and after much outcry and queries as to where her work could be purchased, she opened LambLittleShop in 2016 and has seen an explosion of international success ever since.

She has provided illustrations to two recent major Hachette Book Group publications: *Wild Embrace: Connecting to the Wonder of Ireland's Natural World* by Anja Murray and *Windfall: Irish Nature Poems to Inspire and Connect* edited by Jane Clarke.

# Index